CONTENTS

KW-482-059

100 SMART BOARD™ LESSONS

Interactive whiteboards are fast becoming the must-have resource in today's classroom as they allow teachers to facilitate children's learning in ways that were inconceivable a few years ago. The appropriate use of interactive whiteboards, whether used daily in the classroom or once a week in the ICT suite, will encourage active participation in lessons and should increase learners' determination to succeed. Interactive whiteboards make it easier for teachers to bring subjects across the curriculum to life in new and exciting ways.

'There is a whiteboard revolution in UK schools.'
(Primary National Strategy)

What can an interactive whiteboard offer?
For the **teacher**, an interactive whiteboard offers the same facilities as an ordinary whiteboard, such as drawing, writing and erasing. However, the interactive whiteboard also offers many other possibilities to:
- save any work created during a lesson
- prepare as many pages as necessary
- display any page within the Notebook™ file to review teaching and learning
- add scanned examples of the children's work to a Notebook file
- change colours of shapes and backgrounds instantly
- use simple templates and grids
- link Notebook files to spreadsheets, websites and presentations.

Using an interactive whiteboard in the simple ways outlined above can enrich teaching and learning in a classroom, but that is only the beginning of the whiteboard's potential to educate and inspire.

For the **learner**, the interactive whiteboard provides the opportunity to share learning experiences, as lessons can be delivered with sound, still and moving images, and websites. Interactive whiteboards can be used to cater for the needs of all learning styles:
- kinaesthetic learners benefit from being able to physically manipulate images
- visual learners benefit from being able to watch videos, look at photographs and see images being manipulated
- auditory learners benefit from being able to access audio resources such as voice recordings and sound effects.

With a little preparation all of these resource types could be integrated in one lesson, a feat that would have been almost impossible before the advent of the interactive whiteboard!

Access to an interactive whiteboard
In schools where learners have limited access to an interactive whiteboard the teacher must carefully plan lessons in which the children will derive most benefit from using it. As teachers become familiar with the whiteboard they will learn when to use it and, importantly, when not to use it!

Where permanent access to an interactive whiteboard is available, it is important that the teacher plans the use of the board effectively. It should be used only in ways that will enhance or extend teaching and learning. Children still need to gain practical first-hand experience of many things. Some experiences cannot be recreated on an interactive whiteboard but others cannot be had without it. *100 SMART Board™ Lessons* offers both teachers and learners the most accessible and creative uses of this most valuable resource.

About the series
100 SMART Board™ Lessons is designed to reflect best practice in using interactive whiteboards. It is also designed to support all teachers in using this valuable tool by providing lessons and other resources that can be used on a whiteboard with little or no preparation. These inspirational lessons cover all National Curriculum subjects. They are perfect for all levels of experience and are an essential for any SMART Board users.

Safety note: Avoid looking directly at the projector beam as it is potentially damaging to eyes, and never leave the children unsupervised when using the interactive whiteboard.

Introduction

About the book

This book is divided into four chapters. Each chapter contains lessons and photocopiable activity sheets covering:

- English
- Mathematics
- Science
- Foundation subjects.

At the beginning of each chapter a **planning grid** identifies the title, the objectives covered and any relevant cross-curricular links in each lesson. Objectives are taken from the relevant Primary National Strategy, National Curriculum Programmes of Study (PoS), or the QCA Schemes of Work. All of the lessons should therefore fit into your existing medium-term plans. The planning grids have been provided in Microsoft Word format on the CD-ROM for this purpose.

Lesson plans

The lessons have a consistent structure with a starter activity, activities for shared and independent work, and a plenary to round up the teaching and learning and identify any assessment opportunities. Crucially, each lesson plan identifies resources required (including photocopiable activity sheets **P** and Notebook files that are provided on the CD-ROM 💿). Also highlighted are the whiteboard tools that could be used in the lesson.

Photocopiable activity sheets at the end of each chapter support the lessons. These sheets provide opportunities for group or individual work to be completed away from the board, but link to the context of the whiteboard lesson. They also provide opportunities for whole-class plenary sessions in which children discuss and present their work.

Two general record sheets are provided on pages 170 and 171. These are intended to support the teacher in recording ways in which the interactive whiteboard is used, and where and how interactive resources can be integrated into a lesson.

What's on the CD-ROM?

The accompanying CD-ROM provides an extensive bank of Notebook files. These support, and are supported by, the lessons in this book. As well as texts and images, a selection of Notebook files include the following types of files:

- Embedded Microsoft Office files: These include Microsoft Word and Excel documents. The embedded files are launched from the Notebook file and will open in their native Microsoft application.

- Embedded interactive files: These include specially commissioned interactive files as well as Interactive Teaching Programs (ITPs) from the Primary National Strategy.

- Printable PDF versions of the photocopiable activity and record sheets, as well as the answers to the mathematics activities, are also provided on the CD-ROM.

- 'Build your own' file: This contains a blank Notebook page with a bank of selected images and interactive tools from the Gallery, as well as specially commissioned images. It is supported by lesson plans in the book to help you to build your own Notebook files.

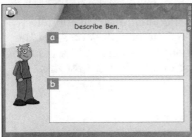

The Notebook files
All of the Notebook files have a consistent structure as follows:

Title and objectives page
Use this page to highlight the focus of the lesson. You might also wish to refer to this page at certain times throughout the lesson or at the end of the lesson to assess whether the learning objective was achieved.

Starter activity
This sets the context to the lesson and usually provides some key questions or learning points that will be addressed through the main activities.

Main activities
These activities offer independent, collaborative group, or whole-class work. The activities draw on the full scope of Notebook software and the associated tools, as well as the SMART Board tools.

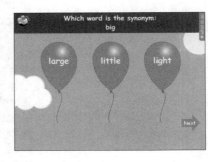

What to do boxes are also included in many of the prepared Notebook files. These appear as tabs in the top right-hand corner of the screen. To access these notes, simply pull out the tabs to reveal planning information, additional support and key learning points.

Plenary
A whole-class activity or summary page is designed to review work done both at the board and away from the board. In many lessons, children are encouraged to present their work.

Whiteboard tools page
The whiteboard tools page gives a reminder of the tools used in the lesson and provides instructions on how they are used.

HOW TO USE THE CD-ROM

Setting up your screen for optimal use
It is best to view the Notebook pages at a screen display setting of 1280 × 1024 pixels. To alter the screen display, select Settings, then Control Panel from the Start menu. Next, double-click on the Display icon and then click on the Settings tab. Finally, adjust the Screen area scroll bar to 1280 × 1024 pixels. Click on OK.

If you prefer to use a screen display setting of 800 × 600 pixels, ensure that your Notebook view is set to 'Page Width'. To alter the view, launch Notebook and click on View. Go to Zoom and select the 'Page Width' setting. If you use a screen display setting of 800 × 600 pixels, text in the prepared Notebook files may appear larger when you edit it on screen.

Viewing the printable resources
Adobe® Reader® is required to view the printable resources. All the printable resources are PDF files.

Visit the Adobe® website at **www.adobe.com** to download the latest version of Adobe® Reader®.

100

SMART Board™

LESSONS

TERMS AND CONDITIONS

IMPORTANT - PERMITTED USE AND WARNINGS - READ CAREFULLY BEFORE USING

Copyright in the Control software contained on this CD-ROM and in its accompanying material belongs to Scholastic Ltd. All rights reserved. © 2007, Scholastic Ltd.

Notebook™, including the Notebook™ artwork (contained within the Gallery), incorporated on this CD-ROM is the exclusive property of SMART Technologies Inc. Copyright © 2007 SMART Technologies Inc. All rights reserved. SMART Board is a registered trademark of SMART Technologies Inc in the UK.

The material contained on this CD-ROM may only be used in the context for which it was intended in *100 SMART Board™ Lessons*. Scholastic Ltd accepts no liability for any adaptation of Scholastic or SMART copyrighted material. School site use is permitted only within the school of the purchaser of the book and CD-ROM. Any further use of the material contravenes Scholastic Ltd's copyright and that of other rights holders.

Save for these purposes, or as expressly authorised in the accompanying materials, the software including artwork or images may not be copied, reproduced, used, sold, licensed, transferred, exchanged, hired, or exported in whole or in part or in any manner or form without the prior written consent of Scholastic Ltd. Any such unauthorised use or activities are prohibited and may give rise to civil liabilities and criminal prosecutions.

This CD-ROM has been tested for viruses at all stages of its production. However, we recommend that you run virus-checking software on your computer systems at all times. Scholastic Ltd cannot accept any responsibility for any loss, disruption or damage to your data or your computer system that may occur as a result of using either the CD-ROM, software, website links or the data held on it.

Due to the nature of the web, the publisher cannot guarantee the content or links of any websites referred to. It is the responsibility of the user to assess the suitability of websites.

IF YOU ACCEPT THE ABOVE CONDITIONS YOU MAY PROCEED TO USE THIS CD-ROM.

Minimum specification:
- PC/Mac with a CD-ROM drive and at least 128 MB RAM
- Microsoft Office 2000 or higher
- Adobe® Reader®
- Interactive whiteboard
- Notebook™ software
- Facilities for printing and sound (optional)

PC:
- Pentium II 450 MHz processor
- Microsoft Windows 2000 SP4 or higher

Mac:
- 700 MHz processor (1 GHz or faster recommended)
- Mac OS X.4 or higher

For all technical support queries, please phone Scholastic Customer Services on 0845 6039091.

YEAR 2

Scottish Primary 3

CREDITS

Author
Karen Mawer

Development Editor
Niamh O'Carroll

Editor
Nicola Morgan

Assistant Editors
Margaret Eaton and Kim Vernon

Illustrators
Jim Peacock (Notebook file illustrations),
Mark Brierley (Notebook file and book illustrations), Theresa Tibbetts
(additional Notebook file illustrations)

Series Designer
Joy Monkhouse

Designers
Rebecca Male, Allison Parry, Shelley Best,
Andrea Lewis, Anna Oliwa and Melissa Leeke

CD-ROM developed in association with
Q & D Multimedia

ACKNOWLEDGEMENTS

SMART Board™ and Notebook™ are registered trademarks of SMART Technologies Inc.

Microsoft Office, Word and Excel are either registered trademarks or trademarks of Microsoft Corporation in the United States and/or other countries.

With grateful thanks for advice, help and expertise to Angus McGarry (Trainer) and Fiona Ford (Education Development Consultant) at Steljes Ltd.

All Flash activities designed and developed by Q & D Multimedia.

Interactive Teaching Programs (developed by the Primary National Strategy) © Crown copyright.

With thanks to Mike Longden for the use of various photographs.

The publishers gratefully acknowledge:
The Royal Mint for the use of images of coins © Crown copyright.

Every effort has been made to trace copyright holders for the works reproduced in this book, and the publishers apologise for any inadvertent omissions.

Designed using Adobe InDesign.

Made with Macromedia is a trademark of
Macromedia, Inc. Director ®
Copyright © 1984-2000 Macromedia, Inc.

Published by Scholastic Ltd
Villiers House
Clarendon Avenue
Leamington Spa
Warwickshire CV32 5PR

www.scholastic.co.uk

Printed by Bell and Bain Ltd, Glasgow

1 2 3 4 5 6 7 8 9   7 8 9 0 1 2 3 4 5 6

Text © 2007 Karen Mawer

© 2007 Scholastic Ltd

**British Library
Cataloguing-in-Publication Data**
A catalogue record for this book is available
from the British Library.

ISBN 978-0439-94538-7

The rights of the author of this work have been asserted by her in accordance with the Copyright, Designs and Patents Act 1988.

Extracts from the Primary National Strategy's *Primary Framework for literacy and mathematics* (2006) www.standards.dfes.gov.uk/primaryframework © Crown copyright. Reproduced under the terms of the Click Use Licence.

Extracts from The National Literacy Strategy and The National Numeracy Strategy © Crown copyright. Material from the National Curriculum © The Queen's Printer and Controller of HMSO. Reproduced under the terms of HMSO Guidance Note 8.

Extracts from the QCA Scheme of Work © Qualifications and Curriculum Authority.

All rights reserved. This book is sold subject to the condition that it shall not, by way of trade or otherwise, be lent, hired out or otherwise circulated without the publisher's prior consent in any form of binding or cover other than that in which it is published and without a similar condition, including this condition, being imposed upon the subsequent purchaser.

No part of this publication may be reproduced, stored in a retrieval system, or transmitted, in any form or by any means, electronic, mechanical, photocopying, recording or otherwise, other than for the purposes described in the lessons in this book, without the prior permission of the publisher. This book remains copyright, although permission is granted to copy pages where indicated for classroom distribution and use only in the school which has purchased the book, or by the teacher who has purchased the book, and in accordance with the CLA licensing agreement. Photocopying permission is given only for purchasers and not for borrowers of books from any lending service.

Due to the nature of the web, the publisher cannot guarantee the content or links of any of the websites referred to in this book. It is the responsibility of the reader to assess the suitability of websites. Ensure you read and abide by the terms and conditions of websites when you use material from website links.

Introduction

Getting started

The program should run automatically when you insert the CD-ROM into your CD drive. If it does not, use My Computer to browse to the contents of the CD-ROM and click on the *100 SMART Board™ Lessons* icon.

When the program starts, you are invited to register the product either online or using a PDF registration form. You also have the option to register later. If you select this option, you will be taken, via the Credits screen, to the Main menu.

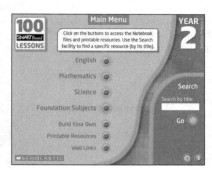

Main menu

The Main menu divides the Notebook files by subject: English, mathematics, science and foundation subjects. Clicking on the appropriate blue button for any of these options will take you to a separate Subject menu (see below for further information). The 'Build your own' file is also accessed through the Main menu (see below). The activity sheets are provided in separate menus. To access these resources, click on Printable resources.

Individual Notebook files or pages can be located using the search facility by keying in words (or part words) from the resource titles in the Search box. Press Go to begin the search. This will bring up a list of the titles that match your search.

The Web Links button takes you to a list of useful web addresses. A help button 📗 is included on all menu screens. The Help notes on the CD-ROM provide a range of general background information and technical support for all users.

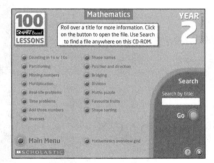

Subject menu

Each Subject menu provides all of the prepared Notebook files for each chapter of the book. Roll over each Notebook file title to reveal a brief description of the contents in a text box at the top of the menu screen; clicking on the blue button will open the Notebook file. Click on Main menu to return to the Main menu screen.

'Build your own' file

Click on this button to open a blank Notebook page and a collection of Gallery objects, which will be saved automatically into the My Content folder in the Gallery. You only need to click on this button the first time you wish to access the 'Build your own' file, as the Gallery objects will remain in the My Content folder on the computer on which the file was opened. To use the facility again, simply open a blank Notebook page and access the images and interactive resources from the same folder under My Content. If you are using the CD-ROM on a different computer you will need to click on the 'Build your own' button again.

Printable resources

The printable PDF activity sheets are also divided by chapter. Click on the subject to find all the activity sheets related to that subject/chapter. The answers to Chapter 2, mathematics, are also provided.

To alternate between the menus on the CD-ROM and other open applications, hold down the Alt key and press the Tab key to switch to the desired application.

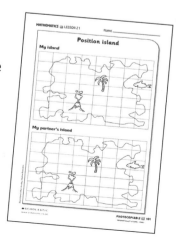

English

The lessons in the English chapter match the objectives in the Primary National Strategy's *Primary Framework for literacy*. These objectives are listed in the curriculum grid below, along with the corresponding objectives from the medium-term planning in the National Literacy Strategy. The curriculum grids in this book are also provided on the accompanying CD-ROM, in editable format, to enable you to integrate the lessons into your planning. The lessons show how the interactive whiteboard can be used to share and introduce new ideas, and actively involve the children in their learning.

Lesson title	PNS objectives	NLS objectives	Expected prior knowledge	Cross-curricular links
Lesson 1: Long vowel phonemes 💿 🅿	Word structure and spelling • Spell with increasing accuracy and confidence, drawing on word recognition and knowledge of word structure, and spelling patterns including common inflections and use of double letters.	W2: To read and spell words containing different spellings of the long vowel phonemes.	• Alternative spellings of long vowel phonemes.	Speaking and listening Objective 15: To listen to each other's views and preferences.
Lesson 2: The *oy* phoneme 💿 🅿	Word structure and spelling • Spell with increasing accuracy and confidence, drawing on word recognition and knowledge of word structure, and spelling patterns including common inflections and use of double letters.	W3: To recognise the common spelling patterns for the vowel phoneme *oy*.	• To use phonic knowledge to read and spell words.	ICT QCA Unit 2A 'Writing stories: communicating information using text'
Lesson 3: The *ow* phoneme 💿	Word structure and spelling • Spell with increasing accuracy and confidence, drawing on word recognition and knowledge of word structure, and spelling patterns including common inflections and use of double letters.	W3: To recognise the common spelling patterns for the vowel phoneme *ow*.	• To use phonic knowledge to read and spell words.	ICT QCA Unit 2A 'Writing stories: communicating information using text'
Lesson 4: Word ending -*ed* 💿	Sentence structure and punctuation • Compose sentences using tense consistently (present and past).	W7: To use the word ending -*ed* (past tense).	• To use the past tense correctly in speech.	History PoS (1a) To place events and objects in chronological order. Speaking and listening Objective17: To tell real and imagined stories using the conventions of familiar story language.
Lesson 5: Linking words	Sentence structure and punctuation • Write simple and compound sentences and begin to use subordination in relation to time and reason.	S2: To find examples of words and phrases that link sentences, such as *after, meanwhile, during*.	• Read text containing linking words.	There are no specific links for this lesson.
Lesson 6: Organisational devices 💿 🅿	Understanding and interpreting texts • Explain organisational features of texts, including layout, diagrams and captions.	S6: To use a variety of simple organisational devices to indicate sequences and relationships.	• Be able to follow simple flow charts.	Design and technology PoS (4b) To understand how mechanisms can be used in different ways.
Lesson 7: Following instructions 💿 🅿	Word recognition Understanding and interpreting texts • Explain organisational features of texts, including layout, diagrams, captions and bullet points.	T13: To read and follow simple instructions.	• Follow verbal instructions.	Design and technology QCA Unit 2B 'Puppets'
Lesson 8: Writing a recount 💿	Sentence structure and punctuation • Write simple and compound sentences and begin to use subordination in relation to time and reason. • Compose sentences using tense consistently (present and past).	T11: To use the language of time to structure a sequence of events.	• Know some language of time.	There are no specific links for this lesson.

Lesson title	PNS objectives	NLS objectives	Expected prior knowledge	Cross-curricular links
Lesson 9: Firework poem	**Creating and shaping texts** • Make adventurous word and language choices appropriate to the style and purpose of the text.	**T12:** To use simple poetry structures and to substitute own ideas, write new lines.	• Know what fireworks are. • Read simple poems.	**RE** QCA Unit 2C 'Celebrations – generic' **History** PoS (6d) To learn about past events from the history of Britain.
Lesson 10: The *air* phoneme	**Word structure and spelling** • Spell with increasing accuracy and confidence, drawing on word recognition and knowledge of word structure, and spelling patterns including common inflections and use of double letters.	**W2:** To recognise the common spelling patterns for the vowel phoneme *air*.	• To use phonic knowledge to read and spell words.	**Speaking and listening** Objective 15: To listen to each other's views and preferences.
Lesson 11: The *er* phoneme	**Word structure and spelling** • Spell with increasing accuracy and confidence, drawing on word recognition and knowledge of word structure, and spelling patterns including common inflections and use of double letters.	**W2:** To recognise the common spelling patterns for the vowel phoneme *er*.	• To use phonic knowledge to read and spell words.	There are no specific links for this lesson.
Lesson 12: The *or* phoneme	**Word structure and spelling** • Spell with increasing accuracy and confidence, drawing on word recognition and knowledge of word structure, and spelling patterns including common inflections and use of double letters.	**W2:** To recognise the common spelling patterns for the vowel phoneme *or*.	• To use phonic knowledge to read and spell words.	There are no specific links for this lesson.
Lesson 13: Compound words	**Word structure and spelling**	**W4:** To split familiar compound words into their component parts.	• Spell simple CVC, CVCC or CCVC words.	There are no specific links for this lesson.
Lesson 14: The prefixes *un-* and *dis-*	**Word structure and spelling** • Spell with increasing accuracy and confidence, drawing on word recognition and knowledge of word structure.	**W8:** To spell words with common prefixes, for example *un* and *dis*, to indicate the negative.	• To spell words that can have *un* or *dis* added.	**Speaking and listening** Objective 15: To listen to each other's views and preferences.
Lesson 15: Antonyms	**Creating and shaping texts** • Make adventurous word and language choices.	**W11:** To use antonyms.	• Give opposites to words.	**Speaking and listening** Objective 23: To work effectively in groups by ensuring each group member takes a turn, challenging, supporting and moving on.
Lesson 16: Past, present and future	**Sentence structure and punctuation** • Compose sentences using tense consistently (present and past).	**S5:** To use verb tenses correctly in speech and writing, such as *catch* and *caught*.	• Speak correctly in the past, present and future.	**Speaking and listening** PoS (4a) To use actions to convey situations.
Lesson 17: Speech marks	**Sentence structure and punctuation**	**S6:** To understand the purpose of speech marks and begin to use them in writing.	• Identify where someone is speaking in a text.	**Speaking and listening** Objective 15: To listen to each other's views and preferences.
Lesson 18: Commas	**Sentence structure and punctuation** • Use commas to separate items in a list.	**S8:** To use commas to separate items in a list.	• Make lists.	**Speaking and listening** Objective 24: To present parts of traditional stories.
Lesson 19: Alphabetical order	**Understanding and interpreting texts** • Explain organisational features of texts, including alphabetical order.	**T16:** To use dictionaries and glossaries to locate words by using initial letter.	• Know the alphabet.	**Geography** QCA Unit 4 'Going to the seaside'
Lesson 20: Cyclical diagrams	**Understanding and interpreting texts** • Explain organisational features of texts, including layout, diagrams and captions. **Creating and shaping texts** • Select from different presentational features to suit particular writing purposes on paper.	**T21:** To produce simple flow charts and cyclical diagrams that explain a process.	• Be able to follow simple flow charts. • Understand the life cycle of an animal.	**Science** QCA Unit 2A 'Health and growth'

Lesson title	PNS objectives	NLS objectives	Expected prior knowledge	Cross-curricular links
Lesson 21: Story setting	**Speaking** • Explain ideas and processes using imaginative and adventurous vocabulary. **Creating and shaping texts** • Make adventurous word and language choices appropriate to the style and purpose of the text. • Select from different presentational features to suit particular writing purposes on paper.	**T13:** To use and re-describe story settings from reading.	• Describe a basic story setting.	**Art and design** QCA Unit 2A 'Picture this!'
Lesson 22: Character profiles	**Creating and shaping texts** • Make adventurous word and language choices appropriate to the style and purpose of the text.	**T14:** To describe characters and write character profiles.	• Create an identity card for a character.	**Speaking and listening** Objective 13: To speak with clarity and intonation when using and reciting texts. **Speaking and listening** Objective 14: To listen to others in class and ask questions.
Lesson 23: Syllables	**Word structure and spelling** • Spell with increasing accuracy and confidence, drawing on word recognition and knowledge of word structure, and spelling patterns including common inflections and use of double letters.	**W2:** To discriminate syllables in multi-syllabic words.	• Hear syllables in words.	**Music** QCA Unit 4 'Feel the pulse – Exploring pulse and rhythm'
Lesson 24: The suffixes -ful and -ly.	**Word structure and spelling** • Spell with increasing accuracy and confidence, drawing on word recognition and knowledge of word structure and spelling patterns.	**W7:** To spell words with common suffixes -ful and -ly.	• To spell words that can have -ful or -ly added.	There are no specific links for this lesson.
Lesson 25: Synonyms	**Understanding and interpreting texts** • Explore how particular words are used, including words and expressions with similar meanings.	**W10:** To use synonyms and other alternative words and phrases that express same or similar meanings.	• Suggest simple alternatives to words with the same meaning.	There are no specific links for this lesson.
Lesson 26: Capital letters and full stops	**Sentence structure and punctuation** • Write simple and compound sentences.	**S5:** Use capital letters and full stops correctly when writing independently.	• Know where to use a full stop and capital letter.	There are no specific links for this lesson.
Lesson 27: Question marks	**Sentence structure and punctuation** • Use question marks.	**S6:** To use wh words typically used to open questions and question marks to write questions.	• Form a question using a question word.	**Science** QCA Unit 2E 'Forces and movement' **Speaking and listening** Objective 16: To adopt appropriate roles in small or large groups and consider alternative courses of action.
Lesson 28: Note taking	**Understanding and interpreting texts** • Draw together ideas and information from across a whole text using simple signposts in the text. **Creating and shaping texts** • Maintain consistency in non-narrative, including purpose and tense.	**T19:** To make simple notes from non-fiction texts. **T21:** To write non-chronological reports.	• Read simple non-fiction texts.	**ICT** QCA Unit 2C 'Finding information'
Lesson 29: Fact or fiction?	**Understanding and interpreting texts** • Draw together ideas and information from across a whole text, using simple signposts in the text. **Creating and shaping texts** • Draw on knowledge and experience of texts in deciding and planning what and how to write.	**T13:** To understand the distinction between fact and fiction and use the terms fact, fiction and non-fiction appropriately.	• Know the difference between fact and story.	There are no specific links for this lesson.
Lesson 30: Riddles	**Creating and shaping texts** • Draw on knowledge and experience of text in deciding and planning what and how to write.	**T11:** To invent own riddles.	• Read and work out simple riddles.	**Speaking and listening** Objective 13: To speak with clarity and use intonation when reading and reciting texts.

Long vowel phonemes

Learning objective
PLS: Word structure and spelling
● Spell with increasing accuracy and confidence, drawing on word recognition and knowledge of word structure, and spelling patterns including common inflections and use of double letters.

Resources
'Phonemes: Part 1' Notebook file; photocopiable page 41 'Long vowel phonemes'; a shared text containing several examples of long vowel phonemes; individual whiteboards and pens; prepared table in five sections (see independent work).

Links to other subjects
Speaking and listening
Objective 15: To listen to each other's views and preferences.
● The children need to listen to each other as they work together to complete the task.

Whiteboard tools
If a microphone is available, use Windows® Sound Recorder (accessed through Start>Programs>Accessories>Entertainment) to record examples of words containing long vowel phonemes. Use the Spotlight tool to focus on words. After you have written words on page 6 of the Notebook file, use the Screen Shade to hide them.

 Pen tray

 Spotlight tool

 Select tool

 Highlighter pen

 On-screen Keyboard

 Screen Shade

Starter
Open the 'Phonemes: Part 1' Notebook file and display page 2. Remind the children of the five long vowel phonemes and give some quick examples of some words that contain them. If a microphone is available, the examples can be recorded using Windows® Sound Recorder.

Read a shared text together (see Resources). Ask the children to listen out for words containing a long vowel phoneme. Invite them to touch their nose every time they think they hear a word containing a long vowel phoneme.

Whole-class shared work
● Ask the children to read the phoneme at the top of each box on page 3. Encourage them to think of other ways to spell these phonemes and to discuss ideas with a partner.
● Take the cards out of the phonemes box in turn. Use voting methods to sort the words. Invite the children to decide what sound each one makes, then drag the phonemes into the correct boxes.
● Using the word wall on page 4, ask the children to read each word. Use the Spotlight tool to focus on one word at a time.
● Pick out the long vowel phoneme in each word, emphasising the sound it makes within the word. Invite volunteers to come to the whiteboard to highlight the long vowel phonemes.
● Sound out some of the words as examples.
● Provide the children with individual whiteboards and, using page 5 which shows pictures of objects whose names contain a long vowel phoneme, challenge the children to spell the words. Invite individuals to use a Pen from the Pen tray to write the words into the boxes beneath the pictures. Then reveal the correct answers by using the Eraser to rub over the area below each white box.

Independent work
● Give each group a set of cards prepared from photocopiable page 41. Ask the children to work together to sort the cards into five groups according to the long vowel sound that they contain.
● Give the children a table divided into five sections: one for each long vowel sound. Ask them to write the words into the correct column of the table.
● Encourage the children to insert the correct spelling of the phoneme into the words.
● Challenge them to think of more words to add to their tables, or to put the words they have sorted into sentences.
● Supply less confident learners with cards that contain only one spelling of each phoneme so that they only have to decide which phoneme to use, and not which spelling.

Plenary
● Read more of the shared text with the children. Ask them to listen out for any words containing a long vowel phoneme. Ask the children to write these on page 6 of the Notebook file and highlight the long vowel phonemes.
● Remove all but five words, then hide the page with the Screen Shade and ask the children to write them on individual whiteboards. Reveal the board again to check spellings.

The *oy* phoneme

Learning objective
PLS: Word structure and spelling
● Spell with increasing accuracy and confidence, drawing on word recognition and knowledge of word structure, and spelling patterns including common inflections and use of double letters.

Resources
'Phonemes: Part 1' Notebook file; photocopiable page 42 'oy wordsearch'; shared text containing examples of the *oy* phoneme; individual whiteboards and pens.

Links to other subjects
ICT
QCA Unit 2A 'Writing stories: communicating information using text'
● Ask the children to make a list of words containing the *oy* phoneme. Show them how to use the return key to put each word on a new line to form a vertical list.

Starter
Open the 'Phonemes: Part 1' Notebook file and display page 7. Introduce the *oy* phoneme to the children and give some quick examples of words that contain it. If a microphone is available, the examples can be recorded using Windows® Sound Recorder.

Ask the children to listen out for words containing the *oy* phoneme as you read the shared text (see Resources) together with the class. Tell them to touch their nose every time they think they hear a word containing the phoneme.

Whole-class shared work
● Go to page 8 and look at the two spellings of the *oy* phoneme.
● In pairs, ask the children to think of five words containing the *oy* phoneme. Tell them to list them on their individual whiteboards.
● Sort the pictures of the *oy* phoneme words on page 8 onto either the *oy* or *oi* spelling tower by dragging and dropping them. (The pictures are: *oil, toy, coins* and *boy*.)
● Challenge the children to write each word on their individual whiteboards as they are sorted. Emphasise the spelling pattern used.
● Invite children to share their examples and add them to the tower.
● Read all of the words on page 9 and ask the children to highlight the words that contain an *oy* phoneme. Focus on individual words with the Spotlight tool .
● Ask the children to sort the words into *oy* or *oi* spellings on their individual whiteboards.

Independent work
● Give each child a copy of photocopiable page 42. Ask them to find ten words that contain an *oy* phoneme. The words are written either left to right or top to bottom.
● Ensure that the children list the words on the right-hand side of the page as they locate them.
● Encourage them to look for places where *oi* and *oy* are together and then see if there is a word around them.
● Provide less confident learners with a list of words to look for.
● Challenge the children who manage to find all ten words to put the words into sentences. Encourage them to check that they are spelling the words correctly when using them in sentences.

Plenary
● Return to the Notebook file and complete the crossword on page 10. Ask the children to read the clues and think of an answer. Explain that all of the answers will be words that contain the *oy* phoneme.
● Tell the children to write their answers on their individual whiteboards, thinking carefully about the spelling of the words. Invite volunteers to complete each answer by dragging the appropriate letters into the boxes.
● Check the answers by pressing the red answer button.

Whiteboard tools
If a microphone is available, record examples of the *oy* phoneme with Windows® Sound Recorder (accessed through Start>Programs>Accessories>Entertainment). Use a Highlighter pen to highlight phonemes, and the Spotlight tool to focus on individual words.

 Pen tray

 Select tool

 On-screen Keyboard

 Spotlight tool

 Highlighter pen

The *ow* phoneme

Learning objective
PLS: Word structure and spelling
● Spell with increasing accuracy and confidence, drawing on word recognition and knowledge of word structure, and spelling patterns including common inflections and use of double letters.

Resources
'Phonemes: Part 1' Notebook file; a shared text containing examples of the *ow* phoneme; some prepared cards with simple sentences including words containing the *ow* phoneme omitted, for the children to complete; individual whiteboards and pens.

Links to other subjects
ICT
QCA Unit 2A 'Writing stories: communicating information using text'
● Let the children carry out the independent activity on screen, deleting the line space gaps and replacing them with suitable words.

Whiteboard tools
If a microphone is available, record examples of the *ow* phoneme with Windows® Sound Recorder (accessed through Start>Programs> Accessories>Entertainment). Use the Spotlight tool to focus on individual words. Use a Pen from the Pen tray to add the answers to the word puzzle on page 14.

 Pen tray

 Select tool

 On-screen Keyboard

 Spotlight tool

 Highlighter pen

Starter
Open the 'Phonemes: Part 1' Notebook file and display page 11. Introduce the *ow* phoneme to the children and give some quick examples of words that contain it. If a microphone is available, the examples can be recorded using Windows® Sound Recorder.

Ask the children to listen out for words containing the *ow* phoneme when reading the shared text (see Resources) together. Invite them to touch their nose every time they think they hear a word containing the phoneme.

Whole-class shared work
● Go to page 12 and look at the two spellings of the *ow* phoneme.
● Working in pairs, challenge the children to think of five words containing the *ow* phoneme. Ask them to list them on their individual whiteboards.
● Sort the pictures of *ow* phoneme words into either the *ow* or *ou* box on page 12. This could be done using voting methods. Drag and drop the pictures into the correct boxes.
● Challenge the children to write each word as they are sorted and emphasise the spelling pattern used.
● Invite children to share their examples. Add these to the appropriate *ow* phoneme box.
● Read all of the words on page 13. Use the Spotlight tool to focus on one word at a time and then ask the children to highlight the words that contain the *ow* phoneme.
● Ask the children to sort the words into *ow* or *ou* spellings on their individual whiteboards.

Independent work
● Give each group a set of prepared cards (see Resources). Tell them that a word containing the *ow* phoneme has been omitted from each sentence and replaced with a gap.
● Ask the children to work in pairs to decide which word has been omitted and then rewrite the sentence with the word included.
● Regularly remind the children that the missing words are all words containing the *ow* phoneme.
● Supply less confident learners with a list of possible words to be placed in the gaps, or supply them with the initial sound for the missing word on the card.
● Challenge more confident learners by including some cards with other phonemes missing (such as the long vowel phonemes) but ensure that it is made clear to them that you have done this.

Plenary
● Return to the Notebook file and complete the wordsearch on page 14. Ask the children to look for words containing the *ow* phoneme in the wordsearch. Explain that there are six words altogether.
● Tell the children to write the words they find on their individual whiteboards, copying the spelling of the word carefully.
● Once they have done this, invite individuals to come to the whiteboard and highlight the words, then write them in the white boxes on the right-hand side of the page.
● Finally, reveal the correct answers by pulling the tab across from the left-hand side of the page.

Word ending -*ed*

Learning objective
PNS: Sentence structure and punctuation
● Compose sentences using tense consistently (present and past).

Resources
'Past tense' Notebook file; prepared cards with sentences written on them in the present tense that can be turned into the past tense; individual whiteboards and pens.

Links to other subjects
History
PoS (1a) To place events and objects in chronological order.
● Ask the children to use the past tense to make a recount of a famous person's life grammatically correct.
Speaking and listening
Objective 17: To tell real and imagined stories using the conventions of familiar story language.
● Ask the children to retell a story and encourage them to use the past tense to retell it.

Starter
Open the 'Past tense' Notebook file and go to page 2. Invite some of the children to talk about what they did last night. As they speak, make a list of the verbs they use (such as *walked*, *played*). Ask the children if they notice anything that the words have in common. Hopefully the children will notice that most of the words end in -*ed*. Tell them that this is because these things happened in the past.

Whole-class shared work
● Explain to the children that verbs (action words) change depending on when the action happened. Demonstrate this with an example.
● Read the six words on page 3. Share the rule that these words follow when they are used in the past tense.
● Ask the children to choose one of the words and write it in the past tense on an individual whiteboard.
● Invite some of the children to move the orange circle over the words to check their answers.
● Encourage the children to try to verbally put the words into past tense sentences.
● Repeat this process with the other rules illustrated on pages 4 to 7.
● Together, read the present tense sentences on page 8 and explain to the children that their task is to put them into the past tense. Ask them to highlight the verbs in each sentence.
● Look closely at the highlighted words and consider whether those words need to be changed to put the sentences in the past tense.
● Double-press on the text and change the correctly highlighted words into the past tense as appropriate using the On-screen Keyboard ▭ . Then move the orange rectangle to reveal the correct answers under each sentence.

Independent work
● Give the children prepared cards (see Resources) with present tense sentences on them. Ask them to rewrite the sentences in the past tense, as though the action happened yesterday.
● Support less confident learners by giving them only verbs that either need an -*ed* adding or an *e* removing and then -*ed* adding.
● Challenge more confident learners by giving them irregular verbs such as *sleep*, *run* and *go*.

Plenary
● Ask every child to write a sentence about something they did last weekend, ensuring that they write the verb correctly in the past tense. On page 9, complete the table of the five rules that a verb can follow in the past tense. For example: add -*ed*, remove the -*e*, and add -*ed*.
● Ask the children to look at the verb in their sentence and decide which rule it follows, then ask them to put their verbs in the correct group in the table.
● Use page 10 to assess whether the children understand the rules. Press on the column headings to go to the appropriate pages (3–7) to remind children of the rules. Return to page 10 by selecting it in the Page Sorter ▭ . Decide on the correct rule for each word and drag the words into the appropriate column.

Whiteboard tools
Double-press on the text and use the On-screen Keyboard, accessed through the Pen tray or the SMART Board tools menu, to put the sentences into the past tense.

 Pen tray

 Select tool

 Highlighter pen

 On-screen Keyboard

▭ Page Sorter

Linking words

Learning objective
PNS: Sentence structure and punctuation
● Write simple and compound sentences and begin to use subordination in relation to time and reason.

Resources
Prepare a Notebook file: type in a passage including lots of linking words. Prepare a set of cards, each with a different linking word written on it; write two sentences which could be joined with a linking word on card (see Starter); blank piece of card; pen.

Links to other subjects
There are no specific links for this lesson.

Starter
On two long pieces of card, write two sentences that may be joined by a linking word. Ask two children to hold them up, side by side. Ask another child to hold up a blank piece of card between the two sentences. Invite the children to think of words that could be written on the card to create one larger sentence.

Whole-class shared work
● Open the prepared file of text (see Resources) and read through the passage as a class. Pause to work out any unfamiliar words and ascertain the meaning of any new words.
● Explain that there is a special type of word called a *linking word* or a *connective* that can be used to join two sentences together.
● Highlight a linking word in the passage that the children have just read and show the two sentences either side of it. For example: *The monkey sat in the tree* **while** *he ate a banana.*
● Explain that although these two sentences could stand alone and make sense, by adding the linking word the sentence is more interesting.
● Ask pairs of children to locate the rest of the linking words in the passage. Give them the opportunity to highlight the linking words on the whiteboard.
● Challenge the children to use the linking words found in a sentence of their own.

Independent work
● Ask the children to retell a story that they have read recently. Set them a challenge to use at least three linking words in their story. Refer back to the linking words highlighted on the whiteboard to provide ideas.
● Invite the children to write or underline the linking words in a different colour, to motivate them to meet their challenge.
● Give less confident learners the prepared cards (see Resources) with linking words written on them. Ask them to pick a card and put the word on the card into a sentence. Show them that their sentences can be split into two smaller sentences if the linking word is omitted.
● Provide an extra challenge for more confident learners by asking them to include at least five linking words.

Plenary
● Encourage the children to check their work to see if they have met the challenge of including at least three linking words. If not, ask them to add them to their work at this point.
● Read out one child's piece of work and invite the others to listen carefully to see if they hear the linking words. Write part of another child's work in your prepared Notebook file and invite individuals to come to the whiteboard and highlight the linking words.

Whiteboard tools

 Pen tray

 Select tool

 Highlighter pen

Organisational devices

Learning objective
PNS: Understanding and interpreting texts
● Explain organisational features of texts, including layout, diagrams and captions.

Resources
'Organisational devices' Notebook file; photocopiable page 43 'Making a pizza'; construction kits; scissors; paper; felt-tipped pens.

Links to other subjects
Design and technology
PoS (4b) To understand how mechanisms can be used in different ways.
● The children can follow plans or instructions to create something that uses a similar mechanism when carrying out their initial research into a new product.

Starter
Display page 2 of the 'Organisational devices' Notebook file. Ask the children to work in pairs. Using a construction kit, ask one child in each pair to create a simple model using only five pieces of the kit – without showing their partner. Ask these children to give verbal instructions to their partner so that they can make a replica of the model.

Invite the children to assess how easy or difficult they found this task. Ask: *Can you think of anything that would have made it easier?* Encourage suggestions (for example, it may have been easier with visual instructions). Write these suggestions on the Notebook page.

Whole-class shared work
● Look at the pictures on page 3 of the Notebook file. Talk about the pictures with the children.
● Explain that the pictures could be used to create a set of instructions for how to make a Plasticine model. Ask the children to consider how to present these instructions.
● Encourage them to use the arrows to show the order of the instructions.
● Let them add numbers if they suggest this.
● Repeat the process on page 4, but this time emphasise the importance of putting the pictures in the correct order.
● Show the children that it is not possible to fit all of the pictures in a line across the page. Show concern that if you put the pictures on two or three lines they may be difficult to follow. Ask the children to suggest what to do so that the instructions are still easy to follow. Did they choose to order and display the pictures in a different way to the previous page?
● Ask the children to evaluate, with a partner, whether the instructions are organised in a useful and easy-to-follow way. Ask them to suggest any improvements.

Independent work
● Give each child a copy of photocopiable page 43. Ask them to cut out and then order the instructions.
● Supply paper and felt-tipped pens. Ask the children to consider how to organise the instructions to show clearly how the pizza should be made.
● Remind them that they could use arrows, numbers and boxes.
● Challenge more confident learners to write their own instructions, as well as organising these clearly on the page.

Plenary
● Discuss some of the work created and evaluate whether it is clear to follow.
● Show the children page 5 of the Notebook file and ask them to read each of the instructions. Invite them to work in pairs to decide the order in which the instructions should be followed. Ask: *How can we show this clearly?*
● Invite individuals to move the instructions on the screen so that they can be clearly followed. The children could vote to decide on the correct place in the order for each instruction.

Whiteboard tools
Use the Select tool to place the arrows and pictures into the correct positions.

 Pen tray

 Select tool

Following instructions

Learning objective
PNS: Word recognition
PNS: Understanding and interpreting texts
● Explain organisational features of texts, including layout, diagrams, captions and bullet points.

Resources
'Following instructions' Notebook file; photocopiable page 44 'How to make a stick puppet'; bread; butter; cheese; plate; knife; white card; sticky tape; straws; felt-tipped pens; scissors; pencils.

Links to other subjects
Design and technology
QCA Unit 2B 'Puppets'
● Develop this lesson by looking at different types of puppets and exploring how they are made.

Starter
Open the 'Following instructions' Notebook file and display page 2. Ask what an instruction is. Give the children simple instructions and let them carry them out. For example, *Put your left hand on your head.* Point out that an instruction is giving an order and it makes you sound bossy!

Ask the children to tell a partner who might need to give instructions, and why. Talk about giving instructions – consider how a teacher gives instructions to tell the children what work to do and how the children might give each other instructions to teach a friend a new game, and so on. Make notes on page 2, if required.

Whole-class shared work
● Read the instructions on page 3. Discuss how the instructions are presented: for example, they are numbered instructions, written in the order they are to be carried out.
● Ask the children to identify the *bossy words* (verbs) in the instructions and invite individuals to come to the whiteboard and highlight them on the Notebook page.
● Read each instruction again, one at a time, and allow a child to carry out each of the steps.
● When the sandwich is made, evaluate the finished product. Ask: *Were the instructions detailed enough? Did the sandwich turn out the way you expected it to?*
● Show the children page 4. Give them the opportunity to read each instruction.
● Challenge them to work out the order in which the instructions should be. Invite children to come to the board to re-arrange them so that they are correct.
● Once they have done this, read the instructions together to check that they are ordered correctly.

Independent work
● Give each child a copy of photocopiable page 44. Ask them to read it carefully to themselves.
● Put white card, sticky tape, straws, scissors, pencils and felt-tipped pens on each table.
● Challenge the children to follow the instructions on their sheet to create a stick puppet.
● Point out key structural features of the instructions as you work with the children (such as *bossy words, numbered points* and so on).
● Support less confident learners with reading any tricky words while encouraging them to have a go at reading key words independently.
● Set a challenge for more confident learners by muddling up the instructions and asking them to put these into the correct order before they begin to follow them.

Plenary
● Ask the children to explain what an instruction sentence needs.
● Show the children page 5 and ask them to read each statement. Challenge them to identify which of the statements are instructions. Allow them to highlight the statements which they believe are instructions. The sentences can then be sorted into two groups.
● Discuss the children's choices together as a class.

Whiteboard tools
 Pen tray

 Select tool

 Highlighter pen

Writing a recount

Learning objectives
PNS: Sentence structure and punctuation
● Write simple and compound sentences and begin to use subordination in relation to time and reason.
● Compose sentences using tense consistently (present and past).

Resources
'Recount' Notebook file; paper; pencils.

Links to other subjects
There are no specific links for this lesson.

Starter
Open the 'Recount' Notebook file and read page 2 together. Introduce the text as a *recount*, explain that a recount gives a chronological account of an event that has taken place. Point out a time connective in the text (such as *next* or *then*) and explain that a time connective is a linking word that can be used to give more information about the time that something happened. Together, identify other time connectives in the text and highlight them.

Whole-class shared work
● Ask the children to describe to a partner how they get ready for school – from waking up, to leaving the house.
● Display the pictures on page 3. Ask the children to describe what is happening in each one.
● Explain to the children that they are going to write a recount of how the boy in the picture (Charlie) got ready for school this morning.
● Discuss how a recount is always written in chronological order, then allow the children time to order the pictures correctly on the board. Talk about the words at the bottom of the page, which will help in writing the recount.
● Work as a class to write a recount of how Charlie got ready for school this morning, using page 4 of the Notebook file.
● Take suggestions from the children and model good recount writing. Emphasise that a recount is written in the past tense, in chronological order and includes time connectives.
● Read back the finished recount and evaluate whether these criteria have been met.

Independent work
● Ask the children to write a recount of a simple, recent event such as planting a seed.
● Suggest that they start by drawing up a simple list of five main events that they are going to include in their recount.
● Refer the children back to the time connectives discovered in the Starter and challenge them to use at least five time connectives in their recount.
● Give less confident learners pictures of the main events that they need to include, and a list of time connectives to support their writing.

Plenary
● Give the children time to check their work and ask them to use a coloured pencil to underline any time connectives they have used. Ask them to check that they have included their target of five time connectives in their work.
● Invite some of the children to read out their recounts. The rest of the class should raise their hands every time they hear a time connective being used. List these on page 5 of the Notebook file. Use this opportunity to assess the children's understanding of time connectives.
● Page 6 offers further opportunities to understand time connectives.

Whiteboard tools
Use a Pen from the Pen tray or the On-screen Keyboard, accessed through the Pen tray or the SMART Board tools menu, to write the class recount on the whiteboard.

 Pen tray

 Highlighter pen

 Select tool

 On-screen Keyboard

Firework poem

Learning objective
PNS: Creating and shaping texts
● Make adventurous word and language choices appropriate to the style and purpose of the text.

Resources
'Poems and riddles' Notebook file; fireworks video; paper; pencils; black paper; chalk or oil pastels.

Links to other subjects
History
PoS (6d) To learn about past events from the history of Britain.
● Carry out this English lesson as part of a project close to Bonfire night or Divali. Use the opportunity to learn about when and why the Gunpowder Plot took place.
Religious education
QCA Unit 2C 'Celebrations – generic'
● Discuss how religions usually involve celebrations and that festivals are occasions for remembering particular events.
● Discuss how light is used as a symbol during festivals.

Starter
With the class, watch a video of some fireworks. Ask the children to observe the different sights and sounds. Suggest that they think of interesting words to describe what they can see (such as *whoosh* and *twinkle*). After they have finished watching the video, invite them to talk about what they saw and heard with a partner. Suggest that they could also describe any firework displays that they have seen to each other.

Whole-class shared work
● Open the 'Poems and riddles' Notebook file. Show the children the shape poem on page 2.
● Ask the children to describe what they can see. If necessary, point out the shape of the Catherine wheel and the launching and exploding rocket.
● Read the poem with the children, encouraging them to add expression. For example, shout the word *bang* and hiss the word *fizz*.
● Move back and forth between pages 2, 3 and 4 to see the poem change to give the effect of fireworks.
● Comment on the type of words used in the poem and how they were used. Ensure that the children realise that the words describe either the sound or appearance of a firework.
● Go to page 5 of the Notebook file. Ask the children to read the words at the bottom of the page. Invite them to sort the words into two boxes: words that describe the sound and words that describe the appearance of the fireworks. If necessary, use voting methods to decide on how to sort the words.
● Clarify the meaning of any words that the children are unsure about.
● Use page 6 to create a class firework poem. Suggest to the children that they could use the words from page 5 and remind them of the shapes and sounds from the video.
● Support the children in rotating, resizing and altering the colour of the text as necessary. Show them how to use the Shapes and Lines tools to illustrate their class poem if they wish to do so.

Independent work
● Tell the children that they are going to produce a firework shape poem. Encourage them to make a list of possible words on some scrap paper.
● Give each child a sheet of black paper and some chalk or oil pastels to create the final poem (make the pastel tips as sharp as possible).
● Suggest that the children use a pencil first to draw a faint outline of the firework shapes that their words are going to follow.
● Support less confident learners with suggestions about appropriate word choices and provide a prepared pencil outline template for them if necessary.

Plenary
● Take a small sample of the children's work and scan it into the computer. Display the work using the whiteboard software; selected examples can be added to page 7 of the Notebook file.
● Invite the class to comment on the poems. Write some of these comments around the pictures.
● Evaluate the shapes and vocabulary used within the poems. Encourage positive comments from the children.

Whiteboard tools
Upload digital pictures of the children's work by selecting Insert, then Picture File, and browsing to where you have saved the images.

 Pen tray

 Select tool

 On-screen Keyboard

 Lines tool

 Shapes tool

The *air* phoneme

Learning objective
PNS: Word structure and spelling
● Spell with increasing accuracy and confidence, drawing on word recognition and knowledge of word structure, and spelling patterns including common inflections and use of double letters.

Resources
'Phonemes: Part 2' Notebook file; photocopiable page 45 'The *air* phoneme' copied onto card and cut up to make individual word cards; shared text containing examples of the *air* phoneme; individual whiteboards and pens; pencils; paper; large sign for each spelling (see Plenary).

Links to other subjects
Speaking and listening
Objective 15: To listen to each other's views and preferences.
● The children are encouraged to use these skills when working as a group to discuss the choices they have made in the independent activity.

Starter
Display page 2 of the Notebook file. Introduce the *air* phoneme to the children and give some quick examples of words that contain it. If a microphone is available, the examples can be recorded using Windows® Sound Recorder.

Read the shared text (see Resources) together and ask the children to listen out for words containing the *air* phoneme as they read. Tell them to touch their nose every time they think they hear a word containing the phoneme.

Whole-class shared work
● Ask the children to think of all the ways that the *air* phoneme can be spelled *(air, ere, ear, are)* and write these on page 2 for them to see.
● Read the sentence on page 3. Ask the children to look carefully at each spelling of the word *bear*. Explain that each word sounds the same but only one is correct.
● Ask the children to discuss with a partner which spelling is correct. Invite a volunteer to come to the board and press on a word to check the answer. This will produce a cheer or a groan, depending on whether they are right or wrong. Alternatively use the Eraser to rub over the space to reveal the missing word in the sentence.
● Repeat this activity on pages 4 to 7.
● With the children in pairs and using page 8, read out the crossword clues, one at a time. Ask the children to write down their answers on their individual whiteboards, considering the spellings carefully.
● Each time, invite a different child to place the answer into the crossword grid by dragging the letters from the foot of the page and dropping them into the appropriate positions in the grid.
● Repeat this until the whole crossword is completed.

Independent work
● Give each group a set of word cards prepared from photocopiable page 45.
● Ask the children to work together as a group to sort the cards into two piles: words that are spelled correctly and words that are spelled incorrectly.
● Encourage the children to discuss choices and work out any disagreements as a group.
● Allow them time to list the correctly spelled words into a table and then ask them to put the words into sentences.
● Give the children regular reminders to check that they have spelled the words containing the *air* phoneme correctly.
● Challenge more confident learners to think of other words containing the *air* phoneme.

Whiteboard tools
Use Windows® Sound Recorder to record examples of the *air* phoneme. Use the Eraser from the Pen tray to reveal the missing words on pages 3 to 7.

 Pen tray

 Select tool

Plenary
● Go into the hall and place a large sign displaying one of the spellings of the *air* phoneme *(air, ere, ear, are)* on each wall.
● Ask the children to move around the hall quietly and when you say a word, choose which spelling of the *air* phoneme the word contains by moving to the wall displaying that spelling.
● Use this game as an opportunity to assess which children are making correct, independent decisions and which require more teaching in this area.

The *er* phoneme

Learning objective
PNS: Word structure and spelling
● Spell with increasing accuracy and confidence, drawing on word recognition and knowledge of word structure, and spelling patterns including common inflections and use of double letters.

Resources
'Phonemes: Part 2' Notebook file; photocopiable page 46 '*er* phoneme crossword'; a shared text containing examples of the *er* phoneme; prepared A5-size cards with single letters on each that can be arranged to spell a word containing an *er* phoneme; individual whiteboards and pens; dictionaries; squared paper for more confident learners.

Links to other subjects
There are no specific links for this lesson.

Whiteboard tools
Use Windows® Sound Recorder (accessed through Start>Programs>Accessories> Entertainment) to record examples of the *er* phoneme. Use the Spotlight tool to focus on individual words.

 Pen tray

 Select tool

 Spotlight tool

 Highlighter pen

Starter
Open the 'Phonemes: Part 2' Notebook file and display page 9. Introduce the *er* phoneme to the children and give some quick examples of words that contain it. If a microphone is available, the examples can be recorded using Windows® Sound Recorder.

Ask the children to listen out for words containing the *er* phoneme when reading the shared text (see Resources) together. Tell them to touch their nose every time they think they hear a word containing the phoneme.

Whole-class shared work
● Look at the three different ways to write the *er* phoneme on page 10.
● Read the sentence on page 10 with the children and ask them to decide, with a partner, which spelling of the *er* phoneme is the correct one to fill the gap in the word.
● Allow a child to press on the yellow box of their choice on the whiteboard to see if their answer was correct. They will hear a cheer or a groan, depending on whether their choice was right or wrong.
● When they have found the correct answer, they can either drag the red box into the word or use the Eraser to check the answer.
● Complete the challenges on pages 11 to 15 in the same way.
● Using the word wall on page 16, ask the children to read each word as you focus on a word at a time with the Spotlight tool .
● Then look at the whole wall and invite a different child each time to highlight the *er* phoneme in each word.
● Go to page 17 and challenge the children to spell words containing the *er* phoneme correctly on their individual whiteboards. Allow some children to use a Pen from the Pen tray to write the words into the boxes beneath the pictures.
● Once they have done this, use the Eraser to reveal the correct answers beneath each box.

Independent work
● Give each similar-ability pair of children a copy of photocopiable page 46 to work on together.
● Remind the children that all of the answers will contain an *er* phoneme. Show them how to use a dictionary to check the spelling of a word if they are unsure which *er* phoneme a word contains.
● Fill in the initial letter of each clue to help support less confident learners.
● Supply more confident learners with squared paper and challenge them to make their own *er* phoneme crossword for a friend.

Plenary
● Give each group a set of prepared cards (see Resources) and ask them to arrange the cards so that they spell out a word containing an *er* phoneme. Tell them to hold up their cards so that the other groups can check the spelling of the word. Discuss any misconceptions or errors.
● Give each group a list of five anagrams of words containing the *er* phoneme to solve. Remind the children to look for the *er* phoneme first to give them a clue.

The *or* phoneme

Learning objective
PNS: Word structure and spelling
● Spell with increasing accuracy and confidence, drawing on word recognition and knowledge of word structure, and spelling patterns including common inflections and use of double letters.

Resources
'Phonemes: Part 2' Notebook file; prepared word cards – most words should contain the *or* phoneme, with a few cards displaying words containing other recently learned phonemes; a shared text containing the *or* phoneme; individual whiteboards and pens; dictionaries; pencils; paper.

Links to other subjects
There are no specific links for this lesson.

Starter
Open the 'Phonemes: Part 2' Notebook file and display page 18. Introduce the *or* phoneme to the children and give some quick examples of words that contain it. If a microphone is available, the examples can be recorded using Windows® Sound Recorder.

Ask the children to listen out for words containing the *or* phoneme when reading the shared text together. Tell them to touch their nose every time they think they hear a word containing the phoneme.

Whole-class shared work
● Look at the five different ways to write the *or* phoneme on page 19.
● Drag a card from the Words box and ask a child to read the word. Ask the children to decide which spelling of the *or* phoneme the word belongs to and then invite an individual to drag the word into the correct place.
● Once all of the cards have been sorted, challenge the children, in pairs, to think of three more words containing an *or* phoneme. Supply individual whiteboards so that the children can record their suggestions. Discuss how to spell the words.
● Show the children a dictionary and ask them what it can be used for. Explain how to locate a word in a dictionary. Look up the meaning of some of the words on the board.
● Challenge a few children to locate words in a dictionary. Ask them to explain to the class what they did to find the word.

Independent work
● Give each group a set of prepared cards (see Resources). Ask the children to sort out the words that contain an *or* phoneme and make sure that they know what each card says.
● Give the children suitable dictionaries and ask them to look up a definition for each of the words containing an *or* phoneme.
● After reading the definition for the word, encourage the children to write down the word with their own definition.
● As an extra challenge for more confident learners, ask them to put the words into alphabetical order before they write the definitions.

Plenary
● Return to the Notebook file and complete the wordsearch on page 20. Ask the children to look for words containing the *or* phoneme in the wordsearch. Explain that there are six words altogether.
● Tell the children to write the words they find on their individual whiteboards, copying the spelling of the word carefully.
● Once they have done this, invite volunteers to come to the whiteboard, highlight the words and write them into the boxes provided on the page. The correct answers can be checked by pressing the red arrow at the top of the screen.

Whiteboard tools
Use Windows® Sound Recorder (accessed through Start>Programs>Accessories> Entertainment) to record examples of the *or* phoneme.

 Pen tray

 Select tool

 Highlighter pen

Compound words

Learning objective
PNS: Word structure and spelling

Resources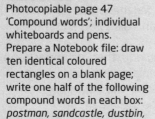
Photocopiable page 47 'Compound words'; individual whiteboards and pens. Prepare a Notebook file: draw ten identical coloured rectangles on a blank page; write one half of the following compound words in each box: *postman, sandcastle, dustbin, newspaper, handbag*; group the boxes and the words that they contain so that they can move together as one object.

Links to other subjects
There are no specific links for this lesson.

Starter
Show the children the following words: *snowman, raincoat, football*. Ask them to explain what each of these objects are. Try to elicit a response such as: *a snowman is a man made of snow*. Ask the children what they notice about each of the words. Point out that all of the words are made by putting two words together. For example: rain + coat = raincoat.

Whole-class shared work
● Introduce the term *compound word* as a word that is made when two smaller words are joined together. Give the children a few examples and ask them if they can think of any ideas of their own.
● Open the prepared Notebook file (see Resources) and read the words with the children.
● Explain that each of the words on the whiteboard is one half of a compound word and that by joining two words together the children can create a set of compound words.
● Ask the children to work in pairs on their individual whiteboards to write down as many of the compound words as they can find.
● If necessary, give less confident learners actual cards with the words on to manipulate.
● Allow some children to drag and drop the words on the whiteboard to create the compound words.
● Encourage the class to explain the meaning of each compound word as it is created.

Independent work
● Provide each pair of children with a set of cards prepared from photocopiable page 47.
● Lay the cards face down on the table in an array of 4 × 5. Tell the children to take turns to reveal two cards and see if they form a compound word. The children may keep the words that create a compound word, or put back words that do not go together.
● To simplify the task for less confident learners, provide fewer cards to begin with. For example, use an array of 3 × 4 cards.
● Challenge more confident learners to write sentences containing the compound words found.

Plenary
● Give each child a card with one half of a compound word on it and ask them to locate the other half of their word. Once the children have paired up to make words, ask the class to vote on whether they think the words created are real compound words or not.
● List the real compound words made. Set the children a challenge to try to add other compound words to the list over the next few weeks.

Whiteboard tools
Use the Shapes tool to draw the rectangles in the prepared Notebook file, and the Text tool to add the compound words. Group the words and rectangles by selecting Grouping>Group from one of the dropdown menus.

 Pen tray

 Select tool

 A Text tool

 Shapes tool

The prefixes *un-* and *dis-*

Learning objective
PNS: Word structure and spelling
● Spell with increasing accuracy and confidence, drawing on word recognition and knowledge of word structure.

Resources
'Prefixes and suffixes' Notebook file; prepared sets of 15 cards containing words that can have the prefixes *un-* or *dis-* added to them to form the negative (such as *lucky* and *agree*); individual whiteboards and pens; pencils; paper.

Links to other subjects
Speaking and listening
Objective 15: To listen to each other's views and preferences.
● The children can practise listening to and taking account of the views of others as they check their own work against the work of others.

Starter
Open page 2 of the 'Prefixes and suffixes' Notebook file. Ask the children to think of words that mean the opposite of *happy*. List all of the ideas given, but ensure that *unhappy* is in the list. Repeat this for the words *kind, honest* and *agree*, again ensuring that *unkind, dishonest* and *disagree* are in their respective lists.

Using these lists, first point out *unhappy* and *unkind*, then *dishonest* and *disagree*, and ask the children if they notice anything in particular about these words. Elicit that *un-* or *dis-* have been added to the beginnings of these words to change them into words of the opposite meaning.

Whole-class shared work
● Tell the children that *un-* and *dis-* are both prefixes that can be added to the beginning of words to create new words. Explain that these particular prefixes create a new word that means the opposite (or negative) of the original word.
● With the class, read the words at the bottom of page 3. Check that all the children understand the meaning of the words. Put the words into context in a sentence if necessary.
● Ask the children to talk with a partner to decide which prefix should be added to which word to create the negative of it.
● Invite individuals to come to the whiteboard and drag the words into the correct boxes to check the answers. When the words are dragged into the boxes the prefixes will magically appear.
● Point out that although *un-* and *dis-* can both be added to *like* and *able*, the two different prefixes give the words two different meanings. Ensure that the children understand that they must choose the correct prefix for the context of the sentence.

Independent work
● Give each group a set of prepared cards (see Resources).
● Ask the children to add an appropriate prefix (*un-* or *dis-*) to the words to create new words with opposite meanings.
● Invite the children to write sentences containing the new words.
● Encourage the children to self-check their work with the rest of their group. Invite them to discuss any words on which they have a difference of opinion.

Plenary
● Show the children page 4 of the Notebook file. Read the sentences with them. Explain that the underlined words need to have a prefix added to them in order to give the sentence the opposite meaning.
● Give the children an opportunity to write down their ideas for each sentence on their individual whiteboards.
● Once they have done this, invite volunteers to come to the whiteboard and drag a prefix into the appropriate space. Discuss any errors and misconceptions together. Then pull the tab on the left-hand side across the screen to reveal the answers.

Whiteboard tools
 Pen tray

 Select tool

Antonyms

Learning objective
PNS: Creating and shaping texts
● Make adventurous word and language choices.

Resources ⊙ Ⓟ
'Antonyms and synonyms' Notebook file; photocopiable page 48 'Antonym dominoes', copied onto card and cut along the dotted lines into a set of 24 dominoes; individual whiteboards and pens.

Links to other subjects
Speaking and listening
Objective 23: To work effectively in groups by ensuring each group member takes a turn, challenging, supporting and moving on.
● The children must work together and take it in turns to play the game. They are encouraged to question the decisions of other players if they do not agree with them.

Starter
Open the 'Antonyms and synonyms' Notebook file and go to page 2. Show the children the picture of the character and work together to make a list of words to describe him. Now ask them to imagine a character that is the opposite of the one on the board and make a list of words to describe this new character.

Whole-class shared work
● Go to page 3 and introduce the word *antonym* as a term for words with an opposite meaning.
● Read the word at the top of page 4 together and ask the children to decide, in pairs, which rocket has the antonym on it.
● Allow a child to press on the rocket to see if their choice is correct. An explosion will be heard if the correct answer is chosen. Alternatively, use the Eraser on the star to reveal whether the answer is correct.
● Repeat this activity on pages 5 to 7, defining any vocabulary as necessary.
● Provide each child with an individual whiteboard. Show page 8 and challenge the children to write down on their boards, in one minute, as many antonyms as they can for the displayed word.
● Once they have done this, invite a volunteer to come to the whiteboard and use the Delete button ✖ to remove the ellipse to reveal one antonym. Then let the children share any other words they have thought of, and add them to the Notebook page.
● Again, address any errors or misconceptions in the children's vocabulary.
● Repeat this activity on pages 9 to 11.

Independent work
● Give a set of antonym dominoes (created using photocopiable page 48) to each group of three children and ask them to share out the dominoes equally.
● Explain that this domino game is exactly the same as normal dominoes, except that the children need to match antonyms together instead of numbers or pictures.
● Encourage the children to challenge the antonym choices of other players if they disagree with them.
● Allow less confident learners to play the game in teams of two so that they can support each other in the decision-making process.
● Challenge more confident learners to create their own antonym domino game once they have played the version supplied.

Plenary
● Go to page 12 and ask the children to explain what an antonym is. Suggest that they explain this to a friend and then share answers as a class. Delete the top yellow ellipse to reveal a congratulatory message to the children.
● Next, delete the lower yellow ellipse. Invite the children to think of an antonym for *fast*. Repeat for several other words to assess which children have grasped the concept.

Whiteboard tools
Use the Eraser to reveal whether the answers on pages 4 to 7 are correct.

 Pen tray

 Delete button

 Select tool

Past, present and future

Learning objective
PNS: Sentence structure and punctuation
● Compose sentences using tenses consistently (present and past).

Resources
'Sorting tenses' Notebook file; photocopiable page 49 'Past, present, future'; individual whiteboards and pens; pencils; prepared cards with written simple actions that the children could mime (such as *catch a fish*; *throw a ball*).

Links to other subjects
Speaking and listening
PoS (4a) To use actions to convey situations.
● The children are asked to mime the action words in the Starter.

Starter
Ask a child to stand at the front of the class and choose an action card (see Resources). Tell the child to act out the action on the card. Ask one of these questions: *What is he doing now? What did he do yesterday? What will he do tomorrow?* Encourage the children to answer in a sentence. For example, *Now he is catching a fish. Yesterday he caught a fish. Tomorrow he will catch a fish.*

Repeat this with a few different action cards. Correct any misconceptions about the use of different tenses. Make a note of the verbs used on page 2 of the 'Sorting tenses' Notebook file.

Whole-class shared work
● Explain that action words often change depending on when the actions took place. Refer the children back to an example from the Starter and remind them how the verb changed as the tense changed.
● Read the sentences on page 3 of the Notebook file. Ask the children to talk with a partner to decide which sentence is about what is happening now, which is about what happened in the past, and which is about what will happen in the future.
● Invite the children to share their ideas with the rest of the class and discuss them. Once they have done this, ask volunteers to come to the whiteboard to drag and drop the sentences into the appropriate boxes.
● Ask: *Do each group of sentences have anything in common?* Encourage answers such as: *All of the future tense sentences have* **will** *in them.*
● Next, go to page 4 and invite the children to complete the sentences using the correct tense.

Independent work
● Give each child an enlarged copy of photocopiable page 49. Discuss what is happening in each picture.
● Ask the children to write three sentences about each picture – one in the past tense, one in the present tense and one in the future tense.
● Give less confident learners a selection of sentences written in the past, present or future tense and read them together. Invite the children to sort the sentences into past, present and future. Ask which words show when the action took place.

Plenary
● Display page 5 of the Notebook file. Ask each child to pick an action word from the page and to write down, on their individual whiteboards, three sentences containing the action word; one in the past, one in the present and one in the future tense.
● Allow the children to share some of their sentences and use this opportunity to assess whether they still have any misconceptions about the way verb tenses are formed or used.
● Finally, move the purple circle around the Notebook page to reveal the correct past and future tense of each verb.

Whiteboard tools
▭ Pen tray

▧ Select tool

▧ On-screen Keyboard

Learning objective
PNS: Sentence structure and punctuation

Resources
'Punctuation' Notebook file; photocopiable page 50 'Speech marks'; individual whiteboards and pens; pencils.

Links to other subjects
Speaking and listening
Objective 15: To listen to each other's views and preferences.
● The children must apply these skills when checking their work with others.

Speech marks

Starter
Display page 2 of the 'Punctuation' Notebook file. Tell the children that they are going to play the 'speech mark' game. You are going to read the text aloud, and when they see an opening speech mark they must make an imaginary sock puppet open its mouth, and when they see a closing speech mark they must make it close its mouth. Read the text aloud together and add the actions.

Whole-class shared work
● Highlight a sentence that is being spoken and highlight the speech marks at the beginning and the end.
● Explain that speech marks are used to show when someone begins to speak (opens their mouth) and when they stop speaking (closes their mouth).
● Go to page 3 and ask the children to highlight the words that one of the characters is actually saying.
● Remind the children that speech marks go around the words that are actually being spoken. Invite volunteers to add the missing speech marks to the text.
● Look at page 4 and remind the children that speech can also be shown in speech bubbles. Ensure that they understand that speech bubbles can only be used where there are pictures of the characters.
● Provide the children with individual whiteboards. Ask them to turn the speech bubbles into story text. For example: *'I am going to meet the Prince,' cheered Cinderella.* Invite a couple of children to write their sentences on the class whiteboard.
● Point out the importance of including who is speaking, and how they spoke in the sentence.

Independent work
● Give each child a copy of photocopiable page 50. Ask the children to underline or highlight all of the words that are actually being spoken by a character, then challenge them to rewrite the sentences with the speech marks in the correct place.
● Encourage the children to check their work with another child so that discussion and self-evaluation can take place.
● As an extension, ask the children to work in pairs to turn the speech bubbles into story text.
● Challenge more confident learners to work in pairs to write a conversation between Cinderella and the Fairy Godmother. Remind them to show who is speaking, and how.

Plenary
● Ask two children to write a conversation between Cinderella and the Fairy Godmother using page 5 of the Notebook file.
● Encourage the other children to check their punctuation, particularly the speech marks. Encourage the children to think of more expressive words than *said* when they are writing who is speaking.

Whiteboard tools

 Pen tray

 Select tool

 Highlighter pen

Commas

Learning objective
PNS: Sentence structure and punctuation
● Use commas to separate items in a list.

Resources
'Punctuation' Notebook file; photocopiable page 51 'Shopping list' with cards cut out; individual whiteboards and pens.

Links to other subjects
Speaking and listening
Objective 24: To present parts of traditional stories.
● Use the opportunity to do some retelling of favourite stories and traditional tales. Find other stories that contain magic spells or lists of ingredients.

Starter
Display page 6 of the 'Punctuation' Notebook file. Give the children individual whiteboards and ask them to make a list of their five favourite television programmes, or their five favourite sweets. (Write the chosen item on the line.) Look at and compare the different ways in which the children present their lists. Some may work down the board and some may work across it. Focus on a list that has been made across the board. Ask: *Are the items in the list clearly separated?* Tell the children that you know of something they can use to separate the items in a list.

Whole-class shared work
● Read the text on page 7 of the Notebook file. Highlight the commas in the two lists and ask the children to consider why they are there and what job they are doing.
● Explain that the commas are used as a substitute for the word *and* in a long list of items. Demonstrate how ridiculous it would sound to keep saying *and* between each item in a long list.
● Emphasise that the last *and* does not get replaced with a comma.
● Show the children page 8 and ask them if they can identify anywhere that commas could be used.
● Emphasise how long-winded the lists are with *and* in between each item.
● Double-press on the text and invite volunteers to use the On-screen Keyboard ▭ to replace the extra *ands* with commas.
● Re-read the list with the commas in, and state how much better it sounds now.

Independent work
● Give each group a set of cards prepared from photocopiable page 51.
● Ask the children to choose a card to find out what to buy at the supermarket, then write a sentence stating what they bought there. For example: *At the supermarket I bought an apple, a banana, a toothbrush, a pizza and some cheese.*
● Tell the children that you are looking for commas separating the items in their lists.
● Give less confident learners a written list with all of the *ands* left in it. Ask them to cross out the *ands* that are not necessary, replacing them with commas.

Plenary
● Ask the children to explain to a partner how to use commas in lists. Listen to some of the explanations and derive a definitive explanation.
● Use page 9 of the Notebook file to make a list of ingredients needed for a magic potion. Give the children individual whiteboards and challenge them to write their own magic spell recipe to turn a frog into a prince. Remind them to use commas in their list of ingredients.
● Once they have done this, invite volunteers to come to the whiteboard to drag and drop the ingredients provided on page 9 into a list.
● Allow the children to share some of their spell ingredients on page 10.

Whiteboard tools
Use the On-screen Keyboard, accessed through the Pen tray or the SMART Board tools menu, to replace the *ands* with commas on page 8.

▭ Pen tray

 Highlighter pen

 On-screen Keyboard

 Select tool

Alphabetical order

Learning objective
PNS: Understanding and interpreting texts
● Explain organisational features of texts, including alphabetical order.

Resources
'Alphabetical order' Notebook file; cards with different letters on them; dictionaries; writing books; pencils; individual whiteboards and pens; prepared cards with topic words that can be defined (try to include some words that begin with the same letter). On page 5 of the Notebook file type six topic-related words (press and drag over a word and its white box, then select Grouping>Group from the dropdown menu so that they can be moved around together).

Links to other subjects
Geography
QCA Unit 4 'Going to the seaside'
● Suggest that the children make individual dictionaries of geographical terms learned during a topic.

Starter
Recite or sing the alphabet as a class. Give each child a card with a different letter from the alphabet on it and ask them to order themselves alphabetically. Read the letters on the cards aloud to check the order. Collect the cards back in and ask the children questions such as: *What letter comes after F? Does K come before or after M in the alphabet?* If required, use page 2 of the Notebook file to show the upper- and lower-case alphabet.

Whole-class shared work
● Go to page 3 and look at the first set of words to be ordered.
● Explain to the children that they must look at the first letter in order to decide which word comes first alphabetically. Highlight the first letters of the words.
● Encourage the children to work in pairs to decide on the correct order for the words.
● Let a child select the order they think is correct on the board and check the answer.
● Open the 'Alphabetical order' activity on page 4. Ask the children to write the answers on their individual whiteboards and show you. Then invite a child to drag and drop the words into the correct order.
● Ask the children to think of ways that alphabetical order is used in books. For example: indexes, glossaries and dictionaries. Talk about how alphabetical order makes it easier to find things in a list.
● Go to page 5 where you placed some words earlier (see Resources). Ask the children to put them in alphabetical order.
● Provide each pair with a dictionary that contains the six words and ask them to look up the definition of each word. Write the definition on the board next to the word.

Independent work
● Give each group a set of words on prepared cards (see Resources) and a dictionary. Ask them to work together to order the words alphabetically.
● Challenge each child to find one of the words in the dictionary and read the definition aloud to their group.
● Ask the children to write down the words in alphabetical order in their books and to write a definition beside each word.
● Challenge more confident learners to make a topic dictionary of their own. Ask them to think of some words to include in their dictionary instead of giving them the prepared cards.

Plenary
● Go to page 6 of the Notebook file. Put the children into pairs and then challenge them to a dictionary race. Say a word and see which pair can find the word the quickest in their dictionary.
● Ask the pairs to read out the definition when they find it, to prove that they have found it. Give less confident learners a simpler dictionary to enable them to participate more easily.

Whiteboard tools

 Pen tray

 Select tool

 Highlighter pen

Cyclical diagrams

Learning objectives
PNS: Understanding and interpreting texts
● Explain organisational features of texts, including layout, diagrams and captions.
PNS: Creating and shaping texts
● Select from different presentational features to suit particular writing purposes on paper.

Resources
'Life cycle of a frog' Notebook file; a children's non-fiction text explaining the life cycle of an animal; individual whiteboards and pens; pencils; coloured card (optional).

Links to other subjects
Science
QCA Unit 2A 'Health and growth'
● This lesson has a clear science link. The children need to understand and present information about a life cycle.

Starter
Ask the children to define what they think a life cycle is. Write their answers on page 2 of the Notebook file. On page 3 open the 'Life cycle of a frog' activity and look carefully at the pictures. Ask the children to place the pictures onto the life cycle diagram in the correct order. Tell them that this diagram illustrates the life cycle of a frog. Explain that it shows where new frogs come from, and how the new frogs eventually grow into an adult and produce more new frogs.

Whole-class shared work
● Use the Area Capture tool 📷 to take a snapshot of the completed diagram of the life cycle of a frog and place it in the centre of page 3 of the Notebook file. Leave space around the image to write.
● Encourage the children to talk about why the diagram is in a circle and not in a straight line across the page. Ensure that they understand the repetitive nature of a cycle.
● Look closely at each stage of the life cycle and ask the children to work in pairs to write an explanation for each stage on individual whiteboards.
● Share some of the explanations and choose one to write next to each stage.
● Use a book to find out about the life cycle of a different animal such as a ladybird or a butterfly.
● Ask the children to decide what stages they would include in the life cycle of this animal and list them so that everyone can see.

Independent work
● Ask the children to work in pairs to illustrate the life cycle of the animal that they have just found out about.
● Refer the children to the list of stages to include in the life cycle diagram.
● Suggest some more creative examples of how to present the life cycle rather than simply drawing the life cycle on plain paper. For example, the children could make a ladybird from red card, and a leaf shape for each stage of the life cycle from green card. Place the leaves in a circular pattern around the ladybird and illustrate each stage of the life cycle on top of the leaves.
● Support less confident learners by giving them prepared pictures of each stage of the life cycle and asking them to arrange the pictures into a diagram that shows the life cycle. Encourage them to add text to each picture to explain the process further.

Plenary
● Share the children's work as a class. Evaluate how effectively the work illustrates the life cycle. Comment on the different ways the children chose to present their work and emphasise how this adds interest. Add notes to page 4, if required.
● Ensure that the children understand that their work does not always have to be done on a piece of paper to be effective.

Whiteboard tools
Use the Area Capture tool to capture the life cycle diagram and place it on page 3 of the Notebook file.

 Pen tray

 Area Capture tool

 Select tool

Learning objectives
PNS: Speaking
● Explain ideas and processes using imaginative and adventurous vocabulary.
PNS: Creating and shaping texts
● Make adventurous word and language choices appropriate to the style and purpose of the text.
● Select from different presentational features to suit particular writing purposes on paper.

Resources
'Story setting' Notebook file; photocopiable page 52 'Story setting' with the cards cut out; individual whiteboards and pens; paint; chalk; felt-tipped pens; paper and card; Big Book with clear illustrations of settings.

Links to other subjects
Art and design
QCA Unit 2A 'Picture this!'
● Encourage the children to evaluate each other's work sensitively and against the specific questions asked.

Whiteboard tools
Use the Spotlight tool or Screen Shade to concentrate on particular parts of the pictures at a time. Upload scanned images of the children's work by selecting Insert, then Picture File, and browsing to where you have saved the images.

 Pen tray

 Spotlight tool

 Select tool

 Screen Shade

Story setting

Starter
Look at a Big Book with clear illustrations that show the setting of the story. Ask the children to think about where the story is set and listen to their ideas. Focus on one of the illustrations and invite the children to describe the setting to a partner. Challenge them to use interesting descriptive vocabulary to do this.

Make notes on page 2 of the 'Story settings' Notebook file. Share some of the children's ideas as a whole class.

Whole-class shared work
● Go to page 3 and look in detail at the pictures of the three settings.
● Focus on one setting at a time using the Spotlight tool 🔦 or the Screen Shade 🔲.
● Ask the children to choose the setting that they are most interested in and describe it to a partner. Share some of these descriptions as a class on page 4.
● Give the children individual whiteboards and ask them to list five words or phrases that could be used when writing a description of their chosen setting. Share some of these ideas as a class.
● Using pages 5 to 7, ask the children to match the setting descriptions to the illustrations and to explain why they think they have chosen the correct one. Discuss any vocabulary that is unfamiliar to them.

Independent work
● Give each group a set of five cards prepared from photocopiable page 52. Ask the children to choose a card and read the story setting description on it. Talk about the type of setting that their card describes.
● Provide the children with materials such as paint, chalk or felt-tipped pens to create a piece of artwork that illustrates the setting description on their card.
● Encourage the children to talk to each other about their setting and discuss ideas about how to illustrate the setting.

Plenary
● Take a few samples of the children's artwork and scan it into the computer. Display the work on page 8 and ask the class to comment on it. Write some of their comments around the picture.
● Ask: *Which setting description do you think this is illustrating?* Evaluate whether the work includes all of the details that were given in the description. Compare different illustrations of the same description. Comment how a more detailed description should give a more accurate picture.

Character profiles

Learning objective
PNS: Creating and shaping texts
● Make adventurous word and language choices appropriate to the style and purpose of the text.

Resources
'Build your own' file; photocopiable page 53 'Character profile'; a set of cards with well-known character names. Open the 'Build your own' file and use it to prepare a Notebook file with images from the English folder under My Content in the Gallery. Insert pictures of two contrasting fairytale characters and place them side by side, typing a selection of descriptive words and phrases for each character at the bottom. On a new page create a template identical to the 'Character profile' photocopiable page; include a picture of one of the previously chosen characters.

Links to other subjects
Speaking and listening
Objective 13: To speak with clarity and use intonation when reading texts.
● Ask the children to read out their profiles in clear voices.
Speaking and listening
Objective 14: To listen to others in class and ask relevant questions.
● Ensure that the children listen carefully to guess which character is being described.

Whiteboard tools
Use the Shapes and Lines tools to create the 'Character profile' template.

 Pen tray

 Select tool

 Text tool

 Shapes tool

 Lines tool

 Gallery

Starter
Open the prepared 'Build your own' file (see Resources) and identify the two characters and the stories they come from. Give the children one minute to describe the two characters to a partner. Read the descriptive words and phrases at the bottom of the page and ask the children to decide which character they think each word or phrase best describes. Drag the words to the character they describe.

Whole-class shared work
● Show the children the 'Character profile' template (see Resources).
● Recap the words and phrases used to describe the character.
● Discuss how to complete the 'Character profile' sheet. Explain that the information does not have to be written in sentences. With the children's help, write in the information. Encourage the use of adjectives.
● When the character profile (or ID card) is complete, read the information on it and then demonstrate how it is possible to use this information to write a passage describing the character.
● Encourage the children to suggest how the information on the card could be turned into proper sentences. Write or type some sentences below the card.
● Evaluate the finished character description for accuracy. Ask: *Would you be able to identify who the character was by listening to this description?*

Independent work
● Give each group a set of the cards displaying a variety of well-known character names (see Resources). Ask each child to choose a card to describe the named character.
● Instruct the children to create an ID card for their selected character using photocopiable page 53 as a template.
● Encourage the children to use descriptive and thoughtful language.
● Provide less confident learners with a bank of useful words to help inspire their initial ideas.
● Challenge more confident learners by asking them to work without using a template.
● When the ID card is complete, ask the children to write a passage to describe the same character. Encourage them to refer back to the key words and phrases that they used on the ID card.

Plenary
● Ask some children to read out their profiles while the others listen. Explain that if a profile has been written well, the listeners should be able to identify the character being described. Ask the listeners if they can identify the character – what words or phrases gave them the biggest clue?
● If the children cannot identify the character, ask the reader to state who the character was. Take suggestions from the listeners about what needs to be included in the description to make it more obvious.
● Scan some of the children's ID cards and display them on a Notebook page. Hide the names and see if the rest of the class can guess who the characters are.

Syllables

Learning objective
PNS: Word structure and spelling
● Spell with increasing accuracy and confidence, drawing on word recognition and knowledge of word structure, and spelling patterns including common inflections and use of double letters.

Resources
Prepare a Notebook file: draw a table with four columns; label the columns as 1, 2, 3 and 4 syllables and lock everything in place (select Locking>Lock in Place from each item's dropdown menu); insert words containing one, two, three or four syllables at the bottom of the page. Prepare some cards: make a set of 15 cards with a one-, two-, three- or four-syllable word on each; prepared table for less confident learners (see independent work); dictionaries for more confident learners; pencils; paper; individual whiteboards and pens.

Links to other subjects
Music
QCA Unit 4 'Feel the pulse – Exploring pulse and rhythm'
● Ask the children to clap the rhythm of the words. Try to fit the words together in a simple composition.

Whiteboard tools
Use the Lines tool to draw columns in the prepared file. Select Locking>Lock in Place from the dropdown menu to prevent items from being moved.

 Pen tray

 Select tool

 Text tool

 Lines tool

Starter
Talk to the children about ways to help spell a tricky word. Listen to ideas, then focus on breaking up a word into chunks. Ask the children to think about how they would spell *butterfly*. Say the word again, emphasising each syllable. For example, *butt-er-fly*. Encourage the children to use their phonic knowledge to spell each chunk.

Whole-class shared work
● Explain to the children that a beat in a word is a syllable. Demonstrate this by saying some words while clapping out the beat.
● Encourage the children to clap the beats (or syllables) of words and ask them to count how many syllables the words have.
● Open the prepared file (see Resources) and help the children to read the words at the bottom of the screen.
● Ask the children to decide, with a partner, how many syllables each word has, and then allow them to sort them into the correct place in the table on the board.
● Suggest to the children that it might help to clap the beats of the word to count the syllables.
● When all of the words are sorted, ask the children to think of one more word for each column. Invite them to use a Pen from the Pen tray to write their suggestions on the table.

Independent work
● Give each group a set of prepared cards (see Resources).
● Ask the children to sort the cards into words containing one, two, three or four syllables and then record these words in a table similar to the one used on the whiteboard.
● Encourage the children to self-check their work with the rest of their group and discuss any words on which they disagree.
● Prepare a table for less confident learners and give them only one- or two-syllable words to begin with.
● Challenge more confident learners to think of four words to add to each column instead of providing them with cards. Provide dictionaries for inspiration.

Plenary
● Remind the children of the spelling strategy discussed at the start of the lesson. Help them to understand that breaking a word into syllables is like breaking a word into chunks to make spelling it easier.
● Give the children individual whiteboards and dictate a longer word to them. Encourage them to use their knowledge of syllables and phonics to break up the word and have a go at spelling it. In addition, ask them to write down how many syllables the dictated word contains.

The suffixes *-ful* and *-ly*

Learning objective
PNS: Word structure and spelling
● Spell with increasing accuracy and confidence, drawing on word recognition and knowledge of word structure and spelling patterns.

Resources
'Prefixes and suffixes' Notebook file; photocopiable page 54 'Suffixes'; individual whiteboards and pens.

Links to other subjects
There are no specific links for this lesson.

Starter
Orally assign a word to each child that contains either the suffix *-ful* or *-ly*. Ask the children to consider how to spell their assigned word, then sort themselves into three groups: *-ful*, *-ly* and *unsure*. Together, help the unsure group to decide. If required, use page 5 of the Notebook file to write the words to show the children how to spell them.

Whole-class shared work
● Explain that *-ful* and *-ly* are both suffixes that can be added to the end of words to create new words.
● Read the words at the bottom of page 6 with the children. Check that they all understand the meaning of the words. Put the words into context in a sentence if necessary.
● Ask the children to talk with a partner to decide which suffix (*-ful* or *-ly*) should be added to each word to create a new word. Then invite volunteers to come to the whiteboard to drag the words into the appropriate box to check the answers.
● Check whether the children understand that the function of the word changes when a suffix is added, by asking them to make sentences on their individual whiteboards incorporating some of the new words. Ask volunteers to write their sentences on page 7 of the Notebook file.
● Read the sentences on page 8. Ask the children to decide which word, from those at the bottom of the page, best fits into each gap.
● Point to a word at the bottom of the page and ask: *In which sentence does this word belong?* Drag the correct word into each sentence.
● Point out that when a word ends in *-y* such as *happy* or *beauty*, the *y* changes to an *i* before the suffix is added.

Independent work
● Give each child a copy of photocopiable page 54. Ask them to fill in the missing word in each sentence, from the selection given.
● Remind the children to check that their sentences make sense.
● Adapt the activity for more confident learners. Simply provide the stems of the words in the word bank (such as *happy* instead of *happily*). They will then need to add the suffix before filling in the missing word.
● As an extension, ask the children to think of more words containing the *-ful* and *-ly* suffix.

Plenary
● Share the answers from the independent work as a class and discuss any differences of choice.
● Go to page 9 of the Notebook file and look at the wordsearch together. Challenge the children to locate the six hidden words in less than three minutes.
● Invite individual children to highlight a word in the grid, then write that word on the lines by the side of the grid. Finally, pull the tab across the screen to reveal the answers.

Whiteboard tools

 Pen tray

 Select tool

 On-screen Keyboard

 Highlighter pen

Synonyms

Learning objective
PNS: Understanding and interpreting texts
● Explore how particular words are used, including words and expressions with similar meanings.

Resources
'Antonyms and synonyms' Notebook file; prepared cards with three words on each one (choose words that have a few different synonyms); a thesaurus; strips of paper; pencils; individual whiteboards and pens.

Links to other subjects
There are no specific links for this lesson.

Starter
Go to page 13 of the 'Antonyms and synonyms' Notebook file. Look at the picture of the character (Ben). Say two sentences that are the same, except for one word – for example: *Ben is kind. Ben is considerate.* Write these next to Ben.

Ask the children to consider the two sentences and decide whether they have the same or a different meaning. Ask the children to vote, then look up the definition of both words in a dictionary. Ask: *Do they have the same or a different meaning?* Use the Undo button to reset the page, then repeat the activity a few times, using different describing words.

Whole-class shared work
● Go to page 14 and introduce the word *synonym* as a term for words with the same or similar meaning.
● Read the word at the top of page 15 together. Ask the children to decide, in pairs, which balloon has the synonym on it.
● Allow a child to press on the balloon. If their choice is correct, they will hear a cheer. Alternatively, use the Eraser to rub over the balloon to reveal the answer.
● Repeat this activity on pages 16 to 19, defining any vocabulary as necessary.
● Provide each child with an individual whiteboard. Display page 20 and challenge the children to write down as many synonyms for the word displayed as they can think of in one minute.
● Choose individuals to write synonyms for the word in the text boxes next to the balloon. Again, address any errors or misconceptions in the children's vocabulary.
● Repeat this activity on pages 21 to 23 of the Notebook file.
● Introduce the children to a simple thesaurus if they have not used one before.

Independent work
● Give each child their own prepared card (see Resources). Check that they are able to read the words and understand their meaning.
● Give each child three strips of paper and ask them to write one of their words on the left-hand side of each piece.
● Encourage the children to write as many synonyms for each word as they can think of on the relevant strips of paper.
● Ask the group to combine all of their completed strips, put them into alphabetical order and stick them onto a sheet of sugar paper or into a scrap book to form a group thesaurus. Encourage the children to add initial letter headings for ease of reference.

Plenary
● Go to page 24 of the Notebook file. In pairs, ask the children to discuss and explain what a synonym is. Share answers as a class. Use the Delete button to delete the top yellow ellipse, revealing a congratulatory message to the children.
● Next, delete the lower yellow ellipse. Challenge the children to think of a synonym for *sad*. Repeat this for several other words until you are sure that they have fully understood.

Whiteboard tools
Use the Undo button to erase any unsaved changes, and the Delete button to reveal hidden information.

 Pen tray

Select tool

 Undo button

Delete button

Capital letters and full stops

Learning objective
PNS: Sentence structure and punctuation
● Write simple and compound sentences.

Resources
'Punctuation' Notebook file; photocopiable page 55 'Capital letters and full stops'; pencils.

Links to other subjects
There are no specific links for this lesson.

Starter
Go to page 11 of the 'Punctuation' Notebook file. Introduce the punctuation game to the children. Explain to them that they are going to read the text aloud, and when they see a capital letter they must put both hands straight up in the air to make themselves tall like a capital letter; and when they see a full stop they must stab the air with their index finger as though they are making a full stop in front of them. Read the text aloud together, combined with the actions.

Whole-class shared work
● Highlight the capital letters in the text on page 11. Ask: *When do we need to use a capital letter?* Remember other uses of capital letters, such as for the beginning of names and for emphasis.
● Ask: *When do we need to use a full stop?* Talk about when a new sentence is needed – for example, when the subject of the sentence changes.
● Show the children page 12 and ask them to read it together. Discuss how it is difficult to read correctly without any punctuation.
● Ask volunteers to come to the whiteboard to add the missing full stops and capital letters to the passage. Show them how to double-press on the text and use the On-screen Keyboard to do this.
● Discuss the children's choices with them and address any errors and misconceptions.
● Demonstrate that reading the sentences created aloud makes it possible to hear if the full stops and capital letters are placed correctly.

Independent work
● Give each child a copy of photocopiable page 55. Challenge them to rewrite the sentences and the paragraph, putting the capital letters and full stops in the correct places – considering all the uses for capital letters.
● Encourage the children to check their work with another child so that discussion and self-evaluation can take place.
● As an extra challenge, ask the children to unjumble the sentences at the bottom of the sheet. Remind them to consider where the capital letter and full stop should be in each sentence.

Plenary
● Display page 13 of the Notebook file. Explain that the sentences have become jumbled. Ask the children to consider if there are any clues about the correct order in the words. Suggest that a word beginning with a capital letter needs to go first and that the full stop will be at the end.
● Invite individual children to unjumble the sentences on the whiteboard.
● Challenge the children to use capital letters and full stops in their independent writing over the next few weeks, and praise evidence of this.

Whiteboard tools
Use the On-screen Keyboard, accessed through the Pen tray or the SMART Board tools menu, to add capital letters and full stops to the text on page 12.

 Pen tray

 Highlighter pen

 On-screen Keyboard

Select tool

Question marks

Learning objective
PNS: Sentence structure and punctuation
● Use question marks.

Resources
'Punctuation' Notebook file; prepared cards with a question word on each to support less confident learners; individual whiteboards and pens; a cardboard crown; paper; pencils.

Links to other subjects
Science
QCA Unit 2E 'Forces and movement'
● Continue the questioning theme in your science work. For example, ask the children to suggest suitable questions to ask such as: *Which car will travel the fastest down the ramp? What does a plant need in order to grow?*
Speaking and listening
Objective 16: To adopt appropriate roles in small or large groups and consider alternative courses of action.
● The children will be using the device of hot-seating as they take the roles of television presenters and the prince in the Plenary activity.

Whiteboard tools
Use the On-screen Keyboard, accessed through the Pen tray or the SMART Board tools menu, to add question marks to the text on page 15.

 Pen tray

 Highlighter pen

 On-screen Keyboard

 Select tool

Starter
Open the 'Punctuation' Notebook file and read the text on page 14. Ask the children to find examples of questions in the text and invite a child to highlight them on the screen. Focus on the question word used at the start of each question.

Ask the children to work with a partner on individual whiteboards to make a list of words that might begin a question. Make a class list of question words including *what, why, who* and so on.

Whole-class shared work
● Read page 15 together and invite children to highlight any question words found in the text.
● Check together that the question words are at the beginning of a question in each instance.
● Explain that there is a punctuation mark called a question mark that is used at the end of question sentences to show clearly that it is a question. Show the children how to write a question mark.
● Ask a child to use the On-screen Keyboard ⌨ to add a question mark to the end of each identified question.
● Next, ask the children to think of a question that the prince might like to ask Cinderella. Invite them to write it down on their individual whiteboards. Share some of the questions as a class and invite a few children to write their questions on page 16.
● Assess whether the children understand how to use a question mark.

Independent work
● Tell the children that they are television presenters and they are going to interview the prince about the ball. Encourage them to think about what questions they would like to ask the prince before they begin to write.
● Invite them to write a list of questions to ask the prince.
● Remind them about using a question word at the beginning of a question and a question mark at the end.
● Provide less confident learners with a bank of question word cards (see Resources) that can be used to begin a question.

Plenary
● Place a cardboard crown on one of the children's heads. Tell the child with the crown that he/she is the prince.
● Ask one child to read out one of their questions to the prince while another child writes the question on the whiteboard using page 17 of the Notebook file.
● Encourage the child playing the prince to try to answer the question in the role of the prince.
● Assess the children's use of question words and question marks during this part of the lesson.

Note taking

Learning objectives

PNS: Understanding and interpreting texts
● Draw together ideas and information from across a whole text using simple signposts in the text.
PNS: Creating and shaping texts
● Maintain consistency in non-narrative including purpose and tense.

Resources P

Photocopiable page 56 'All about penguins'; a children's information text about an animal; an information leaflet about an animal; pencils, highlighters; paper. Prepare a Notebook file: type a factual passage about an animal onto a whiteboard page.

Links to other subjects
ICT
QCA Unit 2C 'Finding information'
● Suggest that the children also find information using a CD-ROM and make notes from it when carrying out their research.

Starter

Share an information text about an animal with the children. Talk about the information that the book communicates and look carefully at the way the information is set out. Ask the children to tell a partner what they have learned after reading each page. Identify whether there is any information on the page that is more or less important than the rest.

Whole-class shared work

● Open the prepared Notebook file (see Resources) and read the text with the class.
● Tell the children that they are going to make an information leaflet. Show them an example of one. Ask them what they may need to do before writing their own leaflet. Suggest that they start by finding out some relevant factual information.
● Explain that reading a text will give us information, but stress that it is not acceptable to copy someone else's work and pretend that it is your own.
● Read the first sentence of the text on the board and ask the children which words they think are key words or phrases. Evaluate their suggestions and highlight the key words.
● Ask the children to identify and highlight key words and phrases in the rest of the text. Double-press on the text, then drag to highlight the words and drag them out of the sentences to copy and paste them as separate text boxes.
● Look over the key words that the children have highlighted and demonstrate how to use these to write new sentences, ensuring that they are different from the original text.

Independent work

● Give each pair of children a copy of photocopiable page 56. Explain that you would like them to produce a leaflet about penguins.
● Encourage them to highlight the key words and phrases in the text.
● Suggest some subheadings that they may want to use in their leaflets, based on the information they have highlighted.
● Allow the children the opportunity to compare notes with others before they begin their leaflet. Comment on any important key words and phrases that have been omitted or any excessive highlighting.
● Challenge them to create an information leaflet using the suggested subheadings and the notes that they have made.
● Remind the children that they should not simply copy sentences straight from the information sheet.

Plenary

● Encourage the children to evaluate the final leaflets for accuracy of information and for layout.
● Scan some particularly effective examples of the children's completed leaflets, display them on a Notebook page and discuss why they are effective.
● You may want to split this lesson across two sessions, with the first session concentrating on the note-taking and the second session concentrating on the making of the leaflet.

Whiteboard tools

Lock the text on the Notebook page by selecting Locking>Lock in Place from the dropdown menu. Upload children's work by selecting Insert, then Picture File, and browsing to where you have saved the images.

 Pen tray

 Select tool

 Highlighter pen

Fact or fiction?

Learning objectives
PNS: Understanding and interpreting texts
● Draw together ideas and information from across a whole text, using simple signposts in the text.
PNS: Creating and shaping texts
● Draw on knowledge and experience of texts in deciding and planning what and how to write.

Resources P
Photocopiable page 57 'Fiction or non-fiction?'; cards containing fiction or non-fiction sentences about ducks; individual whiteboards and pens; information books about ducks and fictional books; pencils. Prepare a Notebook file: on the first page insert two pictures of ducks (copyright permitting) - one a real duck and one a fictional duck; on the second page, draw two boxes on a blank page, labelling one 'Fact' and the other 'Fiction'; type a selection of fact and fiction sentences at the bottom of the page to be sorted.

Links to other subjects
There are no specific links for this lesson.

Starter
Show the children your prepared Notebook page containing the duck pictures - one of a real duck and one of a fictional duck from a story. Ask the children what the two pictures have in common and what is different about them. Write some of these suggestions around the pictures. Draw out that one of the ducks is real whereas the other is a fictional character. Ask the children to suggest the types of book in which they might see each of these pictures.

Whole-class shared work
● Show the children two books - one a story book with a duck as the main character, and one an information book about ducks.
● Ask the children to identify what type of book each is, and explain how they know this.
● Introduce the terms *fiction* and *non-fiction* and explain what each term means.
● Read the first page of each book. Give the children the opportunity to talk about the differences between the two types of text.
● Show the children the sentences at the bottom of your prepared Notebook page (see Resources). Ask them to decide whether the sentences would be found in a non-fiction book or a fiction book, then allow them to drag the sentences into the correct box.
● On their individual whiteboards, ask the children to work in pairs to write one more sentence that can be added into each box.

Independent work
● Provide each child with a copy of photocopiable page 57. Ask them to read each sentence and decide whether it would be found in a fiction book or in a non-fiction book, recording their answers on the sheet.
● Next, challenge the children to write their own fiction and non-fiction sentences.
● Ask more confident learners to write two passages: one passage should be a non-fiction piece about ducks and the other passage should be the beginning of a story about a duck.

Plenary
● Give the children cards containing either a factual sentence about ducks or a sentence from a story where a duck is one of the characters.
● Ask the children to sort themselves into two groups: fiction or non-fiction. Tell any children who are unsure to stand in the middle, and ask the other children to help them make a decision about their sentences.
● Encourage the children to give an explanation as to why the sentence is fiction or non-fiction to help develop the understanding of those who were undecided.

Whiteboard tools
Use the Shapes tool and the Text tool to draw the boxes and type the labels in the prepared Notebook file.

 Pen tray

 Select tool

 Text tool

 Shapes tool

Riddles

Learning objective
PNS: Creating and shaping texts
● Draw on knowledge and experience of texts in deciding and planning what and how to write.

Resources
'Poems and riddles' Notebook file; photocopiable page 58 'Riddles' with cards cut out and prepared.

Links to other subjects
Speaking and listening
Objective 13: To speak with clarity and use intonation when reading and reciting texts.
● Ask the children to read out their riddles for the others to listen to and solve.

Starter
Open the 'Poems and riddles' Notebook file and read the riddles on pages 8 to 10, one at a time, with the children.

Challenge the children to try to work out what the riddles are giving clues for. How did they work out the answers? Point out that each riddle needed to be solved in a different way. After discussion, use the Delete button ☒ to remove the shapes to reveal a picture of the answer.

Whole-class shared work
● Look at each riddle more closely, starting with the most simple riddle on page 8. Highlight the first letter of each clue word to show the children that they spell out *cat*.
● Next look at the riddle on page 9. Highlight the first letter of the first clue word, the second letter of the second clue word and the third letter of the third clue word to spell out *cow*.
● Finally, look at the trickiest riddle on page 10. In this riddle, highlight the letters that are in the first word but not in the second. Show the children that these letters spell out *dog*.
● Explain that the children are going to write a riddle for the word *ant* using the simple riddle template on page 11.
● Challenge them to choose words from the bottom of the page to complete the riddle, or think of their own. Encourage them to think of a final hint and write it on the line provided.
● Check the riddle together to ensure that it can be solved and that no mistakes have been made.

Independent work
● Give each group a set of cards prepared from photocopiable page 58.
● Ask the children to choose a card to determine the animal that they are going to write a riddle for.
● Propose that they use the simplest example from the whole-class work as a template.
● Give less confident learners a writing frame to use, similar to the one shown on page 11 of the Notebook file.
● Challenge more confident learners to use as a template one of the other riddle examples that are trickier to compose. Provide them with support to achieve this challenge.

Plenary
● Look at page 12 of Notebook file together. Challenge the children to choose appropriate words from the bottom of the page to complete the riddle. Encourage them to think of a final hint. Choose one child to write it on the line provided.
● Check the riddle together to ensure that it can be solved, and that no mistakes have been made.

Whiteboard tools
Remove objects by selecting them and pressing the Delete button (or choose the Delete option from the dropdown menu).

 Pen tray

 Delete button

 Highlighter pen

 Select tool

Long vowel phonemes

r _ _ _

s _ _ _ _

p _ _ _ _

t _ _ _

s _ _ _

t _ _ _

p _ _

w _ _ _ _

p _ _

l _ _ _

s _ _

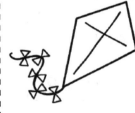

k _ _ _ _

s _ _ _

r _ _ _ _

c _ _ _

b _ _

h _ _ _

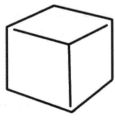

c _ _ _

m _ _ _

c _ _

Illustrations © Mark Brierley / Beehive Illustration

oy wordsearch

e	l	c	b	z	j	o	y	g	d
l	y	o	m	a	f	w	c	u	b
o	x	i	n	s	o	i	l	m	o
y	d	n	h	u	s	b	f	v	i
a	t	x	g	a	w	z	e	c	l
l	o	m	f	o	i	l	s	r	t
e	y	t	u	q	p	b	o	y	e
n	s	b	j	m	e	t	p	r	o
i	k	e	r	o	y	a	l	q	d
j	p	o	i	n	t	h	k	v	i

Words

loyal

_____

_____

_____

_____

_____

_____

_____

_____

◼ Put some of the words that you have found into sentences.

The loyal dog stayed near his master.

_____

_____

_____

_____

_____

SCHOLASTIC
www.scholastic.co.uk

Making a pizza

■ Cut out each instruction and then put them into the correct order. Arrange the instructions on a new sheet of paper so that they can be followed easily. Use numbers and arrows to help organise the instructions more clearly. ✂

Put the plain pizza base onto a plate. 	Take the pizza out of the oven and cut it into slices. 
Place the pizza on a baking tray and put it in the oven for 20 minutes. 	Slice a tomato and lay the slices on top of the cheese. 
Grate some cheese and sprinkle it on top of the tomato sauce. 	Spread some tomato sauce on top of the plain pizza base. 

Extra challenge

■ Create a piece of work that would explain to an alien how to get ready for school in the morning.

■ Remember to use diagrams and arrows as well as words because the alien might not speak any English.

■ Remember to think carefully about how you are going to organise your work on the page before you start.

Illustrations © Mark Brierley / Beehive Illustration

How to make a stick puppet

■ You will need:

a straw   a pencil

a pair of scissors   some sticky tape   a sheet of white card   some felt-tipped pens or crayons

■ Method

1. First choose a favourite character that you would like to make a stick puppet of.

2. Then draw the character you have chosen onto a sheet of white card using a pencil. Make sure that the drawing is a sensible size.

3. Colour in the drawing using felt-tipped pens or crayons.

4. Carefully cut out the drawing with the scissors. You now have a puppet.

5. Next place the puppet face down on the table.

6. Then lay the straw onto the back of the puppet so that the top of the straw is about half way up.

7. Secure the straw to the back of the puppet with sticky tape.

8. Write your name on the back of the puppet.

Illustrations © Mark Brierley / Beehive Illustration

The *air* phoneme

✂

ch<u>air</u>	ch<u>are</u>
c<u>are</u>	c<u>air</u>
f<u>air</u>y	f<u>ear</u>y
wh<u>ere</u>	wh<u>air</u>
b<u>ear</u>	b<u>air</u>
f<u>air</u>	f<u>ere</u>
th<u>ere</u>	th<u>are</u>
bew<u>are</u>	bew<u>ear</u>
st<u>are</u>	st<u>ear</u>
p<u>ear</u>	p<u>ere</u>

er phoneme crossword

Clues

Across

1. Lots of animals have this all over their bodies.

2. The day after Wednesday.

5. A fierce wild cat with stripes.

7. If you fall over you could _____ yourself.

8. The opposite of him.

9. To get water from a tap you need to _____ it on.

Down

1. If you are the winner of a race you must have come _____ .

2. If you need a drink then you are feeling _____ .

3. The opposite of clean.

4. Something you might wear at school.

6. The opposite of boy.

▪ SCHOLASTIC
www.scholastic.co.uk

Compound words

■ Copy this page onto card. Cut along the lines to create individual cards.

light	house	day	dream
sea	shore	cow	boy
fire	fighter	home	work
hair	brush	jelly	fish
skate	board	earth	quake

Antonym dominoes

left	back	thin	poor	back	soft
day	happy	push	short	bumpy	cheerful
night	sad	pull	tall	flat	glum
rough	cold	bottom	freezing	day	push
smooth	hot	top	boiling	night	pull
rich	soft	short	bottom	slim	right
poor	hard	tall	top	plump	left
fat	right	front	hard	rich	front

SCHOLASTIC
www.scholastic.co.uk

Past, present, future

Past	Past
Now	Now
Future	Future

Past	Past
Now	Now
Future	Future

Past	Past
Now	Now
Future	Future

Illustrations © Mark Brierley / Beehive Illustration

Speech marks

■ Underline the words that are being spoken, then put the speech marks in the correct places.

I wish I could go to the ball, sighed Cinderella.

You can go to the ball, replied the Fairy Godmother as she waved her magic wand.

What a beautiful dress, gasped Cinderella happily.

You must be home by midnight, ordered the Fairy Godmother.

■ Turn the speech bubbles into a conversation.

I would like to meet the Prince.

I will make your wish come true.

Can you do magic?

Yes I can. Abracadabra!

_____

_____

_____

_____

_____

Illustrations © Mark Brierley / Beehive Illustration

▪SCHOLASTIC
w w w . s c h o l a s t i c . c o . u k

Shopping list

Illustrations © Mark Brierley / Beehive Illustration

Story settings

A tall Christmas tree stood in the corner of the room. The tree was decorated with red baubles and silver tinsel. Lots of little white lights made the tree shimmer. Under the tree were lots of brightly wrapped presents. Sparkling decorations hung from the ceiling. A log fire crackled in the fireplace and three red stockings hung from the mantelpiece. A little girl sat in a blue armchair cuddling her teddy.

Everywhere looked white and clean. In the distance were three mountains. Each mountain was covered in snow. A row of green fir trees grew in front of the mountains with their branches covered in snow. In front of the trees there was a brown log cabin beside a frozen blue lake. There was smoke rising from the chimney of the log cabin. A robin was perched on a tatty old fence post near the lake.

The bedroom carpet was blue. A bed stood in the middle of the room. The quilt cover was red with bright yellow spots on it. Next to the bed was a small bedside table. A clock and a little red book were on the bedside table. A rocking chair stood in the corner of the room and on the rocking chair were three big brown teddy bears. Hanging from the ceiling of the bedroom were two toy aeroplanes.

It was a cold and misty night. A full white moon peeped out from behind a cloud. On top of a hill at the end of a long winding path there stood a haunted castle. The castle was old with a turret at each corner. The windows were broken and the big wooden door was slightly open. There was an overgrown garden in front of the castle and in the garden were three bare trees and a broken bench.

The town was very busy. Lots of people were hurrying from one shop to another. All of the people were carrying lots of bags of shopping. They were all wearing winter clothes because it was cold. There was a sweet shop in the town with a bright display of sweets in the window. Next door to the sweet shop was a toy shop. The top shop had two teddy bears and a train set in the window.

■ SCHOLASTIC
www.scholastic.co.uk

Character profile

This identity card belongs to _____ _____	Name:
	Address:
	Date of Birth:
	Appearance:
Official Storyland Resident	Occupation:
	Personality:

■ Write a description of your character using the information that you have included on the identity card to help you. Remember to write in sentences!

_____

_____

_____

_____

Name _____

Suffixes

■ Fill in the missing words using the words from the word bank.

1. Shane picked up the glass _____ so he didn't cut himself.

2. Sally looked _____ in her new party clothes.

3. Gran added a _____ of sugar to her tea.

4. The old man shouted _____ at the naughty children.

5. The postman ran _____ because a dog was chasing him.

6. The sun was shining and everyone felt _____.

7. Tess _____ helped Tim to tidy up his toys.

8. The _____ kitten chased the ball of wool.

9. Jill _____ ate all of her sweets instead of sharing them.

10. "What a _____ picture," said Zak's teacher.

Word bank

angrily	wonderful	greedily	spoonful	quickly
playful	kindly	beautiful	carefully	cheerful

Extra challenge

■ Write some more words that end in *-ful* and *-ly* on the back of this sheet.

SCHOLASTIC
www.scholastic.co.uk

Capital letters and full stops

- Put the capital letters and full stops in the correct places.

the ugly sisters were very unkind to cinderella

a mouse lived in the corner of the kitchen

on monday morning the ugly sisters told cinderella to clean the kitchen

- Add the missing capital letters and full stops.

cinderella was very sad she wanted to go to the ball with her sisters the ugly sisters laughed at cinderella they did not want her to go to the ball the ugly sisters gave cinderella lots of horrible jobs to do on monday she had to clean the kitchen on tuesday morning cinderella had to do the laundry on wednesday afternoon she had to make dresses for the ugly sisters on thursday cinderella had to go shopping by friday she was very tired and very weepy

- Re-order these mixed-up sentences. Use the capital letters and full stops to help you.

wanted ball. to go Cinderella the to

_____

sisters The were unkind ugly Cinderella. to

_____

little mouse for felt Cinderella. sorry The

_____

Illustration © Mark Brierley / Beehive Illustration

All about penguins

A penguin is a bird but it cannot fly. A penguin uses its wings as flippers to help it to swim. There are 17 different kinds of penguin in the world and many of these can be found in Antarctica. One kind of penguin that lives in Antarctica is the Emperor penguin. Emperor penguins are the largest penguins in the world. They grow to be over 1m tall and weigh about 30kg.

Appearance

Emperor penguins have black backs, heads and wings and white stomachs. They have orange, yellow and white patches on their necks. Emperor penguins have a thick layer of blubber under their skin. This helps them to keep warm. Emperor penguins have waterproof feathers all over their bodies. These help to keep the penguins dry when they swim in the icy sea.

Keeping warm

It is extremely cold in Antarctica. Emperor penguins keep warm by standing in huddles. The penguins take turns standing in the centre of the huddle. The penguins at the centre of the huddle are warm because they are protected from the icy winds.

Laying eggs

Most penguins lay their eggs in summer but the Emperor penguin is different. The female Emperor penguin lays one egg in winter. She then passes the egg to the male penguin. The male penguin rests the egg on his feet under a thick roll of skin and feathers called a brood pouch. He does this to keep the egg warm and to help the chick to grow. While the male penguin keeps the egg warm, the female penguin goes on a long journey to the sea to find food. When the female penguin returns, the chick has already hatched. The female penguin takes over looking after the chick and the male penguin makes the same long journey to the sea to find food.

SCHOLASTIC
www.scholastic.co.uk

Fiction or non-fiction?

■ What type of book would you find these sentences in?

	Fiction	Non-fiction
Ducks have feathers all over their bodies.		
Mr Duck took his children to school.		
Danny the Duck played with the frogs in the pond.		
Ducks lay eggs.		
"What time is it?" asked the duck.		
Baby ducks are called ducklings.		
Ducks like to swim in water.		
Baby duck wanted to go shopping with his mum.		
A duck has webbed feet to help it to swim.		
The duck stole Granny's sandwich and she was cross.		

■ Write your own fiction and non-fiction sentences about ducks on the back of this sheet or in your book.

Riddles

bird

pig

lion

cow

duck

fish

horse

deer

tiger

sheep

dog

cat

goat

panda

koala

SCHOLASTIC
www.scholastic.co.uk
Illustrations © Mark Brierley / Beehive Illustration

Mathematics

This chapter provides 30 lessons based on the objectives taken from the Primary National Strategy's *Primary Framework for mathematics*, covering all seven strands and a range of objectives. The curriculum grids below are also provided, in editable format, on the accompanying CD-ROM.

The lessons show how the interactive whiteboard can be used to teach and model new mathematical concepts clearly for the whole class to see. The lessons encourage the children to be actively involved in their learning by asking them to make choices by pressing or highlighting text, filling in spaces by writing or typing, and manipulating and sorting numbers and images by dragging or rotating.

Lesson title	PNS objectives	NLS objectives	Expected prior knowledge	Cross-curricular links
Lesson 1: Counting in tens and ones	**Counting and understanding number** • Read and write two-digit numbers in figures and words; describe and extend number sequences.	• To count on and back in tens and ones, starting from any two-digit number.	• Count in tens and ones from 0.	There are no specific links for this lesson.
Lesson 2: Partitioning	**Counting and understanding number** • Explain what each digit in a two-digit number represents, including numbers where 0 is a place holder; partition two-digit numbers in different ways, including into multiples of 10 and 1.	• To know what each digit in a two-digit number represents including zero as a place holder. • To partition two-digit numbers into a multiple of tens and ones.	• Read two-digit numbers.	There are no specific links for this lesson.
Lesson 3: Ordering numbers	**Counting and understanding number** • Order two-digit numbers and position them on a number line.	• To order whole numbers to at least 100 and position them on a number line and 100-square.	• Read whole numbers up to 100.	There are no specific links for this lesson.
Lesson 4: Missing numbers	**Calculating** • Calculate the value of an unknown in a number sentence.	• To recognise the use of a symbol to stand for an unknown number.	• Add and subtract confidently.	**Speaking and listening** Objective 21: To use language and gesture to support the use of models/diagrams/displays when explaining.
Lesson 5: Number facts	**Knowing and using number facts** • Derive and recall all addition and subtraction facts for each number to at least 10.	• To know by heart all addition and subtraction facts for each number to at least 10.	• Partition 10 in different ways using apparatus.	**Speaking and listening** Objective 14: To listen to others in class, ask relevant questions and follow instructions.
Lesson 6: Multiplication (1)	**Calculating** • Represent repeated addition as multiplication.	• To understand the operation of multiplication as repeated addition.	• Count in twos, fives and tens. • Add more than two numbers.	There are no specific links for this lesson.
Lesson 7: Multiplication (2)	**Calculating** • Represent repeated arrays as multiplication.	• To understand the operation of multiplication as describing an array.	• Make groups of up to 10. • Count in twos, fives and tens.	There are no specific links for this lesson.
Lesson 8: Totals and change	**Using and applying mathematics** • Solve problems involving addition and subtraction in context of pounds and pence.	• To find totals and work out which coins to pay.	• Recognise all coins. • Addition strategies.	**PSHE** PoS (2i) To realise that money comes from different sources and can be used for different purposes.
Lesson 9: Measuring length and width	**Measuring** • Read the numbered divisions on a scale.	• To read a simple scale to the nearest labelled division.	• Measure using non-standard units.	**Science** PoS (2f) To make and record measurements.

Lesson title	PNS objectives	NLS objectives	Expected prior knowledge	Cross-curricular links
Lesson 10: Telling the time	**Measuring** • Use units of time (seconds, minutes, hours, days) and know the relationships between them; read the time to the quarter hour.	• To read the time to the hour, half-hour or quarter-hour on an analogue and a 12-hour digital clock.	• Read o'clock times. • Recognise minute and hour hand.	**English** PNS: Understanding and interpreting texts
Lesson 11: Odds and evens	**Counting and understanding number** • Recognise odd and even numbers.	• To recognise odd and even numbers to at least 30.	• Read whole numbers up to at least 30.	**PE** PoS (4a) To know how important it is to be active.
Lesson 12: Estimating	**Counting and understanding number** • Estimate a number of objects. • Count up to 100 objects by grouping them.	• To give a sensible estimate of at least 50 objects. • To count reliably up to 100 objects by grouping them.	• Count in twos, fives and tens. • Count up to 100 accurately.	**Speaking and listening** Objective 15: To listen to each other's views, agree the next steps to take and identify contributions by each group member.
Lesson 13: Adding three small numbers (1)	**Knowing and using number facts** • Derive and recall all addition facts for each number to at least 10, all pairs with totals to 20. • Use knowledge of number facts.	• To add three small numbers by putting the largest number first.	• Order whole numbers up to 20.	**Speaking and listening** Objective 13: To speak with clarity and use intonation when reading and reciting texts.
Lesson 14: Adding three small numbers (2)	**Knowing and using number facts** • Derive and recall all addition facts for each number to at least 10.	• To add three small numbers by finding a pair totalling 10.	• Number bonds that make 10.	There are no specific links for this lesson.
Lesson 15: Addition by partitioning	**Counting and understanding number** • Partition two-digit numbers in different ways, including into multiples of 10 and 1.	• To partition additions into tens and units, then recombine.	• Place value of the digits in a two-digit number.	There are no specific links for this lesson.
Lesson 16: Inverses	**Calculating** • Understand that subtraction is the inverse of addition and vice versa, and use this to derive and record related addition and subtraction number sentences.	• To understand that subtraction is the inverse of addition. • To state the subtraction corresponding to a given addition and vice versa. • To use the relationship between addition and subtraction.	• Understand addition and subtraction confidently.	There are no specific links for this lesson.
Lesson 17: Multiplication (3)	**Knowing and using number facts** • Derive and recall multiplication facts for the 2- and 10-times tables.	• To know by heart the multiplication facts for the 2- and 10-times tables.	• Multiply using repeated addition.	**Speaking and listening** Objective 13: To speak with clarity and use intonation when reading and reciting texts.
Lesson 18: How can we work it out?	**Using and applying mathematics** • Identify and record the information or calculation needed to solve a puzzle or problem. • Present solutions to puzzles and problems in an organised way; explain decisions, methods and results in spoken form, using mathematical language and number sentences.	• To choose and use appropriate operations and efficient calculation strategies to solve problems. • To explain how a problem was solved orally.	• Addition and subtraction strategies.	**Speaking and listening** Objective 15: To listen to each other's views and preferences and agree the next steps.
Lesson 19: Money problems	**Using and applying mathematics** • Solve problems involving addition, subtraction, multiplication or division in context of pounds and pence.	• To use mental addition and subtraction, simple multiplication and division, to solve simple word problems involving money.	• Addition, subtraction, multiplication and division strategies. • Use correct notation when writing money amounts.	**Speaking and listening** Objective 16: To adopt appropriate roles in small or large groups and consider alternative courses of action.

Lesson title	PNS objectives	NLS objectives	Expected prior knowledge	Cross-curricular links
Lesson 20: Shape names	**Understanding shape** • Visualise common 2D shapes and 3D solids.	• To use the mathematical names for common 2D and 3D shapes.	• Name some shapes.	**Art and design** PoS (4a) To have a knowledge and understanding of line, shape, form and space.
Lesson 21: Position	**Understanding shape** • Follow and give instructions involving position.	• To use mathematical vocabulary to describe position.	• Use simple positional vocabulary.	**Geography** QCA Unit 5 'Where in the world is Barnaby Bear?'
Lesson 22: Rounding	**Counting and understanding number** • Round two-digit numbers to the nearest 10.	• To round numbers less than 100 to the nearest 10.	• Read whole numbers up to 100. • Understand what a multiple of 10 is.	**PE** PoS (7a) To send and receive a ball.
Lesson 23: Adjusting	**Calculating** • Add or subtract mentally a single-digit number or a multiple of 10 to or from any two-digit number; use practical and informal written methods to add and subtract two-digit numbers.	• To add/subtract 9 or 11 by adding/subtracting 10 and adjusting by 1.	• Add and subtract 10 mentally.	**Speaking and listening** Objective 15: To listen to each other's views and preferences, agree the next steps to take and identify contributions by each group member.
Lesson 24: Bridging	**Calculating** • Add or subtract mentally a single-digit number or a multiple of 10 to or from any two-digit number; use practical and informal written methods to add and subtract two-digit numbers.	• To bridge through 10 or 20, then adjust.	• Addition and subtraction facts for each number to 10. • Add a single-digit number to a multiple of 10.	**Speaking and listening** Objective 14: To listen to others in class, ask relevant questions and follow instructions.
Lesson 25: Division (1)	**Calculating** • Represent sharing as division.	• To understand the operation of division as sharing.	• Share into equal groups.	**Speaking and listening** Objective 14: To listen to others in class, ask relevant questions and follow instructions.
Lesson 26: Division (2)	**Calculating** • Represent repeated subtraction (grouping) as division.	• To understand the operation of division as grouping.	• Subtract.	There are no specific links for this lesson.
Lesson 27: Worm catching	**Using and applying mathematics** • Describe patterns and relationships involving numbers or shapes. **Counting and understanding number** • Recognise odd and even numbers.	• To solve mathematical problems or puzzles. • To recognise odd and even numbers to at least 30.	• Recognise odd and even numbers.	**Speaking and listening** Objective 15: To listen to each other's views and preferences and agree the next steps.
Lesson 28: Favourite fruits and favourite drinks	**Handling data** • Answer a question by collecting and recording data in lists and tables; represent the data as pictograms to show results.	• To solve a given problem by sorting, classifying and organising information in simple ways.	• Sort objects into groups according to given criteria.	**Science** QCA Unit 2A 'Health and growth'
Lesson 29: Shape sorting	**Understanding shape** • Sort, make and describe shapes, referring to their properties.	• To sort shapes and describe some of their features.	• Describe some shape properties.	**Speaking and listening** Objective 13: To speak with clarity and use intonation when reading and reciting texts.
Lesson 30: Moving along a route	**Understanding shape** • Follow and give instructions involving position, direction and movement.	• To give instructions for moving along a route in straight lines and round right-angled corners.	• Give simple directions.	**ICT** QCA Unit 2D 'Routes: controlling a floor turtle' **Speaking and listening** Objective 14: To listen to others in class, ask relevant questions and follow instructions.

Counting in tens and ones

Learning objective
PNS: Counting and understanding number
● Read and write two-digit numbers in figures and words; describe and extend number sequences.

Resources
'Counting in tens and ones' Notebook file; prepare cards with number sequences counting on and back in tens and ones – leave blank spaces in the sequences for the children to fill in (for example: 6, 16, 26, 36, _, _, _, 76); a bag containing 0-100 number cards; a bag containing four instructions: *count on in ones; count back in ones; count on in tens; count back in tens.*

Links to other subjects
There are no specific links for this lesson.

Starter
Open page 2 of the 'Counting in tens and ones' Notebook file. Press on the thumbnail image to open the *Number grid* ITP and highlight two numbers. Count in ones from the lower to the higher number and back again. Challenge more confident learners to complete the task without looking at the grid. Now choose two numbers that are an exact multiple of 10 apart (for example, 24 and 84) and count in tens from the lower to the higher number and back again. Ask: *What pattern do the numbers follow on the 100-square?* Show that they go vertically down a column.

Whole-class shared work
● Use the *Number grid* ITP to highlight patterns in the numbers when counting forwards and backwards in ones and tens.
● Ask: *What patterns can you see in the numbers?* Illuminate that, when counting in ones, the units digit increases or decreases by one every step but the tens digit remains constant – except when the count passes a multiple of 10. Also explain that, when counting in tens, the units digit remains constant but the tens digit increases or decreases by one every step.
● Check that the children understand that when counting forwards in ones or tens you are adding 1 or 10, and when counting backwards in ones or tens you are subtracting 1 or 10.
● Go to page 3 and look at the number sequence. Ask the children to tell you which number is missing from the sequence. How do they know? Highlight the numbers on the 100-square grid, if required.
● If desired, use voting methods to decide on the correct answer. Drag the chosen number to the sequence to check whether it is correct or not.
● Repeat this process for pages 4 to 12. Use these sequences to assess understanding and tackle any misconceptions.

Independent work
● Give each group a set of prepared cards with number sequences and blank spaces. For example: 6, 16, 26, 36, ___, ___, ___, 76.
● Ask the children to copy the sequences, filling in the missing numbers.
● Remind them to use their findings about the patterns created by counting on and back in tens and ones to help them check their answers.
● Ensure that less confident learners are working within a range of numbers they recognise and understand.
● Make the task more challenging by using numbers over 100 in the sequences.

Plenary
● Sit in a circle and pass around the two bags of cards to music (see Resources).
● When the music stops, the child holding the bags takes out a card from each bag and reads it to the class. Explain that the number card gives the starting number and the instruction states how to count until the child has walked around the circle once and then retaken his/her place.
● During this activity, take the opportunity to assess the children's understanding.

Whiteboard tools
Use a Highlighter pen to draw attention to patterns in the 100-square.

 Pen tray

 Select tool

 Highlighter pen

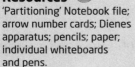

Partitioning

Learning objective
PNS: Counting and understanding number
● Explain what each digit in a two-digit number represents, including numbers where 0 is a place holder; partition two-digit numbers in different ways, including into multiples of 10 and 1.

Resources
'Partitioning' Notebook file; arrow number cards; Dienes apparatus; pencils; paper; individual whiteboards and pens.

Links to other subjects
There are no specific links for this lesson.

Starter
Open the 'Partitioning' Notebook file and go to page 2. Read the number words and numerals together. Order the numerals down the page from smallest to largest. Ask: *How do we know that this is the smallest/largest number?* Establish that to order the numbers you need to look at the first digit; the second digit is only looked at if two numbers have the same first digit. Finally, match the words to the numerals by dragging and dropping them into position on the screen.

Whole-class shared work
● Show the children a 10 and a 1 from the Dienes apparatus. Ensure that they understand what both pieces are worth.
● Display page 3. Explain partitioning as *splitting a number into parts*. Tell the children that they are going to learn how to partition numbers into tens and ones.
● Ask a child to move ten of the orange unit squares to the middle of the screen to build a tower.
● Let two other children repeat the exercise. Count the three sticks of 10 to show that there are 30 ones. Elicit that 30 ones make 3 tens. Ask: *How do we make the number 36?* Reveal the answer on page 4 once everyone has shared their ideas.
● Give out Dienes apparatus and instruct the children to make the number 52. Ask a child to choose the correct answer on page 5. Press on the image that you think is right to produce a groan or cheer depending on whether you are correct or not. Repeat this for number 37 on page 6.
● Give out arrow number cards and instruct the children to make the numbers displayed on page 7. Invite a child to move the arrow cards on the board.
● As an assessment, allow the children to investigate the numbers on page 8 using the Dienes apparatus and the arrow cards. Allow the children to demonstrate their working on page 8. Press the button to be taken to the answers on page 9.

Independent work
● Give each group a set of two-digit numbers to investigate partitioning into tens and ones. Suggest ways that they could record their work, either as a sum or pictorially (for example: 35 = 3 tens + 5 ones).
● Let less confident learners work practically with support, making two-digit numbers with Dienes apparatus and arrow cards.
● Challenge more confident learners to partition three-digit numbers into hundreds, tens and ones.

Plenary
● Look at the numbers on page 10. Ask the children to partition one of the numbers on their individual whiteboards.
● Address any errors made. Look at the number 30. Ask: *How many tens and ones is this number made from?* Explain the importance of the zero: it changes the value of the 3 from 3 ones to 3 tens.

Whiteboard tools
 Pen tray

 Select tool

Ordering numbers

Learning objective
PNS: Counting and understanding number
● Order two-digit numbers and position them on a number line.

Starter

Begin by counting from 0 to 100 to reinforce number order. Open the first page of the prepared Notebook file (see Resources) and ask one child to read out the first set of five numbers. Ask the children to order the numbers, from smallest to largest, on their individual whiteboards. Ask one child to order the numbers on the class whiteboard. Invite another child to locate the numbers on a number line to check the answers. Repeat this for the other two sets of numbers. Challenge more confident learners by giving them numbers up to 200 (or beyond) to order.

Whole-class shared work

● Clearly demonstrate the relationship between a 100-square and a number line to the children as follows:
  ● Show a large 100-square that can be cut up.
  ● Slice the top row (1–10) from the 100-square and hold it up.
  ● Slice the second row (11–20) from the 100-square and hold it up next to the first row so that it creates a 0–20 number line.
  ● Continue this until all of the rows have been separated and a 0–100 number line has been created.
● Show the blank 100-square on the second page of the prepared Notebook file and ask the children to state what numbers would be in the empty squares you highlight. Ask: *How did you work that out?*
● Challenge the children to locate the position of certain numbers on the 100-square and write the numbers into the empty squares.

Independent work

● Supply each child with a blank 100-square and a list of numbers. Let the children locate and shade the numbers from their list on the 100-square to create a simple picture.
● Differentiate the task for less confident learners by giving them the 100-square with some numbers labelled as clues (such as 1, 11, 21, and so on).

Plenary

● Make groups of four or five children. Give each child a number card with a number from 0 to 200 on it. Ask each group to order themselves from the smallest to the largest number.
● Next, merge two groups together and ask the children to order themselves again.
● Finally, merge all of the groups together and ask the children to put themselves in order as a whole class.

Resources

Prepare blank 100-squares and lists of numbers that when shaded will make pictures on the square; number lines; 0–200 number cards; pencils; individual whiteboards and pens. Prepare a Notebook file: open the whiteboard software and use the Text tool to insert three sets of five numbers from 0 to 100 (use different colours for each set and make separate text boxes for each number); on the next page insert a blank 100-square.

Links to other subjects

There are no specific links for this lesson.

Whiteboard tools

Insert a blank 100-square into the prepared file from the Mathematics folder in My Content in the Gallery.

 Pen tray

 Select tool

 Text tool

 Highlighter pen

 Gallery

Learning objective
PNS: Calculating
● Calculate the value of an unknown in a number sentence.

Resources
'Missing numbers' Notebook file; individual number lines; prepared cards with 'missing number' problems on them; coloured pencils. (Microsoft Excel is required to view the embedded spreadsheet in the Notebook file.)

Links to other subjects
Speaking and listening
Objective 21: To use language and gesture to support the use of models/diagrams/displays when explaining.
● Let the children acting as a teacher in the Plenary use the *Number line* ITP as a visual aid to their explanation.

Missing numbers

Starter
Open page 2 of the 'Missing numbers' Notebook file. Press the thumbnail image to open the *Number line* ITP. Set the number line from 0 to 100 and place the markers on two numbers. Let the children work out the difference between the two numbers. Show the difference span to check the answer. Show the addition and subtraction sum and relate it to the numbers on the number line. Repeat this activity for different numbers.

Whole-class shared work
● Go to page 3 and press the button to open the Microsoft Excel file. (Prior to opening the Excel file, ensure that your Excel security level is set to Medium [Tools menu, Macro submenu, Security command]. You will be prompted to enable or disable macros when you open the 'Missing numbers' Excel file; choose Enable macros for this file to work properly.) Select the tab at the bottom of the Excel spreadsheet labelled *addition 2*. Use the up and down arrow buttons beneath the numbers to create a sum, for example: 15 + ? = 23.
● Ask: *What do you need to do to work out the missing number?* (The children need to calculate what must be added to 15 to make 23).
● Demonstrate this calculation on a number line – start on 15 and count the steps on to 23.
● Next, choose the tab labelled *addition 3* and confirm that this type of missing number sum can be calculated in the same way as the previous one, because addition can be done in any order.
● Then, choose the tab labelled *subtraction 2* and show that to calculate the missing number in a sum such as ? – 11 = 7 you need to calculate what you start with if taking away 11 leaves 7.
● Demonstrate this calculation on a number line: to find the answer, start on 7 then add the 11 that were taken away back on.
● Finally, choose the tab labelled *subtraction 3* and show that to calculate the missing number in a sum such as 24 – ? = 16 you need to calculate how many to take away from 24 to leave 16.
● Demonstrate this calculation on a number line: start on 24 and count the steps back to 16.
● You may wish to visit each type of problem in separate lessons initially.

Independent work
● Give each group a set of prepared 'missing number' problem cards (see Resources).
● Ask the children to write the completed problems, using a different colour for the missing number. Give out number lines to enable the children to check their answers.
● Give less confident learners just one type of missing number sum at a time and ensure that they are working within a range of numbers that they are very comfortable with.
● Extend the task by asking the children to use their new skills to work out missing numbers in word problems. For example: *Kate has 23p. How much more does she need in order to buy a book for 50p?*

Plenary
● Return to the Notebook file and use the *Number line* ITP on page 2 (with the addition or subtraction sum and the difference span showing) to work through some of the problems that the children found tricky.
● Invite some of the more confident learners to act as teacher and explain how to work out a problem to the rest of the class.

Whiteboard tools
Use the On-screen Keyboard, accessed through the Pen tray or the SMART Board tools menu, to input numbers in the spreadsheet cells.

 Pen tray

 Select tool

 On-screen Keyboard

Number facts

Learning objective
PNS: Knowing and using number facts
● Derive and recall all addition and subtraction facts for each number to at least 10.

Resources
'Missing numbers' Notebook file; photocopiable page 92 'Four in a row'; counters; individual whiteboards and pens; cards with subtraction and addition symbols; cards with sums with the answers from 0–20; whistle. (Microsoft Excel is required to view the embedded spreadsheet in the Notebook file.)

Links to other subjects
Speaking and listening
Objective 14: To listen to others in class, ask relevant questions and follow instructions.
● The children must work together and listen to each other to play the game in the independent activity.

Starter
Open the 'Missing numbers' Notebook file. Go to page 3 and press the icon to launch the Excel file. (Prior to opening the Excel file, ensure that your Excel security level is set to Medium [Tools menu, Macro submenu, Security command]. You will be prompted to enable or disable macros when you open the 'Missing numbers' Excel file; choose Enable macros for this file to work properly.) Choose the tab at the bottom of the spreadsheet labelled *addition 4*. Set the number after the equals sign to any number between 0 and 10 using the arrows beneath the number. On their individual whiteboards, ask the children to write down two numbers that would make the number sentence correct. Type some answers on the whiteboard to check them.

Next, choose the tab at the bottom labelled *subtraction 4* and repeat the activity, this time finding two numbers to subtract to make the number sentence correct.

Whole-class shared work
● Return to the Notebook file and go to page 4. Press the thumbnail image to open the *Number spinners* ITP and set it up so that it is displaying two six-sided spinners.
● Let one child press the centre of each spinner, then ask another child to read the two numbers spun.
● Show the children an addition or subtraction symbol on a card to let them know whether to add or subtract the two numbers. Encourage them to show the answers using their fingers. Give them only a few seconds before you ask for an answer.

Independent work
● Provide each pair of children with an enlarged copy of photocopiable page 92, together with a prepared spinner and two different-coloured sets of counters.
● Explain that the object of the game is to be the first player to get four counters in a row on the board, horizontally, vertically or diagonally. Show examples of winning lines so that there is no confusion.
● Explain the rules as given on the sheet.
● Let the children check their opponent's calculations and encourage them to contest dubious answers.
● Allow less confident learners to use cubes or a number line to help check their addition and subtraction.
● As an extension, provide more confident learners with an adapted game that uses the results of two spinners added together to make the target number and includes numbers up to 20 on the game board.

Plenary
● Hold up cards showing addition and subtraction sums with answers from 0–20. Give the children a few seconds to work out the answer, then blow a whistle to signal that the children need to get into groups of that amount. This activity needs a large space for the children to move around safely.
● As an added challenge, ask any group that did not manage to find enough children how many more children they need in their group.

Whiteboard tools
Use the On-screen Keyboard, accessed through the Pen tray or the SMART Board tools menu, to input numbers in the spreadsheet cells.

 Pen tray

 Select tool

 On-screen Keyboard

Multiplication (1)

Learning objective
PNS: Calculating
● Represent repeated addition as multiplication.

Resources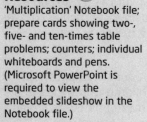
'Multiplication' Notebook file; prepare cards showing two-, five- and ten-times table problems; counters; individual whiteboards and pens. (Microsoft PowerPoint is required to view the embedded slideshow in the Notebook file.)

Links to other subjects
There are no specific links for this lesson.

Starter
Go to page 2 of the 'Multiplication' Notebook file. Open the *Number grid* ITP and ask the children to highlight all of the multiples of 2. Use the grid to count in twos from 0 to 100. Next, ask the children to highlight all of the multiples of 5. Use the grid to count in fives from 0 to 100. Finally, ask the children to highlight all of the multiples of 10. Use the grid to count in tens from 0 to 100.

Whole-class shared work
● Tell the children that they are going to learn how to do a new operation called multiplication and explain that when you multiply, you are adding a number to itself a certain number of times.
● Open the slideshow on page 3 of the Notebook file. Use slides 1–4 to introduce the multiplication symbol, the terminology used to read a multiplication sum and the term *repeated addition*.
● Show the children how to create a repeated addition from a multiplication using slides 5 and 6.
● Supply counters for the children. Display slide 7 and ask them to work out the answers to the multiplication sums by making groups. Translate the groups of counters into number sentences and ask some children to type the number sentences into the boxes.
● Show the children slides 8 and 9 so that they can check their answers.
● Use the Area Capture tool 📷 to take screenshots of any of the slideshow pages, if necessary.

Independent work
● Give each group a set of prepared cards (see Resources). Tell the children to choose a card, read the sum and then write it as a repeated addition.
● Allow the children to use counters and number lines for support during the lesson.
● Work with less confident learners to help them make groups of counters. For example, for 2 × 6, make six groups of 2.
● Challenge more confident learners by including some three- and four-times table problems.

Plenary
● If you have not already done so, return to the Notebook file and display page 4. Drag and drop a number of one type of fruit into the white box on the page.
● Give the children individual whiteboards. Ask them to use their boards to work out how much it would cost to buy the items shown on the Notebook page.
● Once they have done this, use the Undo button ↩ to reset the page. Display another set of fruit and ask the children to calculate the cost of this new set.
● Provide opportunities for the children to explain how they worked out their answers. Ensure that they make the link that they are multiplying the amounts using repeated addition to work out the answers.

Whiteboard tools
Use the On-screen Keyboard, accessed through the Pen tray or the SMART Board tools menu, to input numbers in the spreadsheet cells. Use the Area Capture tool to take screenshots, if required.

 Pen tray

 Select tool

 On-screen Keyboard

 Area Capture tool

↩ Undo button

Learning objective
PNS: Calculating
● Represent repeated arrays as multiplication.

Resources
'Multiplication' Notebook file; pots; several 2p, 5p and 10p coins; counters; prepare cards showing two-, five- and ten-times table sums; paper; pencils. (Microsoft PowerPoint is required to view the embedded slideshow in the Notebook file.)

Links to other subjects
There are no specific links for this lesson.

Multiplication (2)

Starter
Open the 'Multiplication' Notebook file and go to page 5. Ask the children to work out how much money is on pages 5, 6, and 7. Encourage them to count in twos, fives or tens accordingly. Put a pot of 2p, 5p and 10p coins on each table and ask the children to make given amounts using a particular coin. Ask how many of each coin the children needed to make the given amount.

Whole-class shared work
● Go to page 8 and ask: *What do we already know about multiplication?*
● Open the PowerPoint slideshow. Introduce the children to the idea of an array using slides 1–3. Explain that an array is a set of objects arranged into rows and columns so that they make a rectangle formation.
● Remind the children that columns are vertical and rows are horizontal.
● Support the children in making arrays with counters to show given multiplication sums.
● Make some arrays with counters and ask the children what sum the arrays are describing.
● Slides 4–15 provide an opportunity for assessment. Using slide 4, ask the children to choose which array the sum is describing. Press on the array to check the answer. There are three assessment questions altogether.
● Relate the work on arrays to the work done previously on multiplication using repeated addition. Show that each row/column is identical – so by adding the total number of objects in one row/column to itself a certain number of times, a repeated addition is taking place.

Independent work
● Give each group a set of prepared cards (see Resources) and a pot of counters.
● Tell the children to choose a card, read it and then make the array it describes, using the counters provided.
● Once the children have made the group with counters, tell them to draw the array and work out the answer to the sum.
● Work with less confident learners to help them make the arrays for two-times table problems to begin with.
● Challenge more confident learners by including some three- and four-times table problems.

Plenary
● Supply a pot of counters for each group. Ask one member of each group to choose a card from the set they used during the independent work and show it to the rest of the group.
● Give the children ten seconds thinking time and then challenge them to be the first in their group to use the counters to make the array that the card is describing.

Whiteboard tools
Use a Pen from the Pen tray to write the money totals on the Notebook page.

 Pen tray

 Select tool

Learning objective
PNS: Using and applying mathematics
● Solve problems involving addition and subtraction in context of pounds and pence.

Resources
'Real-life problems' Notebook file; photocopiable page 93 'Find the pairs' (photocopy the money Snap cards onto card and cut them out); coins; pots.

Links to other subjects
PSHE
PoS (2i) To realise that money comes from different sources and can be used for different purposes.
● Use this opportunity to help children understand the value of money.

Totals and change

Starter
Discuss how to add together three numbers. Talk about the two main strategies – put the largest number first; and find pairs that total a multiple of 10.

Open the 'Real-life problems' Notebook file and go to page 2. The box contains three of each of these coin amounts: 1p, 2p, 5p, 10p, 20p, 50p. Ask a child to drag three numbers out of the box and write down the addition number sentence they create. Ask: *What is the answer? How did you work it out?* Move on to four cards if appropriate.

Whole-class shared work
● Go to page 3. Ask the children how they would work out which coins they need to pay for something.
● Give each pair a set of coins from 1p to £2 and ask them to order the coins from smallest to largest. Ask some volunteers to move the coins on page 4 to show their solution. Assess whether all coin values are known.
● Give each pair a pot of coins and show page 5. Ask each pair to make 29p. Share the different ways that the children find.
● Next, ask each pair to make 29p using the least number of coins possible. Compare solutions and ask a child to drag the coins to display their solution on page 5.
● Repeat this for 73p and 67p.
● Talk about how to add a group of coins together to find the total. Refer the children back to the strategies used in the Starter.
● Finally, assess any children you are still unsure about by asking them to match the money boxes to the amounts on page 6.

Independent work
● Give each pair two sets of prepared money Snap cards (see Resources) shuffled together.
● Revise the rules for Snap and explain that in the money version the children need to match the money totals with the coins to make a Snap.
● Encourage the children to take their time to work out the totals on each card before they lay out the next one.
● If the children are too excitable, play a Pelmanism game with one set of the cards instead. This can also help to develop short-term memory.
● Create new cards with smaller or greater amounts to suit different abilities.

Plenary
● Give each pair a pot of coins and specify an amount for each ability level. Challenge the children to be the first to make their amount.
● Add an extra challenge by asking them to use the least number of coins possible.
● Ask: *What would happen if we couldn't make the exact amount? How do we work out what change we would need?* Write the children's responses on page 7.

Whiteboard tools

 Pen tray

 Select tool

Measuring length and width

Learning objective
PNS: Measuring
● Read the numbered divisions on a scale.

Resources
'Build your own' file; prepare sheets of paper with different pictures for the children to measure; centimetre rulers; blank number lines. Prepare the 'Build your own' file as follows: on page 1 insert different length lines and a centimetre ruler from the Mathematics folder under My Content in the Gallery; on page 2 insert different-sized rectangles.

Links to other subjects
Science
PoS (2f) To make and record measurements.
● The children will use their new measuring skills during science investigations.

Starter
Give each pair of children a blank number line with the two ends labelled 0 and 20 and no other markings. Say a number between 0 and 20 and ask the children to decide where that number would be on the number line. Tell the pairs they must agree on their answer. Ask the children to explain how they decided where to put the number. Repeat this several times.

Whole-class shared work
● Open the 'Build your own' file and draw the children's attention to the centimetre ruler on the first page. Demonstrate how to move and rotate the ruler.
● Ask: *How do we use a ruler to measure the length of a line?* Give each pair of children a ruler and a line to measure and allow time for the children to demonstrate to their partner how to measure the line. Discuss their ideas.
● State the teaching points clearly and demonstrate them using the prepared Notebook file:
  ● Place the ruler carefully – directly below the line, making sure 0cm is level with the beginning of the line to be measured.
  ● Take the reading from the point on the ruler where the line stops.
  ● Read measurements to the nearest cm if they are not exact (for example, *about 3cm long*).
● Ask the children to come up and measure the length of the lines on the whiteboard using the ruler on the screen.
● Record the measurements next to the lines. Continue to reinforce the teaching points.
● Move on to measuring the length and width of rectangles on page 2 of your prepared file. Distinguish between the terms *length* and *width*.

Independent work
● Give each child a sheet of paper with lines, shapes or pictures on it for them to measure (see Resources).
● Provide less confident learners with just one simple dimension to measure, such as a line or a worm. Encourage the rest of the children to measure the length and width of pictures and the edges of simple shapes.
● Challenge more confident learners to measure to the nearest half centimetre. Progress to using millimetres.
● Remind the children regularly that they should begin measuring from 0cm on the ruler.

Plenary
● Go to page 2 of the prepared Notebook file, showing different-sized rectangles. Ask a child to pretend to be the teacher and explain to the rest of the class how to measure the length and width of one of the rectangles on the page.
● Encourage the other children to ask questions to clarify what 'the teacher' is explaining.
● Challenge the children to measure the length and width of an exercise book, using the tips that they have been given.

Whiteboard tools
Use the Lines tool to insert lines on the prepared Notebook file, and the Shapes tool to draw rectangles.

 Pen tray

 Select tool

Shapes tool

 Lines tool

 Gallery

Learning objective
PNS: Measuring
● Use units of time (seconds, minutes, hours, days) and know the relationships between them; read the time to the quarter hour.

Resources
'Time problems' Notebook file; photocopiable page 94 'Telling the time'; large teaching clock; apparatus for timed activity (see Starter); individual whiteboards and pens.

Links to other subjects
English
PNS: Understanding and interpreting texts
● Ask the children to create a flow chart of their school day and record the times of each event on an analogue clock.

Telling the time

Starter
Open the 'Time problems' Notebook file and go to page 2. Ask the children to close their eyes when you say *go* and open them again when they think one minute has passed. Start the Timer and share one minute with the children, so that they know how long it actually is. Now ask them to estimate how many times they can do an activity, such as bounce a ball, in one minute. Test these estimates by carrying out the activity. Record the results on the Notebook page.

Whole-class shared work
● Use a large teaching clock, displaying both analogue and digital, to show some times. Go to page 3 which shows an analogue and digital clock.
● Ask: *What time does the clock read?* Revise the function of the hour and minute hands and how these relate to the numbers on a digital clock. To rotate the clock hands, select one and then press and drag the end of the line with the arrow. Use a Pen from the Pen tray to write the corresponding time on the digital clock.
● Practise reading o'clock, half-past, quarter-past and quarter to times. Ensure that both analogue and digital displays are used and compared.
● Open the quiz on page 4. Ask the children to write their answers on their individual whiteboards before inviting a volunteer to press the button next to the answer that they think is correct. Repeat this for all six questions.
● Using the clock on page 5, demonstrate how to work out times that are earlier or later than a given time. Show the hands moving around the clock and ensure that all the children understand that quarter of an hour equates to a quarter turn of the minute hand.
● Do the second quiz, on page 6, in the same way as the one on page 4.

Independent work
● Give each child an enlarged copy of photocopiable page 94. Encourage the children to read the times and write them down in words on the line beneath each clock. Supply a word bank of the time and number words they may need.
● Less confident learners will need to practise reading only o'clock and half-past times to begin with.
● As an extension, ask the children to revisit each clock and work out the challenges beneath each one.

Plenary
● Investigate the children's work to see whether most of their difficulties were with telling the time or with passage of time.
● Ask the children to display given times and to display times that are later or earlier than a given time.
● Encourage the children to talk about how they worked out the answer.
● Use this session to assess the children's progress. Use page 7 to compile a summary of what the children have learned.

Whiteboard tools
Use a Pen from the Pen tray to write the time on the blank digital clock on page 3.

 Pen tray

 Select tool

Odds and evens

Learning objective
PNS: Counting and understanding number
● Recognise odd and even numbers.

Resources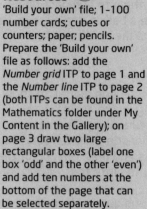
'Build your own' file; 1–100 number cards; cubes or counters; paper; pencils. Prepare the 'Build your own' file as follows: add the *Number grid* ITP to page 1 and the *Number line* ITP to page 2 (both ITPs can be found in the Mathematics folder under My Content in the Gallery); on page 3 draw two large rectangular boxes (label one box 'odd' and the other 'even') and add ten numbers at the bottom of the page that can be selected separately.

Links to other subjects
PE
PoS (4a) To know how important it is to be active.
● Use the Plenary to point out how easy it is to get some exercise every day.

Starter
Challenge the children to count from 1 to 100, alternating between loud and quiet voices as they count. Ask them to say the odd numbers loudly and the even numbers quietly.

Open your prepared 'Build your own' file and display the *Number grid* ITP on the first page. Press on the numbers that the children say loudly as they count so that they can see, as well as hear, the pattern of alternating numbers.

Whole-class shared work
● Look at the *Number grid* ITP with the odd numbers highlighted. Ask: *Can you see a pattern on the number grid?*
● Note that alternating numbers are highlighted. Go to page 2 and circle the highlighted numbers on the *Number line* ITP to emphasise the pattern further.
● If necessary, use the Area Capture tool 🖼 to take screenshots of the ITPs and add them to the Notebook file.
● Ask: *Does anyone know what type of numbers are highlighted/not highlighted?* Introduce the terms *odd* and *even*.
● Invite a child to count out a number of cubes. Demonstrate that if the cubes share exactly into two equal groups, then the number must be even. If they do not share exactly, and there is an odd one left over, the number must be odd.
● Use the prepared Notebook file to sort the ten numbers into either the 'odd' or 'even' box. Check the answers by sharing out cubes.

Independent work
● Give each group a set of 1–30, 1–50 or 1–100 number cards. Ask the children to write odd numbers on the left-hand side of a sheet of paper and even numbers on the right-hand side.
● Allow the children to use cubes or counters to check their answers.
● Support less confident learners by helping them to circle all the odd numbers on a 0–30 number line, using the alternating pattern. Let them use this as a reference.
● Challenge more confident learners to work out a rule for how to determine whether a number is even, just by looking at it. They should notice that even numbers end with a 2, 4, 6, 8 or 0.

Plenary
● Take the children into a large space such as the hall. Assign one end of the hall as odd numbers and the other end as even numbers.
● Stand the children in the middle of the hall and call out a number. Tell the children to run to the correct end of the hall, according to the number you say. Watch carefully for children who are just following the crowd – they will require more work on this objective.

Whiteboard tools
Use the Shapes tool to draw the rectangular boxes in the prepared file, and the Text tool to add the numbers to the page. Use the Area Capture tool to take screenshots, if required.

 Pen tray

 Select tool

A Text tool

 Shapes tool

 Area Capture tool

 Gallery

Estimating

Learning objectives
PNS: Counting and understanding number
● Estimate a number of objects.
● Count up to 100 objects by grouping them.

Starter

Challenge the children to count to 100 in different ways. Open your prepared 'Build your own' file and display the *Number grid* ITP on the first page. Highlight the multiples of 2 using the multiples button. Use the grid to count in twos up to 100, then challenge the children to count again with their eyes closed. Teach them to put a clap between each number so that they have some thinking time. Repeat this activity with multiples of 10 and 5.

Resources
'Build your own' file; photocopiable page 95 'Estimating'; bags of up to 50 objects to be estimated (for example, counters, 1p coins, cubes). Prepare the 'Build your own' file as follows: add the *Number grid* ITP to page 1 and on page 2 add images of, for example, a mouse; resize the animal and copy and paste it randomly around the page between 20 and 50 times; repeat this on a few pages, with different numbers of different animals on each page. (The ITP and animal images are all available in the Mathematics folder under My Content in the Gallery.)

Whole-class shared work
● Working in pairs, ask the children to discuss a meaning for the word *estimate*. Conclude that estimates do not need to be exact and that this is to be expected.
● Tell the children that they are going to estimate how many objects are on a page.
● Go to page 2 of your prepared file. Ask the children to write down an estimate of the number of animals that they can see on the screen. After five seconds enable the Screen Shade ▭ to hide the page from the children's view.
● Share some of the children's estimates. Ask: *Did anyone manage to count the animals?*
● Repeat this for all the prepared pages, ensuring that the children keep their previous estimates.
● Go back to page 2 and explain that the children are now going to assess their estimating skills.
● Pull down the Screen Shade to reveal the page and count how many items there actually are. Drag the images into groups before counting, to show how they can be counted more easily.
● Refer back to the earlier counting practice.
● Repeat this procedure for each page, comparing the estimates to the actual number of images.
● Reinforce that estimates are rarely exact.

Links to other subjects
Speaking and listening
Objective 15: To listen to each other's views, agree the next steps to take and identify contributions by each group member.
● The children need to work collaboratively to share their findings.

Independent work
● Give each group a set of six bags labelled A to F with differing numbers of objects in them. Differentiate by varying the number of objects.
● Ask the children to look at each bag in turn and estimate the total amount. Give them each a copy of photocopiable page 95 to record their answers.
● Ensure that the children are not counting the objects. Talk about how it might be helpful to compare each of the bags to ensure that the bag that appears to hold the most objects has the largest estimate. Remind the children to consider the size of the objects when doing this.

Plenary
● Assign a bag to each child and empty the contents for counting. Remind everyone that grouping objects may make counting easier.
● Invite the children to share the actual totals with their group and to complete their sheets by writing down the totals. Ask each child to raise or lower their thumbs to indicate how good they think their estimating skills are.

Whiteboard tools
Use the Screen Shade to hide or reveal the contents of each page in the prepared Notebook file.

 Pen tray

 Select tool

 Screen Shade

🖼 Gallery

Adding three small numbers (1)

Learning objectives
PNS: Knowing and using number facts
● Derive and recall all addition facts for each number to at least 10, all pairs with totals to 20.
● Use knowledge of number facts.

Resources
'Adding three numbers' Notebook file; 0-20 number cards for each group; individual whiteboards and pens.

Links to other subjects
Speaking and listening
Objective13: To speak with clarity and use intonation when reading and reciting texts.
● The children will have the opportunity to speak clearly when explaining how they worked things out to the class.

Starter
Open the *Number spinners* ITP from page 2 of the 'Adding three numbers' Notebook file, and set it so that it is displaying two six-sided spinners. Invite a volunteer to spin both spinners and ask the children to add the two numbers together as quickly as they can. Talk about the strategies they can use to work out the answers quickly if they do not know the number fact by heart. Encourage them to use known facts to work out the answers more quickly - for example, work out 5 + 6 by using their knowledge that double 5 is 10, then adding one more.

Whole-class shared work
● Use page 3 to introduce the strategy of adding three numbers by putting the largest first. Move the numbers into the correct order.
● Emphasise that putting the largest number first is a useful strategy because it means there is less to add on and therefore less room for errors to be made in calculating the answer.
● Ask the children to write the sum on individual whiteboards and then work out the answer. Invite a child to come to the whiteboard to write the answer on the screen in the space provided. Once they have done this, use the Eraser from the Pen tray to rub over the white box to show whether they are correct.
● Repeat this activity on page 4.
● Use pages 5 and 6 to assess the children's understanding. On page 5, ask the children to rewrite the addition number sentences with the largest number first and then solve them. Invite one of the children to come to the whiteboard to move the numbers into the correct order.
● Go to page 6 to confirm the order of the numbers. Invite children to come to the board to complete the addition sentences on screen. Then use the Delete button 🗙 to remove the red boxes to show the correct answers.

Independent work
● Give each group a set of 0-20 number cards. Ask the children to pick three numbers and add them together. (Give less confident learners a set of 0-10 cards and more confident learners a set of 0-30 cards.)
● Encourage the children to order the three chosen number cards from largest to smallest, write the addition sum and work out the answer.
● Challenge more confident learners by asking: *Is putting the largest number first always the most effective way to find the answer?* For example: 7 + 12 + 7 = ? could be solved more efficiently by knowing that double 7 is 14 then adding 12 more.

Plenary
● Display page 7 of the Notebook file and ask a child to read out the sum. Instruct the children to explain to a partner how they would work out the answer to the sum.
● Share some of these ideas. Ask a child to re-arrange the sum to show the largest number first. Invite another child to share their strategy for working out the sum and let them write in the answer.

Whiteboard tools
Use the Delete button to reveal the answers on page 6 of the Notebook file.

 Pen tray

 Select tool

 Delete button

Adding three small numbers (2)

Learning objective
PNS: Knowing and using number facts
● Derive and recall all addition facts for each number to at least 10.

Resources
'Adding three numbers' Notebook file; photocopiable page 96 'Ladybird flip flap'; prepare a worksheet of sums adding three small numbers (see independent work); individual whiteboards and pens.

Links to other subjects
There are no specific links for this lesson.

Starter
Give a 'Ladybird flip flap' to each child (see photocopiable page 96). Say a number between 0 and 10 and ask the children to show that amount of ladybirds using their flip flap. When the children are comfortable with this, ask them to show the number that needs to be added to the number you say, in order to make 10. For example, if you say *7*, the children show three ladybirds.

Whole-class shared work
● Open the 'Adding three numbers' Notebook file and go to page 8.
● Show the children the sum. Ask: *What could you do to find the answer?*
● Use the Delete button ⊠ to reveal the clue. Remind the children of the Starter activity, where they were finding numbers that equal 10.
● Point out that totalling 6 and 4 gives 10, and explain that it is easier to add a number onto 10. Highlight the 6 and the 4.
● Invite a child to come to the whiteboard to move the third number down to add to the 10 to complete the sum. Let them write in the answer. Once they have done this, delete the red box to reveal the correct answer.
● Practise the new strategy together on page 9. Ask the children to rewrite the sum on their individual whiteboards. Delete the red box to reveal the new sum. Invite one of the children to complete the sum.
● Use page 10 for assessment. Give the children one minute to solve two problems from those given, using the new strategy. Provide them with individual whiteboards to record their answers.
● Invite the children to come to the whiteboard and highlight the numbers they added together first to get 10 or 20. Invite others to write in the answers. Reveal the answers by using the Eraser from the Pen tray to rub over the red boxes beneath the number sentences.

Independent work
● Give each child a worksheet displaying 15 sums that require three small numbers to be added together to solve the problem. Make ten of the problems of the type that can be solved by finding a pair totalling 10.
● Ask the children to identify, and mark on the sheet, the problems they can solve using the strategy of finding a pair totalling 10.
● Tell the children to put a circle around the two numbers that total 10 in each of these sums and then work out the answers.
● Give less confident learners just ten problems, five of which can be solved using the strategy of finding a pair totalling 10.
● Challenge more confident learners to look for pairs totalling 20, then any multiple of 10.

Plenary
● Talk with the children about which sums they solved using the strategy of finding a pair totalling 10 and which ones needed a different strategy. Ask: *How could we solve the other sums?* Make a note of the children's responses on page 11.
● Demonstrate that it is possible to look for any multiple of 10 when adding three numbers, so the strategy can also be useful when adding three larger numbers.

Whiteboard tools
Use the Delete button to reveal the clues and answers.

 Pen tray

 Highlighter pen

 Select tool

 Delete button

Addition by partitioning

Learning objective
PNS: Counting and
understanding number
● Partition two-digit numbers
in different ways, including
into multiples of ten and one.

Resources
'Partitioning' Notebook file;
place number arrow cards;
0-100 number cards;
individual whiteboards and
pens; Dienes apparatus;
prepare some addition cards
for each group; six numbers
between 0-100 on large
paper (see Plenary).

Links to other subjects
There are no specific links for
this lesson.

Starter
Open the 'Partitioning' Notebook file and go to page 11. Remind the children about the previous work done on partitioning two-digit numbers into tens and ones (see page 8 of the Notebook file). Give each child a set of arrow cards and set challenges of making specific two-digit numbers. Ask questions such as: *How many tens are there in 35? How many ones are there in 54? Can you think of a number that has three tens?* Make notes on the Notebook page, if required.

Whole-class shared work
● Explain to the children that partitioning is a good strategy to use when adding two-digit numbers together because they can be added in parts.
● Use page 12 of the Notebook file to demonstrate and talk through the partitioning and recombining strategy. Drag the arrow cards into place, firstly to 10 + 3 + 10 + 6 and then to 10 + 10 + 3 + 6.
● Write the sum of the tens and units numbers in the orange and green arrows respectively. With the children, work out and write the answer.
● Reinforce the strategy with the additions on pages 13 and 14. Give the children individual whiteboards so that they can attempt to work out the answers themselves before completing the process on screen.
● Encourage the children to ask questions and ensure that they are following what is happening by asking them to explain the strategy.
● If the children are finding the strategy difficult, use Dienes apparatus to show the two numbers being partitioned into tens and ones and then recombined as a group of tens and a group of ones.
● Invite a child to come to the whiteboard and drag the arrow cards on the screen, firstly to partition them and then to recombine as a group of tens and a group of ones. Invite another child to write in the answer.
● Use pages 15 and 16 to assess the children's understanding. Take this opportunity to address any errors and misconceptions. Time the children to add an extra challenge to the activity.

Independent work
● Give the children prepared cards with addition sums on them that can be solved using the new strategy. Allow them to use their arrow cards to help them.
● Talk with the children about how they are working out the answers and regularly refer back to the whole-class work.
● Supply less confident learners with Dienes apparatus so that they can practically partition and recombine the numbers.
● Challenge more confident learners by giving them additions that cross the tens boundary, such as 36 + 48. Extend further to additions that cross the 100 boundary, such as 72 + 54.

Plenary
● In the hall, stick six different numbers between 0 and 100 on the wall so that all of the children can see them. Sit the children in the middle and read out an addition sum that gives one of the answers displayed on the wall.
● Give the children adequate thinking time and then ask them to go to the number they think is the answer. Provide individual whiteboards for the children to use during their working out if they need to.

Whiteboard tools
Use the Delete button to
reveal the answers on pages
15 and 16.

 Pen tray

 Select tool

 Delete button

Learning objectives
PNS: Calculating
● Understand that subtraction is the inverse of addition and vice versa, and use this to derive and record related addition and subtraction number sentences.

Resources
'Inverses' Notebook file; photocopiable page 97 'Number triplets'; individual whiteboards and pens; prepare 'inverse partner' game cards (see Plenary). (Microsoft PowerPoint is required to view the embedded slideshow in the Notebook file.)

Links to other subjects
There are no specific links for this lesson.

Inverses

Starter
Open page 2 of the 'Inverses' Notebook file. Talk about different strategies for solving additions and subtractions. Provide each child with an individual whiteboard. Read out five additions and subtractions. Allow sufficient time after reading each question for the children to work out and record the answers on their boards. Share the answers and strategies used to find them.

Whole-class shared work
● Show page 3. Pull the tabs and read the text. Explain that the term *inverse* means *reverse* or *opposite*.
● Press the link at the top of the page to open the PowerPoint presentation to demonstrate that addition is indeed the inverse of subtraction and vice versa. Investigate further on a number line.
● Return to the Notebook file and show page 4. Give the children one minute to write down as many inverses of the number sentences as they can.
● Once the children have a clear understanding of inverses, move on to page 5 to introduce the idea that this understanding can be used to solve problems.
● Using the ladybird on page 6 with a number of spots on each wing, show the children how the spots give two addition sums. Write the addition sums on the page. Encourage the children to use their knowledge of inverses to work out the corresponding subtraction sums. Once they have done this, pull out the tab to reveal the answers.
● Provide the children with an opportunity to repeat this task independently on page 7.
● Go to page 8. Show the children how a set of three numbers can make two addition sums and two subtraction sums. Pull out the tab to reveal the answers.
● Provide the children with an opportunity to repeat this procedure independently on page 9.

Independent work
● Provide each group with a set of number triplets from photocopiable page 97. Alter the numbers on the cards, if necessary, so that they are within a range that the children are comfortable working with.
● Ask the children to create two addition and two subtraction number sentences from the three numbers given on each card.
● Remind the children that if they find two addition sums then they can use their knowledge of inverses to find the subtraction sums.
● Give less confident learners pictures of ladybirds with different spots on each wing and ask them to create two addition sums from each. Support them in finding two subtractions from these additions, using their knowledge of inverses.

Plenary
● Talk about any problems that the children encountered during their work and solve them together, using page 10 for notes.
● Give each child a card with either an addition or subtraction on it. Ensure that each addition card has a corresponding subtraction card (for example, 12 + 16 = 28 and 28 − 16 = 12). Take the children into a large space and ask them to find their inverse partners.

Whiteboard tools

 Pen tray

 Select tool

Learning objective
PNS: Knowing and using number facts
● Derive and recall multiplication facts for the 2- and 10-times tables.

Resources
'Multiplication' Notebook file; photocopiable page 96 'Ladybird flip flap'; individual whiteboards and pens; counters; calculators. Prepare bingo cards by creating 4 × 4 grids using multiples of 2 and 10; prepare question cards with 2- and 10-times tables questions on them. (Microsoft PowerPoint is required to view the embedded slideshow in the Notebook file.)

Links to other subjects
Speaking and listening
Objective 13: To speak with clarity and use intonation when reading and reciting texts.
● The child reciting the questions will be practising speaking clearly.

Multiplication (3)

Starter
Open the 'Multiplication' Notebook file and display page 9. Show the children a ladybird flip flap (see photocopiable page 96 for instructions of how to make one) with some ladybirds hidden. Ask: *How many legs can you see?* Point out that each ladybird has six legs and show how the children can count the legs in twos.

Give each child a flip flap. Invite the children to show a given number of ladybirds. Ask: *How many legs can you see?* Repeat, this time asking the children for the number of spots they can see.

Whole-class shared work
● Go to page 10 and open the PowerPoint slideshow. Press on the star to practise the 2-times table.
● Say the 2-times table as a class, using the terminology: *one two is two; two twos are four* and so on. Use the slideshow to support this activity.
● Repeat for the 10-times table, also using the slideshow.
● Press Escape to exit the slideshow and return to the Notebook file. Show the children page 11 and complete the table together. Filling in the boxes out of order makes this more challenging.
● On individual whiteboards, ask the children to write down the answers to each of the questions on page 12. Afterwards, invite volunteers to come to the whiteboard and use the Eraser from the Pen tray to reveal the answers.

Independent work
● In small groups, assign a caller and give them a pot of prepared question cards. Give the rest of the group a prepared bingo card and some counters each.
● Ask the caller to choose a question card, read it clearly and give the group time to work out the answer.
● Tell the group to work out the answer to each question and cover it up on their bingo card with a counter, if it is present.
● Give the caller a calculator so that they can check the answers to each question. Any wrongly covered answers can then be uncovered.
● Explain that the winner is the first person to get a line either horizontally, vertically or diagonally.
● Change the caller after each game.
● Give less confident learners 2-times table problems only; more confident learners may also be given 5-times table problems.

Plenary
● Display page 13 of the Notebook file and ask: *How much money can you see?* Count the money in twos with the children. Write down the corresponding multiplication sum. For example, five coins: 2p × 5 = 10p.
● Using page 14, ask the children to state the multiplication and the answer. Repeat this with 10p coins on page 15.

Whiteboard tools

 Pen tray

 Select tool

How can we work it out?

Learning objectives
PNS: Using and applying mathematics
● Identify and record the information or calculation needed to solve a puzzle or problem.
● Present solutions to puzzles and problems in an organised way; explain decisions, methods and results in spoken form, using mathematical language and number sentences.

Resources
'Real-life problems' Notebook file; photocopiable page 98 'Work it out'; a set of cards with operations or phrases on them, such as: *shared by, plus, the difference between, groups of.*

Links to other subjects
Speaking and listening
Objective 15: To listen to each other's views and preferences and agree the next steps.
● The children need to work together and listen to each other's ideas in order to solve the problems.

Starter
Open the 'Real-life problems' Notebook file and go to page 8. Ask the children to work in pairs to sort a set of cards with operation words or phrases on them (see Resources) into the type of operation they represent. Ask: *Are there any words or phrases that could represent more than one operation?* Talk as a class about how each pair sorted their cards. Explain that looking out for these words and phrases in word problems helps us to know which operation to use to work out the answer.

Ensure that the children understand the terms *operation* (the type of problem) and *strategy* (a method for working out the answer). Write any notes or key words on page 8, if required.

Whole-class shared work
● Go to page 9. Explain that Jo is a maths detective who loves to solve maths problems and wants the children to help her.
● Read the question on page 10 and ask a volunteer to come to the whiteboard and use the Lines tool to draw the hands on the clocks to show the two times in the question.
● Ask: *What is the question asking us? What operation do we need to use, and why? What strategies could we use to work out the answer?* Highlight any key words in the question (such as *7 o'clock, half past 9* and *how long?*).
● After modelling one strategy on the board, invite some children to share their strategies. Discuss their recording methods.
● Repeat with the questions on pages 11 to 14. Encourage the children to talk about their thinking. Remind them to check that they have actually answered the question being asked at the end.
● Use apparatus from the Gallery such as on-screen teaching clocks, counters and coins to help model questions. This is particularly useful for the less confident learners.

Independent work
● Put the children in pairs of similar ability. Provide each pair with a copy of photocopiable page 98.
● Encourage the pairs to highlight the key words in each problem and discuss what is being asked. Tell them to show their strategies and the answers in the spaces provided. Supply a choice of apparatus for the children to use, if required.
● Ensure that less confident learners are working within the range of numbers that they can comfortably calculate with.
● Talk further about different methods of recording with the more confident learners.

Plenary
● Draw the class together throughout the lesson (as well as at the end) to talk about each question. Ask: *What was each question asking us? What operations did we need to use, and why? What strategies did we use to work out the answer?* Use page 15 to note key points, if required.
● Address any misconceptions and ask for alternative strategies where appropriate.

Whiteboard tools
Use the Lines tool to add hands to the clocks. Use the Gallery to provide apparatus to support questions, if required.

 Pen tray
 Select tool
 Lines tool
 Highlighter pen
 Gallery

Money problems

Learning objective
PNS: Using and applying mathematics
● Solve problems involving addition, subtraction, multiplication or division in context of pounds and pence.

Resources
'Real-life problems' Notebook file; photocopiable page 99 'Money problems'; purses containing different amounts of money (one for each child); cards with different amounts written on each (one each for half the class); cards with corresponding coins on (one each for half the class); highlighters; pencils; items for a role-play shop (see Plenary).

Links to other subjects
Speaking and listening
Objective 16: To adopt appropriate roles in small or large groups and consider alternative courses of action.
● Use the Plenary to extend the children's role-play skills within the context of the shop scenario.

Starter
Give each child a purse of money and ask them to find the total amount of money in the purse. Tell the children to swap purses with a friend to check their answers.

Give half of the class cards with different amounts written on each, and the other half of the class cards with the corresponding coins on. Ask the children to find their partners.

Whole-class shared work
● Open the 'Real-life problems' Notebook file and go to page 16. Look at the symbols (+ – × ÷) and revise what each of them are.
● Read the problem on page 17 and talk with the children about what the question is asking, and what operation they will need to use. Highlight any key words that help to identify the operation needed.
● Drag the pictures and symbols into the white box to illustrate the problem. For example, attach the 15p label to the apple.
● Make duplicate copies of the pictures and symbols if they are needed by selecting the Clone option from an object's dropdown menu.
● Ask: *What strategy could we use to work out this answer?* Discuss different ways to work out the answer as a class.
● Look at pages 18 and 19 in the same way, all the time talking about the operation needed and the strategies that could be used to work out the answer.
● As an assessment, ask the children to work in similar-ability pairs to solve the problems on page 20. Share the answers as a class, talking about which operations were needed and which strategies worked well.

Independent work
● Provide each similar-ability pair with a copy of photocopiable page 99. Encourage the pairs to highlight the key words in each problem and discuss what is being asked.
● Ask the children to record the problem and answer as a number sentence. Encourage the use of pictures and jottings to aid understanding.
● Ensure that less confident learners are working within the range of numbers that they can comfortably calculate with.
● Challenge more confident learners by asking them to work with amounts of money over £1.

Plenary
● Set up a role-play shop and ask the children to invent questions surrounding the role play for their peers to answer.
● Discuss what information, operations and strategies will be needed to solve each problem.
● Encourage the children who answer the questions to act out their solutions using the shop role-play equipment.

Whiteboard tools
To duplicate objects, select them and choose the Clone option from the dropdown menu.

 Pen tray

Select tool

Highlighter pen

Shape names

Learning objective
PNS: Understanding shape
● Visualise common 2D shapes and 3D solids.

Resources
'Shape names' Notebook file; photocopiable page 100 'Find the shapes'; prepared sets of cards, each with a picture of a different 3D shape on it; a selection of 3D shapes (commercial, or a variety of packaging boxes); coloured pencils.

Links to other subjects
Art and design
PoS Art (4a) To have a knowledge and understanding of line, shape, form and space.
● Encourage the children to use their awareness and understanding of shape and space when creating their own artwork.

Starter

Divide the class in two groups according to ability. Give the less confident half of the class a solid 3D shape and ask them to describe it to a partner. Give the more confident half of the class a prepared card (see Resources) and ask them to describe the shape drawn on it to a partner. If required, write words on page 2 of the 'Shape names' Notebook file to help the children in their descriptions.

Explain to the children that each of the cards can be matched to a solid 3D shape. Ask them to find their new partners by matching the cards to the shapes. Use the Shapes tool 🖼 to add shapes to page 2, if required.

Whole-class shared work

● Look at the 2D shapes on page 3. Ensure that the children can read all of the shape names.
● Ask: *Do you know any of the names of these shapes?* Allow the children to match the shape names to the shapes.
● Give a description for each shape as they are labelled, to help consolidation. For example: *A triangle always has three corners and three straight sides.*
● Repeat the activity for 3D shapes on page 4. If possible, supply solid 3D shapes for the children to handle, as they may find it difficult to visualise a drawn 3D shape.
● Show page 5 of the Notebook file and challenge the children to find the listed shapes in the picture. Emphasise the difference between a square and a cube (this is a common misconception when they are drawn). Highlight the shapes as found, if required.

Independent work

● Give each child a copy of photocopiable page 100. Ask them to find how many of each shape are in the picture.
● Tell the children to mark or colour the shapes once they have counted them, to prevent repetition. Encourage them to compare answers regularly with a partner.
● Invite less confident learners to use 2D shape stencils to draw a picture of something, or use 3D shapes to build a model. Ask them to label their creations.
● Challenge more confident learners to match 3D shape names to the nets of shapes as well as the actual shape. Talk about the number and shape of the faces on these 3D shapes.

Plenary

● Ask a child to choose a shape from a range of 2D and 3D shapes.
● Encourage the rest of the children to ask yes/no questions to determine the identity of the chosen shape. For example: *Does it have any square faces?* By the process of elimination, the children can work out which shape is the chosen shape. If required, use page 5 to display the chosen shape and to discuss its properties.
● Be strict about the use of accurate terminology and correct shape names during the game.

Whiteboard tools
Use the Shapes tool to add images of appropriate shapes to the Notebook page.

 Pen tray

 Select tool

 Shapes tool

 Highlighter pen

Learning objective
PNS: Understanding shape
● Follow and give
instructions involving position.

Resources
'Position and direction'
Notebook file; photocopiable
page 101 'Position island';
individual whiteboards and
pens.

Links to other subjects
Geography
QCA Unit 5 'Where in the
world is Barnaby Bear?'
● Encourage the children to
use positional vocabulary to
describe the position of places
on a map or on a photograph
of a place.

Position

Starter
Open page 2 of the Notebook file. Ask the children to work out the answer to additions and subtractions that they can complete mentally. Share the answers and strategies used to work them out. Ask a child to write the answer in a defined place on the grid. For example, say: *Write the answer two spaces below the circle.*

Whole-class shared work
● Use page 3 to introduce the objective.
● In pairs, give the children one minute to make a list on their individual whiteboards of as many *position* phrases as possible (such as *beneath* and *far away from*). Share these ideas as a class and define the meaning of any less obvious phrases.
● Go to page 4 and ask the children to name the objects on the grid.
● Point to the star in the pink square. Ask the children to tell a partner the position of the star in two different ways. For example: *The star is next to (or to the right of) the frog* and *The star is two squares above the strawberry.* Write the children's position vocabulary in the box on the right-hand side of the page.
● Repeat until the location of all the stars has been identified.

Independent work
● Put the children in pairs and give each child an enlarged copy of photocopiable page 101.
● Out of view of their partners, ask each child to design their own island in the top map grid by placing five things on it, such as a haunted castle or a golden chicken's nest. Ensure that each item is drawn in only one square on the grid.
● Ask the children to take turns to describe to their partners what they have added to their own island and the position they have put it in. The child listening must draw their partner's described island on the bottom map grid in the position their partner described.
● Encourage the children to compare their maps at the end and discuss any errors made.
● Less confident learners will need adult support to scaffold their language and to ensure that they remain on task without getting frustrated.

Plenary
● Ask a child to choose an object in the classroom and describe where it is, so that the other children can guess what it is. Explain that they must be precise if they want the other children to be able to identify the object that they have chosen.
● Encourage the use of more adventurous language to describe the position of the object.
● Use page 5 of the Notebook file to record the description.

Whiteboard tools

⬚ Pen tray

▦ Select tool

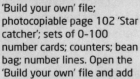

Learning objective
PNS: Counting and understanding number
● Round two-digit numbers to the nearest 10.

Resources
'Build your own' file; photocopiable page 102 'Star catcher'; sets of 0-100 number cards; counters; bean bag; number lines. Open the 'Build your own' file and add the *Number line* ITP (from the Mathematics folder under My Content in the Gallery) to the first page.

Links to other subjects
PE
PoS (7a) To send and receive a ball.
● The children will need to use accurate throwing and catching skills in the Starter.

Rounding

Starter
Stand the children in a circle and count round the circle in tens from 0 to 100. Next, throw a bean bag randomly around the circle – the child catching the bean bag has to say the next number in the sequence. Explain that these numbers are all multiples of 10 and point out that they all end in zero.

Whole-class shared work
● Explain the term *rounding* as a skill that we might use to make numbers easier to work with in our heads.
● Tell the children that they are going to learn to round numbers to the nearest multiple of 10 (ensure they can recall what a multiple of 10 is).
● Open your prepared 'Build your own' file and show the *Number line* ITP. Set it as a 0-60 number line and point out the multiples of 10.
● Drag one marker to show 37, leave the other on 0.
● Ask: *Which multiple of 10 is 37 nearest to?* Set the other box to 30, then to 40, with the difference span displayed to see which has the smallest difference.
● Repeat this exercise so that the children can practise and reinforce this new skill.
● Include one number that ends in 5 and ask the children for suggestions about what you can do now. Share the rule that whole numbers ending in a 5 are always rounded up.
● Use the Area Capture tool 📋 to take screenshots from the ITP, if required.

Independent work
● Put the children into pairs and give out the required resources to play the game on photocopiable page 102. Read the rules of the game together.
● Provide number lines to support the children's decision-making. Reiterate that the closest multiple of 10 is the one they should round to. Highlight the multiples of 10 on the number line for less confident learners.
● Encourage the children to check their partner's answers and dispute any decisions that they do not agree with.

Plenary
● Show random flash card numbers up to 100 and ask the children to give two claps, and then say the number rounded to the nearest 10.
● Demonstrate how rounding numbers can be useful for checking calculations.
● Ensure that the children know that rounded numbers are only approximate, and if they use them in calculations they will only get an approximate answer.

Whiteboard tools
Use the Area Capture tool to take screenshots, if required.

 Pen tray

 Select tool

 Gallery

 Area Capture tool

Adjusting

Learning objective
PNS: Calculating
● Add or subtract mentally a single-digit number or a multiple of 10 to or from any two-digit number; use practical and informal written methods to add and subtract two-digit numbers.

Resources
'Build your own' file; place value cards; two-digit number cards; instruction cards (see independent work); pots. Open the 'Build your own' file and add the *Number grid* ITP (from the Mathematics folder under My Content in the Gallery) to the first page.

Links to other subjects
Speaking and listening
Objective 15: To listen to each other's views and preferences, agree the next steps to take and identify contributions by each group member.
● The children will use their speaking and listening skills to share ideas with others and to deepen understanding.

Starter
Remind the children that, when adding or subtracting 10, the tens digit increases or decreases by 1 but the units digit remains constant. Open your prepared 'Build your own' file and use the *Number grid* ITP to revise visually adding and subtracting 10. Give the children place value cards and ask them to make a number. Next, ask them to add or subtract 10 and show the answer. Emphasise that they are only changing the tens card.

Whole-class shared work
● Highlight five different numbers on the *Number grid* ITP.
● Add 11 to each number by counting on 11 on the number grid. Highlight the answers in a different colour.
● Ask: *What patterns are there between the two sets of numbers?* Explain that the diagonal pattern is created by moving vertically down one space, then horizontally right one space. Say: *Add on 10, then add on 1 more* as you make the movements.
● Introduce the term *adjusting*. Convey that it involves doing an easy calculation of adding on 10 and then adjusting the answer slightly to make it correct.
● Repeat for adding 9, explaining the strategy as *adding on 10 then subtracting 1*.
● If the children seem comfortable with addition by adjusting, move on to subtracting 9 and 11 in the same way.
● If required, use the Area Capture tool 🖼 to take screenshots of the ITP screen.

Independent work
● Give each group a pot of two-digit number cards to choose from, and a pot of instruction cards stating some or all of the following: *add 9, subtract 9, add 11* and *subtract 11*.
● Tell the children to choose a card from each pot and carry out the instruction on the card using the adjusting strategy. Ask them to record their calculations as a number sentence.
● Give less confident learners only one instruction card at first.
● Challenge more confident learners to determine a way of using adjusting to add or subtract any near multiple of 10. Give them some of these problems to solve.
● Question the children regularly about how they worked out answers.

Plenary
● Ask the children to explain to a partner how to add 11, using adjusting. Encourage the children to correct or add to their partner's explanations if necessary.
● Share some explanations as a class.
● Sensitively discourage statements such as *you go down 1 and then across 1* and encourage statements such as *you add 10 and then you add 1 more*. Do the same for adding 9 and subtracting 9 and 11.

Whiteboard tools
Use the Area Capture tool to take screenshots, if required.

 Pen tray

 Select tool

 Gallery

 Area Capture tool

Learning objective
PNS: Calculating
● Add or subtract mentally a single-digit number or a multiple of 10 to or from any two-digit number; use practical and informal written methods to add and subtract two-digit numbers.

Resources
'Bridging' Notebook file; individual whiteboards and pens; cubes or other counters; prepare cards with ten additions bridging 10 or 20 on each. (Microsoft PowerPoint is required to view the embedded slideshow in the Notebook file.)

Links to other subjects
Speaking and listening
Objective 14: To listen to others in class, ask relevant questions and follow instructions.
● The children will communicate how they solve problems to a partner and will ask questions to reinforce understanding.

Bridging

Starter
Refresh and build on the children's knowledge of number bonds for 10, and addition facts for numbers up to 10. Record the number bonds to 10 on page 2 of the 'Bridging' Notebook file, and use page 3 to revise the children's understanding of partitioning.

Ask the children to list their ideas for each task on their individual whiteboards. Then invite volunteers to come to the board and write their answers on the Notebook page.

Whole-class shared work
● Ensure that the children know what a multiple of 10 is.
● Launch the PowerPoint slideshow on page 4 of the Notebook file to explain and demonstrate the method of addition by bridging (see pages 1 to 4 of the slideshow).
● Demonstrate clearly that 8 + 6 is still the same amount as 10 + 4. Give one child eight cubes and another six cubes. Ask the child with six cubes to give two of them to the child with eight cubes and then point out that this now shows 10 + 4 = 14. Ask: *Has the number of cubes changed?*
● Use the PowerPoint slideshow (slides 5 to 10) to solve three additions using the method of bridging. Encourage the children to work in pairs on their individual whiteboards to work out each step.
● On page 4 of the Notebook file, demonstrate how the children should record each step of their working. Encourage them to practise this on their individual whiteboards. For example: 8 + 6 = 8 + 2 + 4 = 10 + 4 = 14.
● Encourage the children to use their preferred method (such as counting on) to check the answer, to increase their confidence in the reliability of the new method.
● Finally, use page 5 to assess understanding. Let each child choose a problem to solve independently.

Independent work
● Give each child a prepared card (see Resources). Differentiate as follows: less confident learners bridging 10; more confident learners bridging any multiple of 10.
● The children choose five of the sums on the card to solve using the method of bridging and then solve them, recording their answers as demonstrated.
● Provide less confident learners with place value equipment or a number line and additional teacher support.
● Encourage the children to explain to a partner how they solved each of the five questions.
● Allow the children to check their work using their preferred method of addition.

Plenary
● Ask the children to share any successes and difficulties they have experienced and work through an example as a class.
● Use page 6 of the Notebook file or look again at the last two slides of the slideshow (slides 9 and 10: *What is 16 + 7?*) to help the children to assimilate their new knowledge. Drag and drop the blocks and change the numbers on the arrow cards.
● In a subsequent lesson, when the children are comfortable with addition by bridging, use pages 7 to 8 to introduce the method of subtraction by bridging.

Whiteboard tools
 Pen tray

 Select tool

Division (1)

Learning objective
PNS: Calculating
● Represent sharing as division.

Resources
'Division' Notebook file; photocopiable page 103 'Sharing'; sweets; individual whiteboards and pens; counters.

Links to other subjects
Speaking and listening
Objective 14: To listen to others in class, ask relevant questions and follow instructions.
● While the children are explaining their answers in pairs, encourage them to listen to each other carefully and question the explanations.

Starter
On page 2 of the Notebook file, open the *Number grid* ITP and shade all the multiples of 5. Ask the children to count in fives from 0 to 100. Tell them that these numbers are all multiples of 5 because they can all be shared into five equal groups with none left over. Show a range of numbers from 0 to 100 and ask them to say whether or not each number is a multiple of 5.

Whole-class shared work
● Explain *division* as *sharing a number into equal parts*. Take 20 sweets and share them equally between yourself and three children. Say: *I have divided the sweets equally between each of us; we have five each.* This can be modelled on page 3. Introduce the division symbol.
● Read the problem on page 4 with the children and ask them to suggest ways to solve it. After listening to their ideas, invite a child to share out the cabbages on screen, using division by sharing.
● Once they have done this, use the Delete button ☒ to remove the red box to reveal the correct answer.
● Explain the number sentence to the children. Say: *We started with 14 cabbages. Then we shared them equally between two tortoises, giving each tortoise seven cabbages.*
● Repeat this for the problem on page 5.
● Read the questions on page 6. Ask the children to choose a problem to solve, and to write their answers on their individual whiteboards. Start the Timer (30 seconds).
● Ask the children to tell a partner their answer and explain how they worked it out. Address any misconceptions by working through both examples practically.

Independent work
● Give each child a copy of photocopiable page 103. Ask them to work out the answers to the problems (they may use counters).
● Encourage the children to have a go at writing a division number sentence for each problem.
● Support less confident learners by working alongside them to solve simple sharing problems practically.
● Challenge more confident learners by asking them what to do with $7 \div 2$. Talk about being able to halve the extra one, or leave a remainder of 1.
● Help the children to realise that the way they deal with the remainder depends on what is being shared.

Plenary
● Display page 7 of the Notebook file. Ask: *How many bananas can each monkey have?* Let the children move the bananas to show the answer.
● Invite a volunteer to write the corresponding division calculation on the Notebook page.

Whiteboard tools
Use the Delete button to reveal hidden answers.

 Pen tray

 Select tool

 Delete button

Division (2)

Learning objective
PNS: Calculating
● Represent repeated subtraction (grouping) as division.

Resources
'Division' Notebook file; photocopiable page 104 'Grouping'; number line; counters; individual whiteboards and pens; ball; biscuits or cakes (real or plastic).

Links to other subjects
There are no specific links for this lesson.

Starter
Sit the children in a circle with you in the centre holding a ball. Tell them that they are going to practise counting backwards in different steps. Give them a starting number and a step size. For example, say that you are going to start at 57 and count back in tens. Roll the ball to a child and ask the child to roll the ball back to you, stating the first number of the count. Roll the ball to another child and he or she must state the next number in the count. Continue this until zero (or a number smaller than 10) has been reached.

Whole-class shared work
● Open the 'Division' Notebook file and go to page 8. Explain division as *making groups of equal amounts from a larger amount*. Take 30 biscuits or cakes (real or plastic) and stack them into groups of five. Say: *I have divided the biscuits into groups of five and there are six groups*. This can be modelled on page 8. Revise the division symbol.
● Read the problem on page 9 and ask the children to suggest ways to solve it. Help them to work out the answer using *division by grouping*. Invite a volunteer to come to the whiteboard to group the sweets on screen and to write in the answer. Then use the Delete tool ⊠ to remove the red box to reveal the number sentence.
● Explain the number sentence to the children. Say: *We started with 12 sweets, then we made groups of three sweets until they had all been used, making four groups*. Show the calculation on a number line by starting on 12 and counting how many backward jumps of 3 it takes to get to 0.
● Repeat this procedure for the problem on page 10.
● Give out individual whiteboards and read the questions on page 11. Ask the children to choose a problem to solve, then start the Timer (30 seconds). Check for any misconceptions.

Independent work
● Provide each child with a copy of photocopiable page 104. Ask the children to work out the answers to the problems. Let them use counters if required.
● Encourage the children to have a go at writing a division number sentence for each problem.
● Support less confident learners by working alongside them to solve simple grouping problems practically.

Plenary
● Go to page 12 of the Notebook file. Write a division number sentence and ask the children to work out the answer.
● Give the children time to work with a partner to invent a problem that the number sentence shows. For example, 8 ÷ 2 = 4 could be: *A bread loaf was cut into eight slices; sandwiches were made using two slices for each one. How many sandwiches were made altogether?*

Whiteboard tools
Reveal answers using the Delete button.

 Pen tray

 Select tool

 Delete button

Learning objectives
PNS: Using and applying mathematics
● Describe patterns and relationships involving numbers or shapes.
PNS: Counting and understanding number
● Recognise odd and even numbers.

Resources
'Maths puzzle' Notebook file; counters; pots.

Links to other subjects
Speaking and listening
Objective 15: To listen to each other's views and preferences and agree the next steps.
● Encourage the children to listen carefully to the various explanations of the other investigations.

Worm catching

Starter
Revise the definition of odd and even numbers. Remind the children that even numbers can be shared into two equal groups whereas odd numbers have an odd one left over. On page 2 of the 'Maths puzzle' Notebook file, make two lists of the digits that are at the end of odd and even numbers.

Take the children into a large space. Assign one end of the space as *odd* and the opposite end as *even*. Call out a number and tell the children to move quickly to the correct end of the space.

Whole-class shared work
● Share the problem on page 3 of the Notebook file with the class.
● List all of the odd numbers up to 11 so that everyone is clear about what these are. State clearly that 0 is neither an odd nor an even number.
● Display page 4 of the Notebook file. Ask one child to drag and drop the worms below the three birds so that one arrangement of the answer is displayed. Use the Area Capture tool 🔲 to save the arrangement to the end of the Notebook file, if required.
● Check the arrangement as a class to ascertain that there are 11 worms altogether and that all the birds have an odd number of worms.
● Record the answer in the table on page 5, using page 4 as a reminder.
● Go back to page 4. Use the Undo button 🔄 to reset the page, and ask another child to find a different arrangement. Record this new arrangement in the table on page 5.
● Repeat this until the children believe that all of the arrangements have been found.
● Ask: *How do we know all of the arrangements have been found?* Suggest that we could arrange the answers in the tables more systematically (such as: 1–1–9, 1–3–7, 1–5–5 and so on). Explain that this can help with checking to see if any arrangements have been missed out.

Independent work
● Show the children the problem on page 6 of the Notebook file. Encourage them to have a go at solving the problem in pairs, in the same way as the worm problem.
● Give the children counters to represent the mice, and pots to represent the cats.
● Challenge the children to be systematic, as discussed in the whole-class shared work.
● Supply less confident learners with a copy of the table on page 8 of the Notebook file to help them record their findings.

Plenary
● Invite the children to share the answers to their investigations. Talk about any differences in the children's answers. Invite a child to move the mice on page 7.
● Work out a definitive set of answers as a class and invite a child to record it in the table on page 8.

Whiteboard tools
Use the Area Capture tool to take a snapshot of the pages where the sharing has taken place, as a reminder to the children.

 Pen tray

 Select tool

 Area Capture tool

 Undo button

Learning objective
PNS: Handling data
● Answer a question by collecting and recording data in lists and tables; represent the data as pictograms to show results.

Resources
'Favourite fruits' Notebook file; photocopiable page 105 'Favourite drinks'; a selection of fruits; A4 paper; coloured pencils; glue.

Links to other subjects
Science
QCA Unit 2A 'Health and growth'
● Emphasise the health aspects of eating lots of fruit, and in drinking the right type of drinks.

Favourite fruits and favourite drinks

Starter
Ask the children to sort themselves in a variety of ways (such as length of forename, age and shoe size). Ask questions about how they are sorted. For example: *How many letters does the longest name have? How many people have size 13 shoes?* Suggest grouping the children to make it easier to count them.

Whole-class shared work
● Go to page 2 of the 'Favourite fruits' Notebook file. Read the question at the top of the page. Explain that you would like the class to investigate this. Then open the linked 'Favourite fruits' pictogram by pressing the thumbnail image on the screen.
● Give the children an opportunity to taste some fruit. (**Safety note:** Check for any allergies beforehand.) Ask them to consider which of the fruits they most preferred.
● Ask: *How can we find out which fruit our class likes the most?* Take suggestions from the children and give constructive feedback about their ideas.
● Explain that the information can be used to create a pictogram. Ensure that everyone understands what a pictogram is, and how it works.
● Ask each child to place their vote for their favourite fruit on the pictogram displayed on the screen. Keep stopping to ask questions. For example: *Which fruit is most popular now? Are there any fruits that nobody likes? How many children like apples best?*
● When the pictogram is complete, use the Area Capture tool 🖼 to take a snapshot of it. Place the image beneath the original question on page 2.
● Write the answer underneath the pictogram and save the page.

Independent work
● Open page 3 of the Notebook file and read the question at the top. Explain that the children are going to investigate this in pairs.
● List six suggestions of favourite drinks in the space provided, then ask the children to vote for their favourite by raising their hand. Record the number of votes next to each drink.
● Supply each pair with a plain sheet of paper, a copy of photocopiable page 105, colouring pencils and glue.
● Ask the children to create a pictogram to show the answer to the investigation. Suggest using one glass to represent one child and colouring each type of drink a different colour.
● Challenge more confident learners to use one glass to represent two children (so a glass will need to be cut in half to deal with an odd number of votes).

Plenary
● Encourage the children to add titles and labels to their work. Ask them to make sure that they have answered the question.
● Scan in some of the children's work on page 4 and evaluate its effectiveness in communicating the answer.
● Ask other questions about the data to assess the children's understanding.

Whiteboard tools
Use the Area Capture tool to take a snapshot of the completed pictogram. Upload scanned images of the children's work by selecting Insert, then Picture File, and browsing to where you have saved the images.

 Pen tray

 Select tool

 Area Capture tool

Learning objective
PNS: Understanding shape
● Sort, make and describe shapes, referring to their properties.

Resources
'Shape sorting' Notebook file; a selection of 2D and 3D shapes; prepared Venn diagrams, Carroll diagrams and shapes to cut out (see independent work).

Links to other subjects
Speaking and listening
Objective 13: To speak with clarity and use intonation when reading and reciting texts.
● Encourage the children to speak clearly when they are describing the shapes to the class.

Shape sorting

Starter
Put a selection of 2D and 3D shapes on each group's table and ask the children to spend one minute, as a group, discussing the shapes and their properties. Remind them what faces, edges and corners are.

Choose a mystery shape and give the children clues to identify that shape. For example: *This shape has 12 edges.* Encourage them to discard the shapes they know it cannot be after every clue and ask them to explain how they eliminated these shapes. Key words can be added to page 2 of the 'Shape sorting' Notebook file.

Whole-class shared work
● Go to page 3 and confirm with the children that a pentagon is any shape with five straight sides and five corners, while a hexagon is any shape with six straight sides and six corners.
● Sort the shapes, using the drag-and-drop method. Count the sides each time to check.
● Move on to page 4. Ask the children to describe and name some of the shapes they can see. Explain that the overlapping part of the Venn diagram allows for shapes to be a member of both sets (those with both curved and straight edges). Sort the shapes together.
● Look at page 5 and explain how to use a Carroll diagram. Ask the children to determine what shape properties each section of the Carroll diagram can contain. Sort the shapes together.

Independent work
● Give most of the children a Venn diagram with two overlapping sets. Label one set as '3D shapes' and the other set as 'curved edges'.
● Supply the children with a range of 2D and 3D shape pictures and ask them to sort these into the correct places on the diagram.
● Give less confident learners a Venn diagram with two separate sets and ask them to sort two shapes that they find it difficult to distinguish between, such as cubes and cuboids. Provide actual shapes rather than pictures for any 3D shape sorting.
● Challenge more confident learners with a Carroll diagram. Label the top as 'pyramid' and 'not a pyramid'. Label the side as 'square base' and 'not a square base'. Ask the children to sort 3D shapes. Once completed, ask them to comment on the shapes that have ended up together.
● Working in pairs will stimulate conversation about the properties of the shapes and may prove more beneficial than working alone.

Plenary
● Put shapes into feely bags and ask the children to describe them to the class so that they can try to guess what they are. Make a note of good shape vocabulary on page 6 of the Notebook file.
● Sort the revealed shapes into a large Venn diagram, created with hoops or ropes on the classroom floor.

Whiteboard tools

⌨ Pen tray

🖰 Select tool

Moving along a route

Learning objective
PNS: Understanding shape
● Follow and give instructions involving position, direction and movement.

Resources
'Position and direction' Notebook file; photocopiable page 106 'Robot directions'; counters; pencils; simple maze marked out on floor (see Plenary).

Links to other subjects
ICT
QCA Unit 2D 'Routes: controlling a floor turtle'
● Allow the children to program a floor turtle to travel through a simple maze.
Speaking and listening
Objective 14: To listen to others in class, ask relevant questions and follow instructions.
● The children must listen carefully to the instructions given to them by their partner in the Plenary.

Starter
Take the children into a large space. Demonstrate what a quarter turn is and describe this as a right-angled turn. Show the children which way is clockwise and anti-clockwise. Ask them questions such as: *If you make three quarter turns clockwise and then two quarter turns anti-clockwise, which way will you be facing?*
  Try out the instructions to test the children's answers.

Whole-class shared work
● Open the 'Position and direction' Notebook file and use page 6 to introduce the commands needed to make a rabbit move around the screen. Invite the children to come and move the rabbit on the grid in the various directions. Explain that they are not completing the maze at this stage.
● Ensure that all the children are confident in their use of left and right.
● Go to page 7 and give the children a few minutes to describe, to a partner, the route the rabbit will need to take to the end of the maze. Point out the key words: *up, down, left* and *right*. Write the first instruction in the first box, *Up 6*, to get the discussion started. Invite the children to write the subsequent instructions in the boxes provided.
● Once they have done this, use the Eraser from the Pen tray to rub over the blue boxes to reveal the hidden instructions.
● Invite a volunteer to come to the whiteboard to move the rabbit according to the instructions.
● Move on to page 8, with a ladybird on a grid. This ladybird moves in a different way to the rabbit. Instead of moving forwards and sideways to go round corners, this ladybird needs to turn on the spot and travel in the direction that it is facing. It can only make quarter turns. Invite the children to move and turn the ladybird.
● Look at page 9 and work as a class to determine the route that the ladybird will need to take to the end of the maze. Invite the children to drag and drop the required instructions and then to move the ladybird.

Independent work
● Give each child a copy of photocopiable page 106 and a counter.
● Ask each child to find a route for the robot (counter) through the maze and draw it with a pencil.
● Ask the children to write the instructions that the robot must follow on the lines beneath the maze.
● Support less confident learners by scribing their directions for them or allowing them to record their directions orally using a tape recorder.
● Challenge more confident learners by giving them a robot that can only move forward and make quarter turns. Draw an arrow on the counter to support the children in recalling in which direction the robot is travelling. Suggest that they move the counter along the route as they write their instructions.

Plenary
● Mark out a simple maze on the playground or hall floor.
● Put the children in pairs and assign one child in each pair as the robot and the other as the controller. Blindfold the robot and ask the controller to lead the robot through the simple route by giving clear directional instructions. Ensure that there are no tripping hazards nearby.
● Make an assessment of each child's ability to give and understand instructions during this activity.

Whiteboard tools
Use the Eraser from the Pen tray to reveal the hidden instructions.

 Pen tray

 Select tool

Four in a row

- You will need: counters in two different colours (one colour for each player), game board, spinner.

Instructions

- Take it in turns to spin the spinner. Find two numbers on the board that can be either added or subtracted to make the number on the spinner and use the counters to cover them both. The first player to get four counters in a row (horizontally, vertically or diagonally) wins the game.

6	10	3	7	1	5	4
1	7	1	9	3	8	9
4	3	7	5	4	2	0
6	3	9	10	8	7	10
0	8	2	5	6	2	5
10	4	7	1	9	3	10
8	3	4	10	7	0	9
5	2	6	1	4	2	1

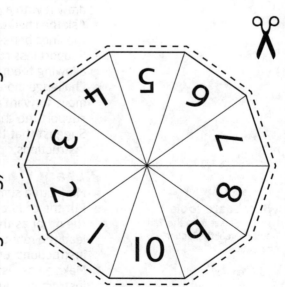

■ SCHOLASTIC
www.scholastic.co.uk

Find the pairs

80p	43p	28p	64p	32p
25p	16p	37p	42p	65p
36p	74p	49p	30p	51p

Coins © The Royal Mint

Telling the time

The time is
_____

What time will it
be in 3 hours?
_____

The time is
_____

What time will it
be in 5 hours?
_____

The time is
_____

What time was it
2 hours ago?
_____

The time is
_____

What time was it
6 hours ago?
_____

The time is
_____

What time will it
be in 4 hours?
_____

The time is
_____

What time was it
7 hours ago?
_____

The time is
_____

What time will it
be in half an hour?
_____

The time is
_____

What time will it
be in half an hour?
_____

The time is
_____

What time was it
half an hour ago?
_____

The time is
_____

What time was it
one and a half
hours ago?
_____

The time is
_____

What time was it
a quarter of an
hour ago?
_____

The time is
_____

What time will it
be in a quarter of
an hour?
_____

SCHOLASTIC
www.scholastic.co.uk

Estimating

▪ Estimate how many objects are in each group that your teacher has given to you.

	Estimated total	Actual total	Difference
A			
B			
C			
D			
E			
F			

▪ Count the actual number of objects in each group and compare your estimated total to the actual total.

▪ How close were your estimates?

Quick finisher

▪ Estimate how many there are in each of these groups.

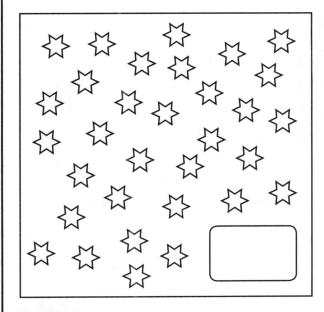

Ladybird flip flap

- Instructions for how to make a flip flap.

1. Cut out each square above individually.

2. Stick the 16 individual cards face down onto a sheet of clear sticky-backed plastic. Arrange the cards in the order they are displayed above. Leave a small, even gap (about 2 or 3mm) on all sides between each card.

3. Stick clear sticky-backed plastic over the top of the cards so that the cards are encased between the two layers. Trim the edges to neaten it.

4. Fold the 'flip flap' along each of the gaps between the cards to establish a crease.

Illustrations © Mark Brierley / Beehive Illustration

Number triplets

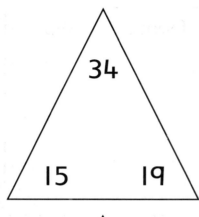
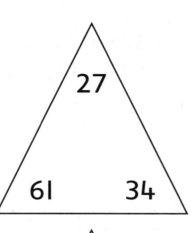
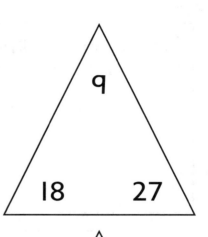

34   15   19

27   61   34

9   18   27

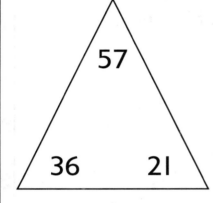
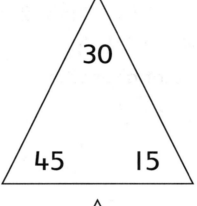
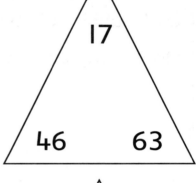

57   36   21

30   45   15

17   46   63

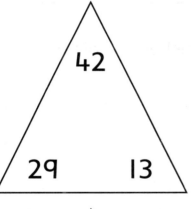
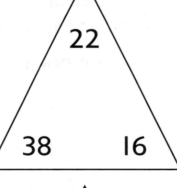
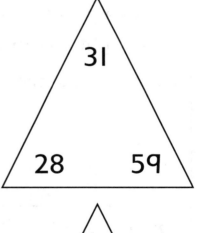

42   29   13

22   38   16

31   28   59

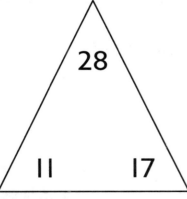
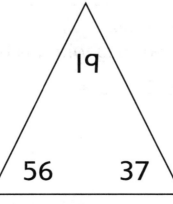
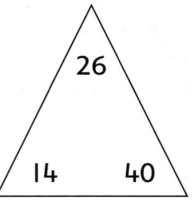

28   11   17

19   56   37

26   14   40

Work it out

Jon bought an apple for 32p and a bottle of water for 49p.
He paid for his shopping with a £1 coin.

How much change did he get?

Jon, Mel, Des, Gav and Shaz all have 2 rabbits each.
Each rabbit eats 5 carrots a day.

How many carrots is that altogether?

Jon had 57 stickers in his collection.
He bought 13 more stickers then gave 9 stickers to his friend.

How many stickers has Jon got now?

Jon had a bag of 24 sweets.
He shared the sweets equally with his best friend Sal.

How many sweets did Sal have?

📖 **SCHOLASTIC**
www.scholastic.co.uk

Money problems

Kat bought 3 apples and 4 bananas.
Each apple cost 5p and each banana cost 10p.

How much did the apples and bananas cost altogether?

Tim had 37p.
He spent 24p on a comic and then his Gran gave him 15p.

How much money has Tim got now?

Mum made £18 at a car boot sale.
She shared the money equally between Kay and Dom.

How much money did Kay and Dom get each?

Lucy bought a pen for 48p and a rubber for 26p.
She paid for them with a £1 coin.

How much money did Lucy have left over?

Find the shapes

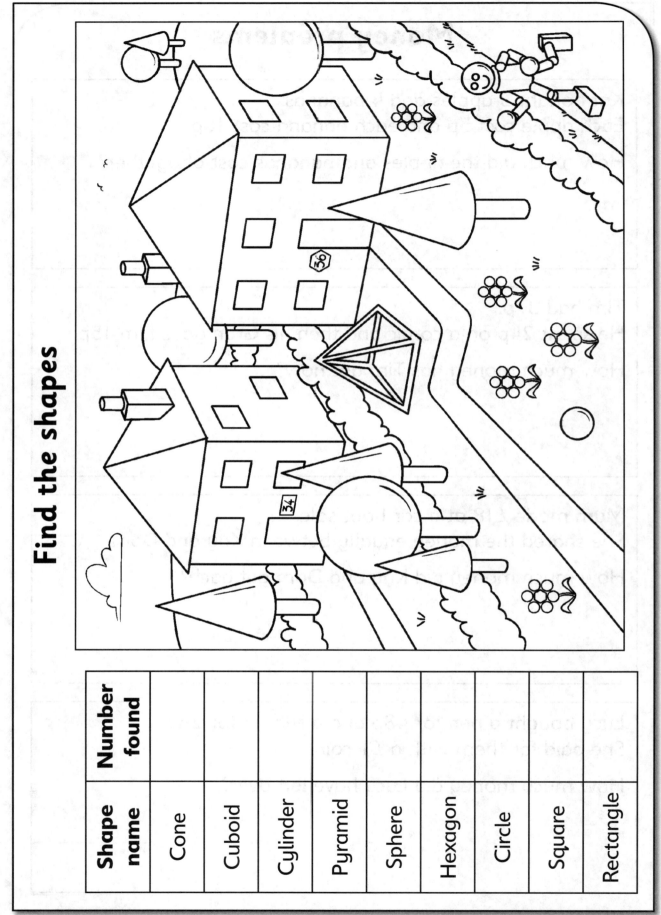

Shape name	Number found
Cone	
Cuboid	
Cylinder	
Pyramid	
Sphere	
Hexagon	
Circle	
Square	
Rectangle	

Illustrations © Mark Brierley / Beehive Illustration

Position island

My island

My partner's island

Illustrations © Mark Brierley / Beehive Illustration

Star catcher

A rounding game for 2 players.

- **You will need:** 2 game boards, 11 counters each, a set of 0–100 number cards.

- **Object of the game:** To be the first player to cover all of the stars on their board.

- **Rules:** Players take it in turns to pick a number card. Players must round the number on their card to the nearest 10 and cover up the star on their board displaying that number. If the star is already covered, the player does nothing. The winner is the first to cover all of their stars.

▲SCHOLASTIC
www.scholastic.co.uk

Sharing

1. Two children shared 8 sweets. How many sweets did they each get?

_____

2. Ten dogs shared 50 treats. How many treats did each dog get?

_____

3. A piece of rope measures 18m. If it is cut into 2 equal pieces, how long would each piece be?

_____

4. If 20 stickers are shared between 5 boys, how many stickers will each boy get?

_____

5. A bag of seed holds 10g. If the bag is shared between 5 birds, how much seed can each bird have?

_____

6. Jan's mum made 20 cakes for Jan's party. Ten children were at the party, how many cakes did each child have?

_____

7. A mother bird has 5 babies. How many worms can they each eat if the mother bird collects 30 worms altogether?

_____

8. Tom cooked 6 sausages. He shared the sausages with Jill. How many sausages did they have each?

_____

Quick finisher

Work out the answer to these divisions.

$15 \div 5 =$ _____ $12 \div 2 =$ _____ $60 \div 10 =$ _____

$18 \div 2 =$ _____ $40 \div 10 =$ _____ $25 \div 5 =$ _____

Grouping

1. How many groups of 2 children can be made from a class of 20 children?

_____

2. How many bags of 10 apples can be made from a box of 60 apples?

_____

3. How many 5p sweets can be bought with 25p?

_____

4. How many 2m ropes can be made from a 14m rope?

_____

5. How many 10g bags of sweets can be made from a 50g box of sweets?

_____

6. How many 2-litre bottles of water can be filled from an 18-litre barrel?

_____

7. How many packets of 5 cream cakes can be made from a box of 45 cream cakes?

_____

8. How many 5-a-side football teams can be made from a group of 30 children?

_____

Quick finisher

Work out the answer to these divisions.

$35 \div 5 =$ _____ $14 \div 2 =$ _____ $50 \div 10 =$ _____

$12 \div 2 =$ _____ $90 \div 10 =$ _____ $40 \div 5 =$ _____

◖**SCHOLASTIC**
www.scholastic.co.uk

Favourite drinks

Illustrations © Mark Brierley / Beehive Illustration

Robot directions

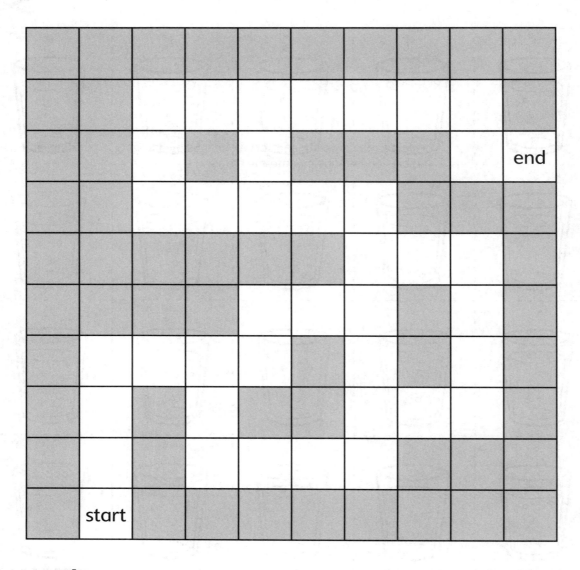

Instructions

_____

_____

_____

_____

_____

Science

This chapter provides 20 lessons based on objectives taken from the QCA Schemes of Work for Science. The lessons cover a range of objectives from each of the six schemes of work for Year 2. The lessons show how the interactive whiteboard can be used to teach and model new scientific concepts clearly for the whole class to see. They support the children in developing their investigative skills by allowing them to share and discuss ideas and conclusions as a class. The lessons encourage the children to be actively involved in their learning by asking them to make choices by pressing or highlighting the text on screen, filling in spaces by writing or typing, manipulating and sorting images by dragging or rotating, and creating tables and graphs by entering data.

Lesson title	Objectives	What children should know	Cross-curricular links
Lesson 1: Food groups	QCA Unit 2A 'Health and growth' • To know that there are many different foods. • To record information in drawings and charts. • To know that we eat different kinds of food. • To be able to collect information and present the results in a block graph.	• Know the names of different foods.	**Mathematics** PNS: Handling data
Lesson 2: Keeping healthy	QCA Unit 2A 'Health and growth' • To understand that humans need water and food to stay alive. • To understand that humans need exercise to stay healthy. • To make and record observations and make simple comparisons.	• Know the basic needs of humans. • Understand simple changes that happen to the body when they exercise.	**PSHE** PoS (3a) To know how to make simple choices that improve their health and well-being. **Art and Design** QCA Unit 2A 'Picture this!' **PE** QCA Unit 4 'Games activities'
Lesson 3: Animals and their young	QCA Unit 2A 'Health and growth' • To know that animals (including humans) produce young and these grow into children and new adults. • To understand that babies and children need to be looked after while they are growing. • To ask questions in order to make simple comparisons of babies and children.	• Know that animals grow. • Be able to ask questions.	**Citizenship** QCA Unit 3 'Animals and us'
Lesson 4: Medicine safety	QCA Unit 2A 'Health and growth' • To know that medicines help us to get better but are drugs and not food and can be dangerous. • To understand that some people need medicines to keep them alive and healthy. • To recognise hazards and risks in medicines and how to avoid these.	• Know that medicines are taken when they are ill to make them feel better.	**Citizenship** QCA Unit 1 'Taking part' **Citizenship** QCA Unit 2 'Choices'
Lesson 5: The local environment	QCA Unit 2B 'Plants and animals in the local environment' • To know that there are different kinds of plants and animals in the immediate environment. • To observe and make a record of animals and plants found. • To present results in a table.	• Know some names of plants and animals. • Know what is a plant and what is an animal.	**English** PNS: Understanding and interpreting texts
Lesson 6: The life cycle of plants	QCA Unit 2B 'Plants and animals in the local environment' • To know that flowering plants produce seeds. • To know that seeds produce new plants.	• Know the names of parts of a flowering plant.	**ICT** QCA Unit 2C 'Finding information'

Lesson title	Objectives	What children should know	Cross-curricular links
Lesson 7: Investigating plants ⚫ P	**QCA Unit 2B** 'Plants and animals in the local environment' • To turn ideas about what plants need to grow, into a form that can be tested. • To observe and make a day-to-day record of observations. • To use the results to draw a conclusion about what seeds need to grow. • To recognise when a comparison is unfair.	• Be able to make simple observations. • Understand the term *fair*.	**Speaking and listening** Objective 15: To listen to each other's views and preferences; agree the next steps to take.
Lesson 8: Sorting plants and animals ⚫	**QCA Unit 2B** 'Plants and animals in the local environment' • To observe and recognise some simple characteristics of animals and plants. • To know that the group of living things called animals includes humans.	• Know some names of plants and animals. • Know what is a plant and what is an animal.	**ICT** QCA Unit 2E 'Questions and answers'
Lesson 9: Categorising animals ⚫	**QCA Unit 2C** 'Variation' • To know that living things in the locality can be grouped according to observable similarities and differences. • To present results in a block graph.	• Know some names and characteristics of animals.	**ICT** QCA Unit 2E 'Questions and answers'
Lesson 10: Human variation ⚫	**QCA Unit 2C** 'Variation' • To know that humans are more like each other than they are like other animals. • To know that humans are similar to each other in some ways and different in others. • To explore human variation making observations and comparisons.	• Be able to compare.	**Art and design** QCA Unit 2A 'Picture this!'
Lesson 11: Investigating differences between children ⚫ P	**QCA Unit 2C** 'Variation' • To know that some differences between themselves and other children can be measured. • To measure hand span in standard units of length, make comparisons and present measurements in a block graph. • To raise questions about differences between themselves, test them and decide whether their predictions were correct.	• To measure in centimetres (cm).	**Mathematics** PNS: Measuring
Lesson 12: Natural or man-made ⚫	**QCA Unit 2D** 'Grouping and changing materials' • To know that some materials occur naturally and some do not. • To know the names of some naturally occurring materials. • To know that some naturally occurring materials are treated before they are used.	• Be able to name the material objects are made from.	**Art and design** QCA Unit 2B 'Mother Nature, designer' **Speaking and listening** Objective 15: To listen to each other's views and preferences, agree the next steps to take and identify contributions by each group member.
Lesson 13: Squashing, bending, twisting, stretching ⚫	**QCA Unit 2D** 'Grouping and changing materials' • To know that objects made from some materials can be altered by squashing, bending, twisting and stretching. • To describe ways of making materials or objects change, using appropriate vocabulary. • To explore materials using appropriate senses and make observations and simple comparisons. • To construct a table to record observations.	• Be able to describe the properties of some materials.	**Art and design** QCA Unit 2A 'Picture this!'

Lesson title	Objectives	What children should know	Cross-curricular links
Lesson 14: Heating materials ● ▣	**QCA Unit 2D** 'Grouping and changing materials' • To know that materials often change when they are heated. • To make observations and simple comparisons. • To use a table to make a record of observations. • To decide whether what happened was what they expected.	• Know some materials that change when heated.	**Science** QCA Unit 3A 'Teeth and eating'
Lesson 15: Investigating different vehicles ● ▣	**QCA Unit 2E** 'Forces and movement' • To suggest questions about ways in which different objects move. • To make measurements of distance and record these in a prepared table. • To use the results in a table to draw a block graph. • To decide whether their comparison was fair.	• To measure in centimetres (cm).	**Mathematics** PNS: Handling data
Lesson 16: Investigating ramp height ● ▣	**QCA Unit 2E** 'Forces and movement' • To suggest a question to test and predict what will happen. • To decide what to do and what measurements to take. • To make measurements and record these in a prepared table. • To use the results in a table to draw a block graph. • To say whether the prediction was correct and try to explain the results.	• To measure in centimetres (cm).	**Mathematics** PNS: Handling data
Lesson 17: What does electricity do? ●	**QCA Unit 2F** 'Using electricity' • To know that everyday appliances use electricity (including things that light up, heat up, produce sounds and move).	• Know that some appliances use electricity to make them work.	**Mathematics** PNS: Handling data
Lesson 18: Dangers of electricity ●	**QCA Unit 2F** 'Using electricity' • To know that everyday appliances are connected to the mains and that they must be used safely. • To know that some devices use batteries which supply electricity; these can be handled safely.	• Know electricity can be dangerous.	**PSHE** PoS (3g) To understand rules for, and ways of, keeping safe, including basic road safety, and about people who can help them to stay safe. **Art and design** QCA Unit 2A 'Picture this!'
Lesson 19: Building a circuit ●	**QCA Unit 2F** 'Using electricity' • To make a complete circuit using a battery, wires and bulbs. • To explore how to make a bulb light up, explaining what happened, and using drawings to present results.	• Know electricity can come from a battery.	**PSHE** PoS (3g) To understand rules for, and ways of, keeping safe, including basic road safety, and about people who can help them to stay safe.
Lesson 20: Testing circuits ● ▣	**QCA Unit 2F** 'Using electricity' • To know that an electrical device will not work if there is no battery or if there is a break in the circuit. • To make and test predictions about circuits that will work. • To say whether the evidence supports the predictions. • To explain what happened, drawing on their knowledge of circuits.	• Know how to build a complete circuit to light a bulb.	**English** PNS: Creating and shaping texts

Food groups

Learning objectives
QCA Unit 2A 'Health and growth'
● To know that there are many different foods.
● To record information in drawings and charts.
● To know that we eat different kinds of food.
● To be able to collect information and present the results in a block graph.

Resources
'Keeping healthy' Notebook file; photocopiable page 130 'Food groups'; a few days prior to the lesson, ask the children, as homework, to keep a food diary for one day and return it for the lesson; supply a template similar to the diary on page 4 of the 'Keeping healthy' Notebook file.

Links to other subjects
Mathematics
PNS: Handling data
● The children will use their mathematical skills to record information in a pictogram or block graph.

Starter
Ask the children to look at their food diary (see Resources) and talk with them about what they eat. Find out what they already know about food, particularly with regard to staying healthy. Ask: *What would happen if we didn't eat or drink? What would happen if we only ate one sort of food? What do you understand by the term 'healthy'?* Record the children's responses on page 2 of the 'Keeping healthy' Notebook file.

Whole-class shared work
● Consider the pull-out question on page 2 and then look at page 3 with the children. Check that they know what the different foods are.
● Explain that different types of food do different jobs in our bodies and that this is why it is important to eat a variety of foods to remain healthy.
● Support the children in sorting the food pictures into the correct food groups. Talk about their decisions and give definitions for any new vocabulary.
● Show the children Jack's food diary on page 4. Ask them to identify the food groups that the foods in the diary belong to.
● Go to page 5 and tell the children that you will be working together to use the tally chart to sort the food in Jack's diary into the five food groups. Refer back to page 4 to look at what Jack ate and record the results in the tally chart on page 5. Highlight the foods on page 4 as they are recorded in the tally chart. Print out the results on page 5.
● Go to page 6. Using the printout of page 5, show the children how to drag and drop the coloured boxes from the bottom of the page into the appropriate place on the block graph to illustrate the tally chart data (about Jack's food).

Independent work
● Give each child a copy of photocopiable page 130. Ask them to transfer the information from their own food diary onto the tally chart.
● Provide plenty of support at this stage, as some foods (such as a ready meal) can be difficult to classify into one particular group.
● Ask the children to use tally chart data to create a block graph using the template on the sheet.
● Encourage more confident learners to attempt to create their own tally chart and block graph on squared paper instead of using the photocopiable sheet.

Plenary
● Look at the block graph created earlier on page 6 of the Notebook file. Ask the children what they think it shows about Jack's diet.
● Ask questions about the chart such as: *Is Jack eating a healthy diet? Has Jack eaten five portions of fruit and vegetables? Is Jack a vegetarian?* Write the children's responses on page 7.
● Give the children an opportunity to evaluate their own eating habits with a partner. Ask some children to give feedback on their discussions to the rest of the class.

Whiteboard tools

 Pen tray

 Select tool

 Highlighter pen

Keeping healthy

Learning objectives
QCA Unit 2A 'Health and growth'
● To understand that humans need water and food to stay alive.
● To understand that humans need exercise to stay healthy.
● To make and record observations and make simple comparisons.

Resources
'Keeping healthy' Notebook file; posters about healthy living; outdoor space; plain paper; felt-tipped pens.

Links to other subjects
PSHE
PoS (3a) To know how to make simple choices that improve their health and well-being.
● Ask the children to investigate ways to live a healthy lifestyle.
Art and design
QCA Unit 2A 'Picture this!'
● In this lesson the children will be drawing images on their posters to promote healthy living.
PE
QCA Unit 4 'Games activities'
● Encourage the children to recognise the changes that take place in their bodies as they exercise.

Starter
Ask the children to talk with a partner about what things they think humans need to do to keep healthy. Listen to some of their ideas and then open the 'Keeping healthy' Notebook file. Show the list of statements on page 8. Ask the children to decide which statements belong in the box. Talk about their ideas and correct any misconceptions.

Whole-class shared work
● Ask the children to sit quietly for one minute and consider how their bodies feel when they are at rest. Record key words on page 9.
● Take the children into the playground and ask them to play an active game for a few minutes. Ask: *How do your bodies feel now?*
● Encourage the children to think about what changes have occurred in their bodies, and why these may have happened. Record a few sentences on page 9.
● Alternatively, instead of recording ideas as a class on the whiteboard, give the children the opportunity to record individually how they felt before and after exercising, using key words and drawings.
● Ask the children to consider what exercise they do. Ensure that they understand that there are many alternative ways to exercise. Talk about the benefits of exercise.
● Show some posters promoting keeping healthy, particularly those relating to exercise. Talk about their layout and the message they portray.
● There is an example of a simple poster on page 10 of the Notebook file. The poster labels are mixed up; invite the children to drag them to the correct position.

Independent work
● Give the children a plain piece of A4 paper and some felt-tipped pens. Ask them to create a poster to promote the benefits of exercise to other children in the school.
● Encourage the children to talk to a partner about the message they want to get across on their poster.
● Make sure the children consider the layout and content of the poster carefully before they begin – for example, large, bold lettering, using all of the page and appropriate drawings to support the message.

Plenary
● Take samples of the children's posters and scan them into the computer. Display the posters using the whiteboard software and ask the class to comment on them.
● Ask: *What message is the poster giving? Does it motivate you to do some exercise?* Encourage positive comments from the children.
● Ask the children to revise with a partner what humans need to do to stay healthy. Assess how far their learning has moved on during the lesson.

Whiteboard tools
Upload scanned images of the children's work by selecting Insert, then Picture File, and browsing to where you have saved the images.

 Pen tray

 Select tool

Animals and their young

Learning objectives
QCA Unit 2A 'Health and growth'
● To know that animals (including humans) produce young and these grow into children and new adults.
● To understand that babies and children need to be looked after while they are growing.
● To ask questions in order to make simple comparisons of babies and children.

Resources
'Life cycles' Notebook file; paper; pencils. Before the lesson, invite an adult with a baby to visit the class and talk to the children about caring for a baby (encourage the children to ask sensible questions).

Links to other subjects
Citizenship
QCA Unit 3 'Animals and us'
● In this lesson, the children will find out about and appreciate the needs of themselves and others.

Starter

Explain that there are special names for baby animals. Show page 2 of the 'Life cycles' Notebook file. Read the question at the top of the page and encourage the children to discuss the answer. Allow them to press on the animal that they think is correct for each question. If it is correct, they will hear a cheer.

Ask the children to consider whether the young would look like its mother when it is born and also whether it comes from an egg or from its mother's tummy. Repeat this activity on pages 3 to 7.

Whole-class shared work

● Pages 8 and 9 show the life cycles of a chicken and a frog. Page 10 shows the timeline of a human. First, ask the children to explain each life cycle or timeline. Then invite them to drag and drop the pictures into position.
● Discuss how the animals change from being born to becoming a fully grown adult. Explain that some animals look completely different to their parents when they are young and others, like humans, look very similar.
● Discuss how long the parents of these different animals care for their young and what needs they have. Compare these needs to the needs of a human infant.
● Introduce Ellie and Jack on page 11. Relate Jack to the baby that visited the class (see Resources), and Ellie to the children themselves. Talk briefly about ways in which Ellie and Jack's parents might look after them.
● Move on to page 12 and consider the questions. Encourage the children to answer the questions using the knowledge they gained from the baby visit and what they know about themselves. Write the main points into the boxes.

Independent work

● Fold pieces of paper in half, vertically, and give each child a sheet.
● Ask the children to draw a picture of a baby at the top of the first half and a picture of a child at the top of the second half of the divided page.
● Beneath the pictures, ask the children to record their ideas about the needs of each. In what ways do the child and baby need to be looked after? Why is this necessary?
● Supply less confident learners with prompt questions that they can answer about the needs of babies and children. For example: *What do they eat?*
● Extend more confident learners by asking them to write a paragraph comparing the needs of babies and children. For example: babies only drink milk, but children can eat solid food because they have teeth to chew it.

Plenary

● Share some of the children's thoughts from their independent work. Address any errors and misconceptions that are evident in their work. Page 13 can be used for notes.
● Ask the children to explain to a partner two ways that babies have different needs from children.

Whiteboard tools

 Pen tray

 Select tool

Medicine safety

Learning objectives
QCA Unit 2A 'Health and growth'
● To know that medicines help us to get better but are drugs and not food and can be dangerous.
● To understand that some people need medicines to keep them alive and healthy.
● To recognise hazards and risks in medicines and how to avoid these.

Resources
'Keeping healthy' Notebook file; photocopiable page 131 'Medicine safety'; a selection of clearly labelled clean, empty medicine packets and bottles.

Links to other subjects
Citizenship
QCA Unit 1 'Taking part'
QCA Unit 2 'Choices'
● Give the children the opportunity to develop their understanding of drugs and medicines and realise that they have to make informed choices to keep safe.

Starter
Talk with the children about what they know about medicines. Record their ideas on page 12 of the 'Keeping healthy' Notebook file. Ask them to think about times when they have taken medicines.

Encourage children who take regular medication (such as for asthma) to talk about the medicines they take, and why. Introduce the term *drugs* to the children as another term meaning medicines. Explain that drugs can come in different forms such as liquid, tablets, creams, injections and inhalers.

Whole-class shared work
● Share pages 13 and 14 of the Notebook file with the children. Stress to them that it is always acceptable to say no if they are unsure about something. Ensure that they understand the traffic light system (see page 14).
● Read the dilemmas on pages 15 to 18. Ask the children to talk with a partner about what they would do in each case. Remind them about the traffic light system for making decisions.
● Ask the children to share their ideas and talk about them as a class. Immediately correct any errors or misconceptions that they may have. Record important points in the boxes on the Notebook pages, using the correct colours.
● Use pages 15, 17 and 18 to address the importance of correct labelling and packaging.
● Use page 16 to explain that there are some adults who they can trust to help them (such as parents and doctors).
● Use pages 17 and 18 to demonstrate that appearances can be deceptive, so an unknown substance should never be taken.
● Use page 19 to explain that drugs that are good for some people can be harmful to others.

Independent work
● Give each group some empty medicine packets and bottles to inspect closely. Encourage the children to read the labels and safety messages on them.
● Ask the groups to list the instructions they find on the packets. Talk with the groups about why these instructions are important and what might happen if they were ignored.
● Give each child a copy of photocopiable page 131. Ask them to design and make a box for a new headache medicine. Give dosage instructions.
● Refer the children back to the labelling on the real medicine packaging.

Plenary
● Evaluate the boxes that the children made for safety, warnings and instructions on how to take the drugs safely.
● Go back to page 12 of the Notebook file (there is a link on page 20). Ask the children if there are any other ideas that they have learned in the lesson that they would like to add to their list, or any ideas that they now think are wrong and need to be changed. Add their ideas to the page in a different colour.

Whiteboard tools
 Pen tray

 Select tool

The local environment

Learning objectives
QCA Unit 2B 'Plants and animals in the local environment'
● To know that there are different kinds of plants and animals in the immediate environment.
● To observe and make a record of animals and plants found.
● To present results in a table.

Resources P
Photocopiable page 132 'Plants and animals in the local environment'; clipboards; pencils. Prepare a Notebook file: take digital photographs of a variety of plants and animals found around the school grounds, then insert these photographs into the whiteboard software along with their proper names so that they can be moved individually.

Links to other subjects
English
PNS: Understanding and interpreting texts
● The children will learn the names of plants and animals during this lesson.

Starter
Ask the children to think about the plants and animals they might see in their own garden or at the local park. Encourage them to share their ideas. Find out if they know the names of any of the plants and animals that they have seen locally. Ask them to consider whether the same plants and animals can be found in every garden.

Whole-class shared work
● Explain to the children that they are going to be nature detectives and investigate the local environment of the school grounds.
● Open the prepared Notebook file (see Resources). Show the children the photographs of the plants and animals that they might find in the school grounds.
● Ask the children to work with a partner to decide what each photograph shows. Help them to match the photographs to their labels.
● Encourage the children to use the proper names for plants and animals throughout the activity – to extend their understanding of different species. For example, *daffodil* instead of flower and *blue tit* instead of bird.
● Ensure that the children understand that plants and animals are living things that must be treated with care and respect and should not be removed from the habitat in which they were found.
● Remind the children about important safety issues such as not putting things into their mouths and what to do if they find broken glass.

Independent work
● Give every child a copy of photocopiable page 132, together with a clipboard with a pencil attached to it.
● Take the children for a walk around the school grounds to look for plants and animals. Ask them to record what they find and where they find it on their sheet.
● Allow less confident learners to record their findings using pictures, if necessary.
● Challenge more confident learners to record their findings in their own table instead of supplying them with a photocopiable sheet.
● Draw the children's attention to smaller animals such as insects, and larger plants such as trees.
● Make sure that the children wash their hands thoroughly after the walk.

Plenary
● Review what the children found while on their walk. Ask them whether anyone was surprised by what they did or did not find, and why they think particular plants and animals were found in certain places.
● Elicit from the children that certain plants and animals like different habitats. For example: *A caterpillar was found on the lettuces because they like to eat green leaves.*
● Go back to the prepared Notebook file and highlight any plants or animals that the children found on their walk.

Whiteboard tools

 Pen tray

 Select tool

 Highlighter pen

 Text tool

The life cycle of plants

Learning objectives
QCA Unit 2B 'Plants and animals in the local environment'
● To know that flowering plants produce seeds.
● To know that seeds produce new plants.

Resources
'Life cycles' Notebook file; a variety of flowers and fruits with seeds inside them (make sure that you are aware of any children's allergies and check a plant guide to ensure that none of the plants are poisonous); soil and small plant pots; stickers; a plant in flower in a pot; a dandelion in its various stages; magnifying glasses.

Links to other subjects
ICT
QCA Unit 2C 'Finding information'
● Suggest that the children extend their knowledge of life cycles by searching for information using CD-ROMs.

Starter
Show the children a plant in flower in a pot and ask them to explain to a partner where they think the plant came from. Encourage them to add as much detail to their explanations as possible. For example, if the children suggest that the plant grew from a seed, ask them where the seed came from. Make a note of their responses on page 14 of the Notebook file.

Whole-class shared work
● Show the children an apple and ask them where they think it came from.
● Look at page 15 of the Notebook file. Invite the children to drag and drop the labels from the box into place.
● Ask the children to decide where they think you should begin to read the information. Elicit that there is no correct starting point and that is why it is displayed as a cyclical diagram.
● Share the life cycle of an apple with the children, talking about every stage in detail.
● Move on to page 16. Ask the children to label the parts of the plant, dragging and dropping the labels from the red box into the appropriate positions.
● Ask the children to try to describe the life cycle of a dandelion to a partner. Listen to their ideas and then explain the life cycle, showing the children real dandelions at the different stages if possible.

Independent work
● Give each group a variety of different flowers and fruits with seeds on or inside them. Ask the children to have a close look at them.
● Challenge the children to find and harvest the seeds from each of the flowers and fruits. Give them the opportunity to look closely at the seeds with magnifying glasses.
● Ensure that the children know not to eat the seeds and be aware of any allergies that they may have.
● Give the children some soil, plant pots and stickers and ask them to plant the seeds into the pots and label them. Help them to plant the seeds correctly.
● Ask the children to make predictions about what will happen next.

Plenary
● Talk with the children about what they might expect to happen to their seeds now that they have been planted. Ask: *Will the seeds grow if we just leave them on the window sill? What do the seeds need to have so that they will grow into healthy plants?*
● Assess the children's understanding.
● Challenge the children to say what type of plant their seed will grow into to ensure that they understand the concept that the seed can only grow into the same species of plant that it came from.
● Write the children's ideas into page 17 of the Notebook file to provide a record that you can return to.

Whiteboard tools
Use the Eraser from the Pen tray to reveal the hidden answers on page 16.

 Pen tray

 Select tool

Investigating plants

Learning objectives
QCA Unit 2B 'Plants and animals in the local environment'
● To turn ideas about what plants need to grow, into a form that can be tested.
● To observe and make a day-to-day record of observations.
● To use the results to draw a conclusion about what seeds need to grow.
● To recognise when a comparison is unfair.

Resources
'Investigating plants' Notebook file; photocopiable page 133 'Investigating plants'; individual whiteboards and pens; cress and runner bean seeds; soil; sand; cotton wool; paper towel; wool; planting trays or plant pots; water; measuring beakers.

Links to other subjects
Speaking and listening
Objective15: To listen to each other's views and preferences; agree the next steps to take.
● The children need to work and cooperate in a group to carry out the investigation.

Starter
Ask the children to list, on their individual whiteboards, what they think plants need in order to grow. Open the 'Investigating plants' Notebook file and show them page 2. Ask them to sort the pictures into the boxes according to whether a plant needs them to grow.

Whole-class shared work
● Show the children the question that you are going to investigate together on page 3 of the Notebook file.
● Ask them to suggest what they could do to find the answer; what equipment they will need; and how they could make the test fair. Talk in depth about their ideas and record their suggestions on the page.
● Guide the children to the idea of planting cress seeds in different materials (including soil) to see if they will grow. Discuss how to make the test fair.
● Set up the experiment. Involve the children by asking them to put the materials into pots (see Resources), count out seeds and measure out equal amounts of water for each pot. Plant the seeds.
● Go to page 4. Explain that the children need to examine the seeds regularly and record the results in the table.
● Next, show the children the question on page 5 and explain that they are going to investigate this question in groups.
● Use page 6 to help the children to plan their investigation, as with page 3 above.
● Guide the children to the idea of changing the variables of light and water for the same type of seed, and comparing their growth.

Independent work
● Give each group some soil, plant pots, measuring beakers, water and runner bean seeds and support them in setting up their investigation.
● Talk about what steps they are taking to ensure that their investigation is fair.
● Provide opportunities for the children to take and record measurements throughout the next few weeks as necessary.
● Provide each child with a copy of photocopiable page 133 to record their results. Challenge more confident learners to make up their own tables.

Plenary
● Talk to the children about what they have found out and evaluate whether the results were as they expected. Ask for a final answer to each of the questions posed during the original lesson and show how the investigations support these answers. Record their responses on page 7.
● Ask the children to consider whether the investigations that they carried out were fair. What did they need to do to make them fair? (Equal amounts of water and light given to each set of seeds growing on different materials.)

Whiteboard tools

 Pen tray

 Select tool

Learning objectives
QCA Unit 2B 'Plants and animals in the local environment'
● To observe and recognise some simple characteristics of animals and plants.
● To know that the group of living things called animals includes humans.

Resources
'Plants and animals' Notebook file; a selection of images of plants, animals and inanimate objects for the children to sort; paper; scissors; glue; pencils.

Links to other subjects
ICT
QCA Unit 2E 'Questions and answers'
● Invite the children to use the information on plants and animals and inanimate objects to prepare a simple database.

Sorting plants and animals

Starter
Open the 'Plants and animals' Notebook file. Ask the children to define the words *plant* and *animal*. Record these initial ideas on page 2. Save the Notebook file so that these ideas can be looked at again in the Plenary.

Whole-class shared work
● Read the definitions of *plants* and *animals* on page 3 and talk about them. Invite a child to come to the whiteboard and use a Highlighter pen to highlight the important words.
● Show the children page 4. Ask them to name the plants, animals and objects at the bottom of the page.
● Challenge them to sort the pictures into the three groups – *plant, animal* or *neither*.
● Begin by finding pictures to add to the animal group. Remind the children of the definition of an animal. Help them to consider humans as part of this group. Show that humans fit the *animal* definition.
● If children want to place the teddy bear and rocking horse in the animal box, explain that they are not alive, and never have been, so they cannot be animals.
● Next, find pictures to add to the plant group. Remind the children of the definition of a plant. Help them to consider trees for this group. Show that trees fit the *plant* definition.
● Check that the remaining pictures should be added to the *neither* group.
● Help the children to understand that if the objects are not alive and have never been alive, then they are neither a plant nor an animal and can be added to the *neither* group.

Independent work
● Provide the children with sheets of paper and a selection of images to be sorted into three groups: plants, animals and neither (see Resources).
● Ask the children to divide their page into three parts and write the appropriate headings at the top of each section. Supply them with scissors and glue and ask them to cut out and stick the pictures into the correct groups.
● Keep reminding the children of the definitions for plant and animal. Encourage them to check that their sorting choices fit the definitions.
● Challenge more confident learners to think of three more things to add to each group by drawing them.

Plenary
● Return to page 2 of the 'Plants and animals' Notebook file (there is a link on page 5). Re-read the definitions of *plant* and *animal* that the children originally gave. Encourage them to amend the definitions according to what they have learned.
● Show the children some of the pictures that caused discussion during the independent work time, and ask them to decide what group they belong to. Always refer back to the definitions to check the children's decisions.

Whiteboard tools
Use a Highlighter pen to highlight key words to define plants and animals.

 Pen tray

 Select tool

 Highlighter pen

Learning objectives
QCA Unit 2C 'Variation'
● To know that living things in the locality can be grouped according to observable similarities and differences.
● To present results in a block graph.

Resources
'Plants and animals' Notebook file; a selection of images of different animals found in the locality, including humans; plain paper; glue; scissors; pencils; squared paper.

Links to other subjects
ICT
QCA Unit 2E 'Questions and answers'
● Help the children to create a branching (binary tree) database using a selection of animals.

Categorising animals

Starter
Display page 6 of the 'Plants and animals' Notebook file. Sit the children in a circle to play the 'Similar and different' game. Ensure that they know what *similar* and *different* mean. Show pictures of two different animals. Move around the circle, asking the children to think of a way that the two animals are either similar or different; the first person has to say a similarity and the second person has to say a difference. When all ideas are exhausted, show two more animals.

Whole-class shared work
● Explain to the children that the big group called animals can be split up into a number of smaller groups by looking at the similarities between the animals.
● Give the children an example of this by explaining that robins, bees and butterflies can all be grouped together because they can all fly.
● Show the children page 7. Tell them that you have decided to sort the animals into three groups: *walk*, *slither* and *fly*.
● Invite individuals to come to the whiteboard and move the animals into the three different groups.
● When the animals are sorted, count how many there are in each group, to see which method of movement is most common.
● Use page 8 to show how to display the children's findings in a block graph.
● Show the children the pictures that they will be sorting in the independent work (see Resources) and ask them to talk to a partner about the different categories they could sort them into.
● Use page 9 to list the different ideas that children have, and leave these on display when the children begin their independent work.

Independent work
● Give each child a set of pictures to sort. Ask them to decide how they are going to sort the pictures and then separate a piece of paper into the appropriate number of sections. Ensure that they add a heading to each section.
● Provide the children with glue and scissors. Ask them to cut out and stick the pictures into the appropriate groups.
● Less confident learners may benefit from working in pairs so that they can discuss their decisions together.
● Give the children some squared paper or a block graph template and ask them to show their results as a block graph.

Plenary
● Invite some of the children to share their work with the class. Record their responses on page 10 of the Notebook file.
● Ask the children questions about what they found out. Talk with them about some of the terms used to properly classify animals such as *mammal, bird* and *insect*. Work with the children to define these categories of animals.
● Determine which category humans belong to.

Whiteboard tools

 Pen tray

 Select tool

Human variation

Learning objectives
QCA Unit 2C 'Variation'
● To know that humans are more like each other than they are like other animals.
● To know that humans are similar to each other in some ways and different in others.
● To explore human variation making observations and comparisons.

Resources
Mirrors; individual whiteboards and pens; paper; coloured pencils; pictures of different animals (including humans). Prepare a Notebook file: take digital photographs of six of the children in the class (check parental permission first), and make a three-page file with two photographs on each page.

Links to other subjects
Art and design
QCA Unit 2A 'Picture this!'
● The children will need to make careful observations of their partners in order to create good representations of them.

Starter
Show the children pictures of different animals (including humans). Ask them to pick out the humans from the selection of pictures. Discuss how they knew that the pictures they selected were of humans. What features did they look for? Show them a picture of a chimpanzee and ask them to explain how they know it is not a human. Conclude that all humans look similar to each other.

Whole-class shared work
● Ask the children to choose a partner to work with and look closely at. On their individual whiteboards, ask them to write down a (sensitive) detailed description of their partner's appearance.
● Encourage the pairs to find things in their descriptions that are the same, and things that are different. Share these as a class.
● Show the children two of the digital photographs in your prepared Notebook file (see Resources). Ask the class who is depicted in the photographs. Encourage explanations of how they know this. Label the photographs with the children's names.
● Sit the children in a circle and ask them to think of a way that the two children in the photographs are either similar or different; the first child you choose has to give a similarity and the next child has to give a difference. Write down the explanations.
● When all ideas are exhausted, display the second page in your prepared file showing two more photographs, and repeat the procedure.
● Reiterate that the children look more like each other than they look like any other type of animal.

Independent work
● Put the children in pairs. Supply mirrors and request that they take a close look at their own appearance and that of their partner.
● Allow the children time to draw a detailed portrait of their own face on one side of the page and of their partner on the other side of the page.
● Ask them to write detailed descriptions of themselves and their partners beneath the appropriate drawings.
● Encourage the children to list three similarities and three differences between themselves and their partners.
● Challenge more confident learners by putting them into groups of three and supporting them to carry out a three-way comparison.

Plenary
● Listen to some of the similarities and differences between the pairs and reiterate that, even with the differences, the children still look more like each other than they look like any other type of animal.
● As a final observation challenge, ask the class to sort themselves into groups according to different criteria, such as hair or eye colour.

Whiteboard tools
 Pen tray

 Select tool

Investigating differences between children

Learning objectives
QCA Unit 2C 'Variation'
● To know that some differences between themselves and other children can be measured.
● To measure hand span in standard units of length, make comparisons and present measurements in a block graph.
● To raise questions about differences between themselves, test them and decide whether their predictions were correct.

Resources
'Investigating differences' Notebook file; photocopiable pages 134 and 135 'Investigating differences (1) and (2)'; measuring equipment; paper; pencils; rulers; scissors. (Microsoft Excel is required to view the embedded spreadsheet in the Notebook file.)

Links to other subjects
Mathematics
PNS: Measuring
● The children will use their measuring skills to measure parts of their bodies.

Starter
Show the children what is meant by the term *hand span*. Ask them to predict which child will have the largest hand span. Use page 2 of the Notebook file to demonstrate how to measure a hand span. Ask the children to draw around one of their hands on a sheet of paper, then cut out the paper hands and use rulers to measure the span. Tell them to write their hand span on their paper hand. Find out who has the largest hand span.

Whole-class shared work
● Ponder aloud whether the tallest person in the class has the largest hand span. Look at the first question on page 3. Ask: *How can we find out whether the tallest person in the class has the largest hand span?* Scribe the children's ideas in the first box on page 4. Then consider the other two questions and scribe their ideas in the second and third boxes.
● Open the spreadsheet on page 5 and show the children the worksheet labelled *Hand span v height*.
● Choose ten children and measure their heights. Write the heights on cards that the children can hold in front of them. Ask them to stand in order from shortest to tallest.
● Enter the ten children's names (from shortest to tallest) and corresponding heights into the table. A bar chart of the children's heights will appear.
● Now enter the same children's hand span measurements into the table next to their heights. A bar chart of the children's hand spans will appear.
● Look at the two bar charts with the children and ask questions about them.
● Ask the children to answer the original question of whether the person with the largest hand span is also the tallest person. Ask them to explain how the bar chart shows them this.
● Return to page 5 and point out that the children have already answered the first question.

Independent work
● Challenge the children to work in groups of five to answer the second question (ie whether the tallest children have the longest feet).
● Supply paper, measuring equipment and scissors for the children. Ask them to take accurate measurements of foot length and height.
● Supply each child with photocopiable pages 134 and 135. Ask the group to share their measurements to complete the sheets. Encourage the children to use their results to find an answer.
● Arrange the children into mixed-ability groups to support the less confident learners.

Plenary
● Share the results from each group's investigation. Use the Microsoft Excel file link on page 5 to enter the results of ten children's measurements into the worksheet labelled *Foot length v height* and make a final conclusion.
● Ask the children to predict the answer to the third question from what they have learned so far. Ask ten children for their hand span (which they should each have on a paper version of their hand from the Starter) and their foot length (which they will have recorded in their independent work). Enter these into the *Hand span vs foot length* tab on the spreadsheet to form a conclusion.
● Ask the children to suggest other questions that could be investigated involving differences between themselves. Use page 6 for notes.

Whiteboard tools
Use the On-screen Keyboard, accessed through the Pen tray or the SMART Board tools menu, to input data in the spreadsheet cells.

 Pen tray

 Select tool

 On-screen Keyboard

Natural or man-made

Learning objectives
QCA Unit 2D 'Grouping and changing materials'
● To know that some materials occur naturally and some do not.
● To know the names of some naturally occurring materials.
● To know that some naturally occurring materials are treated before they are used.

Resources
'Materials' Notebook file; a variety of objects made from natural and man-made materials; glue; scissors; individual whiteboards and pens.

Links to other subjects
Art and design
QCA Unit 2B 'Mother Nature, designer'
● The children will be using natural and man-made materials to produce a collage.
Speaking and listening
Objective 15: To listen to each other's views and preferences, agree the next steps to take and identify contributions by each group member.
● The children will work as part of a group to decide on the materials to use for their collages.

Whiteboard tools

 Pen tray

 Select tool

Starter
Provide the children with a variety of different objects and ask them to sort them according to the material that they are made from. Encourage them to add labels to each of their groups. Look at some of the objects and talk about the characteristics of the material they are made from. Revise some of the technical vocabulary for materials such as *transparent, rough* and so on. Key words can be recorded on page 2 of the 'Materials' Notebook file.

Whole-class shared work
● Introduce the terms *natural material* and *man-made material*. Explain that a natural material is not produced by humans – it is a material that is made from a plant or an animal, or is found under the ground. Ask the children to think of some examples of natural materials, such as wood and wool.
● Use page 3 to sort materials into natural and man-made. Ensure that the children understand these terms properly.
● Explain the difference between *manufactured* and *not manufactured*. Make sure that the children understand that natural materials can be manufactured into useful objects (such as paper or a knitted jumper) but that the material the object is made from is still natural.
● Explain that a man-made material would not exist if man didn't make it using chemicals in a factory (such as plastic or nylon).
● Go to page 4 and challenge the children to talk to a partner about how to sort the objects using the Carroll diagram. Support their decision-making process with appropriate questioning.

Independent work
● Provide a wide selection of natural and man-made materials that are suitable for use in a collage.
● Put the children into groups of three. Ask each group to choose whether they want to create a collage from natural materials or man-made materials.
● Set the groups a theme for their collage, such as Christmas characters. Challenge them to create it using the material type of their choice.
● Ensure that the groups are of mixed ability so that the less confident learners are supported in their decision making.
● Encourage the children to talk about the origins and properties of the materials that they are using as they work.

Plenary
● Show each collage to the class and ask them to guess whether the group chose to use man-made or natural materials for their collage.
● Challenge the children to find any materials from the wrong group that have mistakenly been included in the collages.
● As a final assessment, ask the children to list on their individual whiteboards five objects in the classroom that are made from natural materials and five that are made from man-made materials. Beside the object name, ask the children to write the name of the material that the object is made from. This can be modelled on page 5 of the Notebook file.

Squashing, bending, twisting, stretching

Learning objectives
QCA Unit 2D 'Grouping and changing materials'
● To know that objects made from some materials can be altered by squashing, bending, twisting and stretching.
● To describe ways of making materials or objects change, using appropriate vocabulary.
● To explore materials using appropriate senses and make observations and simple comparisons.
● To construct a table to record observations.

Resources
'Materials' Notebook file; Plasticine; elastic bands; pebbles; clay; foam balls; play dough. Prepare a sheet: create a table similar to the table on pages 8 and 9 of the 'Materials' Notebook file.

Links to other subjects
Art and design
QCA Unit 2A 'Picture this!'
● The children will use their knowledge of the ways in which different materials can be manipulated to produce artwork.

Starter
Open the 'Materials' Notebook file and go to page 6. Ask the children to work with a partner to think of different ways that a material such as play dough can be changed. Listen to the ideas as a class. Encourage the children to consider whether all materials can be changed in the same ways. For example, can all materials be stretched?

Whole-class shared work
● Go to page 7. Give each child a piece of play dough and ask them to do squash it. Show them what squashing is with your own piece of play dough.
● Next ask the children to bend, twist and stretch the play dough. Ensure that all of the children are happy with this vocabulary.
● Show the children some Plasticine, an elastic band, a pebble, some clay and a foam ball. Talk about the properties of each of them in turn.
● Now show the children the table on page 8 of the Notebook file. Ask them to predict whether each of the materials will squash, bend, twist or stretch. Allow them to record their predictions with a tick or cross in the appropriate box.
● Encourage the children to predict whether the object will return to its original state once a force is no longer being applied to it, or whether it will remain distorted like the play dough.

Independent work
● Supply the children with a copy of the prepared sheet (see Resources) and the five materials to be tested (Plasticine, an elastic band, a pebble, some clay and a foam ball).
● Ask the children to test the materials and complete the table with the actual results.
● Challenge more confident learners to create their own table to record their results.
● Talk to the children about whether the results were as they expected.

Plenary
● Gather the children together and use page 9 of the Notebook file to record the results of their experiments.
● Discuss the results with the children and talk about anything that surprised them. Make a note of interesting observations or comments on page 10.
● Ask some questions about the materials, such as: *Can you keep stretching an elastic band? Once an elastic band has snapped, will it still return to its original state? Is there any way that you could change a pebble? Can anything be squashed but not stretched?* Discuss the children's answers to these questions.

Whiteboard tools
Convert handwritten words to text by selecting them and choosing the Recognise option from the dropdown menu.

 Pen tray

 Select tool

Heating materials

Learning objectives
QCA Unit 2D 'Grouping and changing materials'
● To know that materials often change when they are heated.
● To make observations and simple comparisons.
● To use a table to make a record of observations.
● To decide whether what happened was what they expected.

Resources
'Materials' Notebook file; photocopiable page 136 'Heating materials'; four different types of sweets; a cake; a slice of bread; paper towels. (Check for any food allergies before the children eat or handle the foods.)

Links to other subjects
Science
QCA Unit 3A 'Teeth and eating'
● Use the opportunity to discuss the importance of looking after our teeth, and how we should brush our teeth carefully after eating sugary foods.

Starter
Open the 'Materials' Notebook file and go to page 11. Show the children a cake and ask them if it has always looked like it does now. Encourage them to think about how the cake turned from a bowl of mixed ingredients into a cake. Establish that the ingredients changed as they were heated. Ask the children to consider whether the cake could be turned back into its original separate ingredients.

Whole-class shared work
● Show the children a slice of bread and ask them to describe to a partner what will happen to it as it is heated.
● Display the photographs on page 12 of the Notebook file. Challenge the children to place the photographs in order, according to the amount that the bread has been heated.
● Ask them to think about whether the toast will return to its original state when it is cooled.
● Invite the children to think of other things that change when they are heated. Can they think of any materials other than food? Ask them to consider whether the materials will return to their original state once they have cooled.

Independent work
● Tell the children that they are going to find out what happens to different sweets as they are heated. Explain that they are going to use the heat from their hands to heat the sweets, as it is safer than a candle.
● Start off by asking the children to wash their hands. Supply paper towels to wipe their hands during the experiment.
● Give each child a copy of photocopiable page 136. Show them the four sweets they will be investigating. Ask them to make detailed predictions about what will happen to each sweet as it is heated in their hand.
● Tell the children to hold the first sweet in their closed hand and then use the Timer on page 13 to time three minutes.
● Invite the children to open their hands, describe what has happened to the sweet, eat it and record their observations in the table.
● Repeat this cycle until all of the sweets have been tested.
● As an extra challenge, ask the children to complete the bottom section of the photocopiable sheet.

Plenary
● Add the names of the sweets to the table on page 14 of the Notebook file. Compile the results of the experiment as a class.
● Find out whether the children were surprised by any of the results or whether they made accurate predictions. Address any misconceptions that may arise during the discussion. Page 15 can be used for notes.
● Ask the children to consider what would have happened if the sweets had been heated with a candle instead. Invite them to decide what would have happened to each sweet if it had been left to cool.

Whiteboard tools

 Pen tray

 Select tool

Investigating different vehicles

Learning objectives
QCA Unit 2E 'Forces and movement'
● To suggest questions about ways in which different objects move.
● To make measurements of distance and record these in a prepared table.
● To use the results in a table to draw a block graph.
● To decide whether their comparison was fair.

Resources
'Forces' Notebook file; photocopiable page 137 'Vehicle test'; a range of toy vehicles; measuring equipment. (Microsoft Excel is required to view the embedded spreadsheet in the Notebook file.)

Links to other subjects
Mathematics
PNS: Handling data
● The children will be using their mathematical knowledge to create and interpret a block graph of their results.

Starter
Display page 2 of the 'Forces' Notebook file. Show the children five toy vehicles (see Resources) and ask them to explain how they could make the vehicles move (by pushing them) and how they could make them move faster (by pushing harder). Ask the children to consider if there are any other factors that could affect the speed at which the vehicles move.

Whole-class shared work
● Examine the five toy vehicles closely. Talk about their properties (the heaviest, longest, one with the biggest wheels and so on). Make a note of key words on page 3.
● Ask the children to predict which of the vehicles will travel the furthest and explain why they think this. Write their predictions into the table on page 4.
● Open the spreadsheet by pressing the link on page 4 of the Notebook file. Draw a starting line on a smooth flat surface. Push the vehicles, one at a time, with an equal force from the starting line.
● Support the children as they measure the distance each vehicle travels and record these results in the top table in the spreadsheet (Test 1). A bar chart of the data should appear next to the table.
● Look at the results with the children and encourage them to evaluate whether their predictions were correct. Invite them to suggest reasons why the results are as they are.
● Repeat the same experiment, but this time allow a different child to push each vehicle from the starting line.
● Record the results in the bottom table (Test 2) and compare the two sets of results.
● Ask the children to consider why the results might be different. Ask: *Was the test a fair test? How could we make the test fair?*
● Conclude that the same person needs to push each vehicle with the same force to make the test fair.

Independent work
● Supply each pair of children with five toy vehicles and ask them to make a prediction about which one will travel furthest, and why.
● Support the pairs in independently carrying out the experiment from the whole-class work.
● Ensure that the children consider whether the test is a fair test.
● Give each pair a copy of photocopiable page 137. Ask them to record the distance each vehicle travelled.
● Ask the children to create a block graph using the measurements collected and then evaluate their initial predictions.

Plenary
● Invite the children to talk about their investigations. Ask: *Did any of the results surprise you? Why do you think this vehicle travelled furthest? How did you make the test fair?*
● Return to the Notebook file and record the children's responses on page 5.

Whiteboard tools
Use the On-screen Keyboard, accessed through the Pen tray or the SMART Board tools menu, to enter text into the spreadsheet.

 Pen tray

 Select tool

 On-screen Keyboard

Investigating ramp height

Learning objectives
QCA Unit 2E 'Forces and movement'
● To suggest a question to test and predict what will happen.
● To decide what to do and what measurements to take.
● To make measurements and record these in a prepared table.
● To use the results in a table to draw a block graph.
● To say whether the prediction was correct and try to explain the results.

Resources
'Forces' Notebook file; photocopiable page 138 'Ramp height'; ramps and blocks; rulers; toy cars; measuring equipment. (Microsoft Excel is required to view the embedded spreadsheet in the Notebook file.)

Links to other subjects
Mathematics
PNS: Handling data
● The children will use their mathematical knowledge to create and interpret a block graph of their results.

Whiteboard tools
Use the On-screen Keyboard, accessed through the Pen tray or the SMART Board tools menu, to enter text into the spreadsheet.

 Pen tray

 Select tool

 On-screen Keyboard

Starter
Show the children how to build a ramp. Ask them to roll some different vehicles down the ramp and discuss how they travelled. Ask: *How could you make the vehicle move faster or slower?* Elicit that altering the ramp height could change the speed of the vehicle. Page 6 of the 'Forces' Notebook file can be used to model how a ramp can be built. Select the blue ramp, then press and drag the right-hand white circle to adjust the ramp height.

Whole-class shared work
● Show the children a low ramp and a high ramp. Ask them to predict which ramp would make a vehicle travel fastest, and to explain why they think this. Record their predictions on page 7.
● Explain that if a vehicle travels faster it will also travel further before it stops. Suggest that measuring the distance a vehicle travelled from the end of the ramp will indicate how fast it was travelling.
● Ask: *What factors do we need to consider to make the test fair? Would it be fair to use a different vehicle each time?*
● Open the spreadsheet by pressing the link on page 7. Draw a starting line on the ramp and raise it with one block. Release the vehicle from behind the starting line without pushing it.
● Support the children as they measure the distance the vehicle travels from the bottom of the ramp. Show them how to use the On-screen Keyboard to record the measurement in the table.
● Repeat this with the ramp raised up two, three, four and five blocks.
● Look at the results with the children and encourage them to evaluate whether their predictions were correct. Can they suggest reasons for why the results are as they are?

Independent work
● Supply each pair of children with a ramp, five blocks, a ruler and a toy vehicle. Ask them to carry out the experiment from the whole-class work independently to see if they get the same results.
● Reinforce that it is good to repeat a test as it makes results more trustworthy.
● Ensure that the children consider whether the test they are carrying out is a fair test.
● Give each pair a copy of photocopiable page 138. Tell them to use this sheet to record the distance that each ramp height makes the vehicle travel.
● Ask the children to create a block graph using the measurements collected, and then evaluate their initial predictions.

Plenary
● Compare the children's results with the results found in the whole-class activity. Work with the children to suggest reasons for any discrepancies if they arise.
● Display page 8 of the Notebook file and invite one pair to enter their information on the block graph. They will need to label the axes.
● Ask the children to try to explain the reasons for their results to a partner.

What does electricity do?

Learning objective
QCA Unit 2F 'Using electricity'
● To know that everyday appliances use electricity (including things that light up, heat up, produce sounds and move).

Resources
'Uses of electricity' Notebook file; a variety of electrical appliances that use both mains power and batteries; old catalogues containing pictures of electrical appliances; scissors; glue; paper; individual whiteboards and pens.

Links to other subjects
Mathematics
PNS: Handling data
● Suggest that the children present the results of their sorting in a pictogram or block graph.

Starter
Show the children a variety of electrical appliances (include some that use mains electricity and some that use batteries). Talk about what the appliances are, and what they do. Ask the children to consider what makes them work. Explain that they work because the electricity gives them power. Ensure that the children understand that electricity can come from the mains supply or from a battery. Ask them to decide what supplies the electricity that powers each object. Record their responses on page 2 of the 'Uses of electricity' Notebook file.

Whole-class shared work
● Look again at the electrical appliances. Explain that the electricity provides energy to an appliance in order to make it perform a specific function. For example, the electricity that goes to a lamp makes the bulb light up, meaning that the energy from the electricity is turned into light.
● Ask the children to consider what kind of outputs the energy from the electricity can be turned into. They should suggest heat, light, sound and movement.
● Explain that some appliances turn the energy from the electricity into more than one output. For example, a television turns electricity into light (for the picture) and sound.
● Go to page 3 and open the 'Uses of electricity' interactive quiz. Ask the children to decide what the main output of each appliance is. Some of the appliances may have more than one output, so ensure that the children understand that they are looking for the main output only.
● Use page 4 to summarise the answers to the quiz.

Independent work
● Provide each group with a selection of old catalogues, scissors, paper and glue. Ask the children to find and cut out pictures of things that use electricity from the catalogues.
● Encourage the children to sort the pictures that they gather according to their main output – heat, light, sound or movement.
● Allow the children to choose their own way to record their decisions.
● Encourage more confident learners to use Venn diagrams with intersecting circles. This means that the children can consider those appliances that have two outputs.

Plenary
● Take a sample of the children's work and scan it into the computer. Display the work on page 5 of the Notebook file and ask the children to comment on it. Annotate the work with some of the children's comments.
● Ask: *Have the appliances been sorted correctly? Has the work been recorded in an easy-to-understand way?* Discuss any errors or misconceptions that may arise in the children's work.
● As a final assessment, give the children individual whiteboards and ask them questions about the appliances that they viewed earlier. For example: *How many of the appliances turn the energy from the electricity into heat? What output does the radio give?*

Whiteboard tools
Add scanned images of the children's work to the page by selecting Insert, then Picture File, and browsing to where you have saved the images.

 Pen tray

 Select tool

Dangers of electricity

Learning objectives
QCA Unit 2F 'Using electricity'
● To know that everyday appliances are connected to the mains and that they must be used safely.
● To know that some devices use batteries which supply electricity; these can be handled safely.

Resources
'Dangers of electricity' Notebook file; an electrical safety video; an electrical safety poster; individual whiteboards and pens; felt-tipped pens; A4 paper.

Links to other subjects
PSHE
PoS (3g) To understand rules for, and ways of, keeping safe, including basic road safety, and about people who can help them to stay safe.
● The children will begin to appreciate the dangers of electricity.
Art and design
QCA Unit 2A 'Picture this!'
● The children will be sensitively evaluating each other's work.

Starter
Watch a video about electrical safety together. Discuss the dangers of electricity with the children and answer any questions that they may have. Explain that electricity can be very useful as it allows us to see when it is dark (and watch television!). Stress that although it is useful, it is also deadly if it is not used safely.

Ask the children what they think electricity looks like. Explain that it is actually invisible so it may still be there to hurt them even if they can't see it. Use page 2 of the Notebook file to write notes.

Whole-class shared work
● Give each child an individual whiteboard and ask them to write a list of appliances that use electricity that can be seen around the classroom. Ask them to write beside each appliance whether it is powered by battery or by mains electricity. Remind them that batteries only supply small amounts of electricity so they are safe for us to touch and use.
● Invite the children to share their answers. Make a note of their responses on page 3 of the Notebook file.
● Next, ask the children to take a close look at the picture displayed on page 4. Encourage them to talk to a partner about the electrical hazards that they can see in the picture.
● Invite volunteers to come to the whiteboard to circle or highlight the hazards that they can see, and then talk about them as a class.
● Display page 5. Ask: *Do you think the younger children in the school know about the dangers of electricity? How could you let them know?*
● Show the children an electrical safety poster and talk about its message and design.

Independent work
● Assign partners to act as 'critical friends'.
● Provide the children with sheets of A4 paper and some felt-tipped pens. Ask them to create a poster for the younger children in the school to explain to them the dangers of electricity.
● Encourage the children to use simple text and big bold pictures to illustrate their message.
● Stop the children every few minutes and ask them to look at their partner's poster.
● Encourage the 'critical friend' to point out some positive aspects of the poster and, most importantly, state whether the poster is communicating the desired message.

Plenary
● Take a small sample of the children's work and scan it into the computer. Add the examples to page 5 of the Notebook file and ask the class to comment on them.
● Evaluate whether the posters communicate the desired message. Encourage positive comments from the children and annotate the posters with them.
● As a final reminder, ask the children to tell a partner three ways to stay safe around electricity. Record their observations on page 6.

Whiteboard tools
Add scanned images of the children's work to the page by selecting Insert, then Picture File, and browsing to where you have saved the images.

 Pen tray

 Select tool

 Highlighter pen

Building a circuit

Learning objectives
QCA Unit 2F 'Using electricity'
● To make a complete circuit using a battery, wires and bulbs.
● To explore how to make a bulb light up, explaining what happened and using drawings to present results.

Resources
'Circuits' Notebook file; bulbs; batteries; wires; battery holders; bulb holders; paper; pencils.

Links to other subjects
PSHE
PoS (3g) To understand rules for, and ways of, keeping safe, including basic road safety, and about people who can help them to stay safe.
● Use this lesson as an opportunity to discuss the dangers of playing with electricity.

Starter
Explain that in order to make a bulb light up you need a bulb, a battery and wire. Open page 2 of the 'Circuits' Notebook file. Ask the children to match the objects to the labels. Show them a real battery, bulb and wire.

Whole-class shared work
● Tell the children that they are going to try to build a circuit to light a bulb. Explain the term *circuit* as *a closed loop that electricity travels around*.
● Explain that after the circuit has been made, the children are going to draw a diagram of it.
● Remind the children of the equipment they will be using to build the circuit, and ask them to suggest ideas for how it could be represented in a diagram. Use page 3 to record their ideas.

Independent work
● Supply each pair of children with a number of batteries, bulbs and wires and challenge them to light the bulb. Ensure that all of the equipment is functioning correctly before handing it out.
● Do not give out battery holders and bulb holders at first. Without these, the children can see the path that the current takes more easily, particularly through the bulb.
● If children are struggling to make the connections between the wires and the battery or bulb, supply the holders as appropriate.
● Remind the children about what was discussed earlier – that a complete circuit is needed to light a bulb.
● When the pairs have lit the bulb, ask the children to record their circuit as a labelled diagram.
● Encourage them to think about how and why the bulb lights up when a circuit is made.

Plenary
● Inivte a volunteer to use page 4 of the Notebook file to create a labelled diagram of the circuit they made.
● Make the circuit to test whether it lights a bulb and then compare it to the others that the children created.
● Point out that all the circuits are a closed loop with no breaks in them. Listen to the children's ideas about how and why the bulb lights up, then explain how the bulb actually lights.
● Ensure that the children understand that electricity is made in the battery and then travels around the circuit in one direction towards the bulb. Point out that inside the bulb there is a thin piece of wire that the electricity squeezes through. The electricity gets very hot and it glows. After the electricity leaves the bulb it returns to the battery to get some more energy, completing the circuit.

Whiteboard tools

 Pen tray

 Select tool

Testing circuits

Learning objectives
QCA Unit 2F 'Using electricity'
● To know that an electrical device will not work if there is no battery or if there is a break in the circuit.
● To make and test predictions about circuits that will work.
● To say whether the evidence supports the predictions.
● To explain what happened, drawing on their knowledge of circuits.

Resources
'Circuits' Notebook file; photocopiable page 139 'Testing circuits'; bulbs; batteries; wires; battery holders; bulb holders.

Links to other subjects
English
PNS: Creating and shaping texts
● Suggest that the children write a set of simple instructions to explain how to create and test a circuit.

Starter
Open page 5 of the Notebook file. Revise what the children already know about circuits by asking them to create a circuit that will light a bulb. Show them a complete circuit with the bulb lit and ask them what they could do to make the bulb go out. Listen and respond to their ideas.

Point out that a battery has a positive and negative end. Explain that the electricity flows out of the negative end and into the positive end when it is placed in a circuit.

Whole-class shared work
● Ask the children to consider what a circuit needs in order to work. Remind them of the importance of having a closed circuit if a bulb is to light up. Record their ideas on page 6.
● Go to page 7. Look at the different circuits with the children and ask them to predict whether the bulbs will light or not. Encourage them to explain their predictions, using their knowledge of circuits. Ask them to write the voting letters (**a** or **b**) on their individual whiteboards, then take a tally of their votes.
● Once the children have finished voting, invite volunteers to come to the whiteboard to drag and drop the diagrams into the appropriate boxes.
● Choose one of the circuits and ask the children to explain how they could find out whether their prediction was correct or not. Elicit that they could make the circuit and see if the bulb lights.
● Allow one of the children to make the circuit and test the prediction. Ask the rest of the class to explain why the circuit did or did not work, as appropriate.

Independent work
● Give each child a copy of photocopiable page 139. Ask them look at the picture of each bulb on the sheet, and to record their prediction about whether it will light or not.
● Allow the children access to bulbs, batteries, wires, bulb holders and battery holders. Encourage them to build the circuits on the sheet to test their predictions.
● Tell them to use the sheet to record the results of their tests.
● Challenge the children to explain why the bulb did or did not light. Ask them to record these ideas on the sheet.
● Encourage the children to talk with a partner about their predictions and explanations.

Plenary
● Go through each problem on the photocopiable sheet, one at a time, and ask the children whether the bulb lit up or not. Use page 8 to sort the images into the appropriate columns.
● Encourage the children to give an explanation for each problem. Address any errors or misconceptions they may have along the way.

Whiteboard tools

 Pen tray

 Select tool

Food groups

■ Use your own food diary to create a tally chart of the different types of food you have eaten.

Food group	Tally
Meat, fish and eggs	
Fruit and vegetables	
Cereals, bread and pulses	
Dairy	
Sugar and fats	

■ Use the tally chart you have made to create a block graph of the different types of food you have eaten.

	Meat, fish and eggs	Fruit and vegetables	Cereals, bread and pulses	Dairy	Sugar and fats
10					
9					
8					
7					
6					
5					
4					
3					
2					
1					

■ SCHOLASTIC
www.scholastic.co.uk

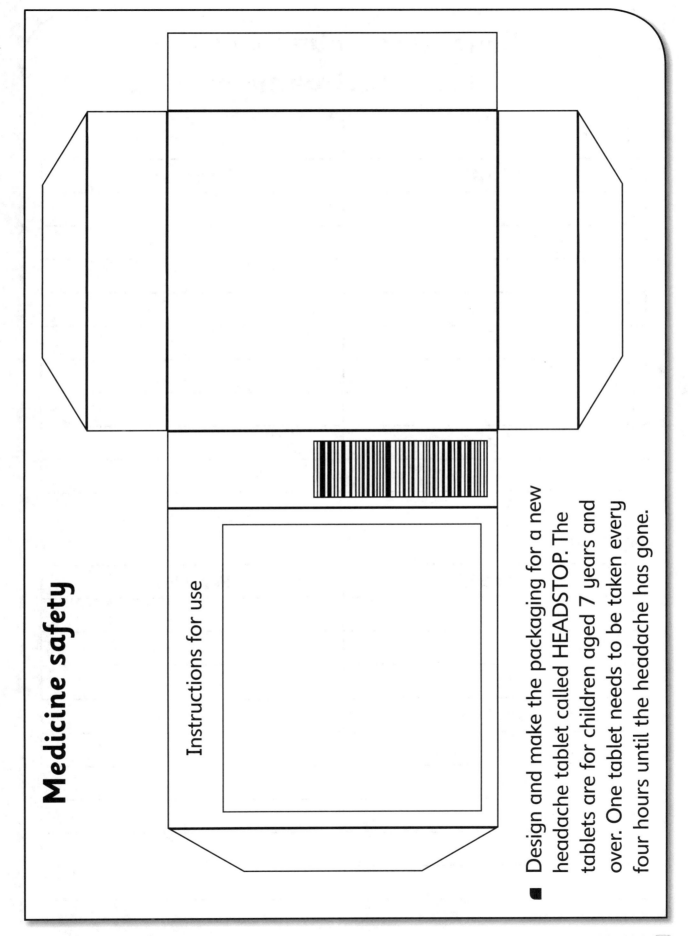

Medicine safety

Instructions for use

● Design and make the packaging for a new headache tablet called HEADSTOP. The tablets are for children aged 7 years and over. One tablet needs to be taken every four hours until the headache has gone.

Name _____

Plants and animals in the local environment

Plants

What?	Where?

Animals

What?	Where?

◖ SCHOLASTIC
www.scholastic.co.uk

Investigating plants

- Record the results of your investigations in this table.
- Each week, use pictures and words to describe the height and colour of your runner bean plants.

	Week 1	Week 2	Week 3	Week 4
Light Water				
Light No water				
No light Water				
No light No water				

Investigating differences (1)

■ Measure the height and foot length of five people.
Record your results in these tables.

Name	Height in cm

Name	Foot length in cm

Does the tallest person have the longest feet?

_____

◖ S C H O L A S T I C
www.scholastic.co.uk

Investigating differences (2)

◾ Use your results to complete this block graph.

Foot length in cm					
26					
25					
24					
23					
22					
21					
20					
19					
18					
17					
16					
15					
14					
13					
12					
11					
10					
9					
8					
7					
6					
5					
4					
3					
2					
1					

Height in cm (shortest to tallest)

Heating materials

■ Predict what will happen when you hold each of the sweets in your hand for 3 minutes. Try it and see what happens.

Name or type of sweet	What do you think will happen when you hold it?	What actually happened when you held it?

■ Think of other materials that will change when they are heated. How will they change?

1. _____   _____

2. _____   _____

3. _____   _____

4. _____   _____

5. _____   _____

◣SCHOLASTIC
www.scholastic.co.uk

Vehicle test

Vehicle	Distance travelled in cm

Block graph _____

Ramp height

Height of ramp	Distance travelled in cm

Block graph _____

📖 S C H O L A S T I C
www.scholastic.co.uk

Testing circuits

Circuit	Prediction Will it work? Yes/No	Result Did it work? Yes/No	Explanation Why did this happen?

Illustrations © Mark Brierley / Beehive Illustration

Foundation subjects

This chapter provides 20 lessons based on objectives taken from the QCA Schemes of Work for the foundation subjects. The lessons cover a range of objectives from the history, geography, ICT, music, art, DT and PE schemes of work. The lessons show how the interactive whiteboard can be used to support the teaching and learning of all of these subjects. The children can share and discuss ideas and evaluate their work as a class. The lessons encourage the children to be actively involved in their learning, by asking them to make choices by pressing or highlighting, filling in spaces by writing or typing, and manipulating and sorting images by dragging or rotating. The lessons provide the class with the opportunity to look at videos and pictures together, which can then be used as a stimulus for other activities.

Lesson title	Objectives	What children should know	Cross-curricular links
History			
Lesson 1: Changes Florence Nightingale made	**QCA Unit 4** 'Why do we remember Florence Nightingale?' • To select information from pictures of the past. • To understand about the conditions in the Crimea. • To know about some of the improvements made by Florence Nightingale and identify reasons for her actions.	• When and where the Crimean war took place and who it was between. • Be able to talk about the conditions in the hospitals in Scutari before Florence arrived.	**ICT** PoS (3a) To share their ideas by presenting them in a variety of forms. **English** PNS: Sentence structure and punctuation
Lesson 2: The life of Florence Nightingale	**QCA Unit 4** 'Why do we remember Florence Nightingale?' • To find out about the life of a famous person from the past. • To recount the main events in the life of Florence Nightingale. • To understand why Florence Nightingale is remembered today.	• Some of the main events in Florence Nightingale's life. • Some of the important work Florence did in Scutari and afterwards.	**ICT** QCA Unit 2A 'Writing stories: communicating information using text' **English** PNS: Understanding and interpreting texts PNS: Creating and shaping texts
Lesson 3: What happened during the Great Fire of London?	**QCA Unit 5** 'How do we know about the Great Fire of London?' • To know why the fire broke out. • To know about the main events of the fire. • To sequence the events correctly. • To know what an eyewitness is.	• Know that the fire happened a long time ago and be able to place the event on a timeline. • Be able to locate London on a map of the British Isles.	**Speaking and listening** Objective 24: To present work from different parts of the curriculum for members of their class.
Lesson 4: What have we learned about the Fire of London?	**QCA Unit 5** 'How do we know about the Great Fire of London?' • To use knowledge and understanding of the Great Fire to make a representation of it.	• The main events, causes and consequences of the fire.	**Art and design** PoS (2c) To represent observations, ideas and feelings, and design and make images and artefacts.
Lesson 5: What were seaside holidays like in the past?	**QCA Unit 3** 'What were seaside holidays like in the past?' • To sequence photographs into a time series of three time periods by identifying differences between present and past times. • To use time-related vocabulary. • To find out about holidays in the past from photographs.	• Be able to talk about their own holidays in the past. • Some simple similarities and differences between today and a long time ago.	**Geography** QCA Unit 4 'Going to the seaside'

Lesson title	Objectives	What children should know	Cross-curricular links
Geography			
Lesson 6: Holiday destinations	QCA Unit 4 'Going to the seaside' • To be able to name and investigate places. • To be able to use geographical terms. • To know how to use maps and atlases. • To be able to conduct a survey.	• Find the countries that make up the British Isles on a map. • Know the difference between countryside, seaside and town.	**Mathematics** PNS: Handling data
Lesson 7: Seaside features	QCA Unit 4 'Going to the seaside' • To investigate a place. • To identify the features of a seaside. • To use geographical terms.	• Names of some features found at the seaside.	**History** QCA Unit 3 'What were seaside holidays like in the past?'
Lesson 8: A different locality	QCA Unit 5 'Where in the world is Barnaby Bear?' • To find places on a map. • To recognise features of a place. • To identify types of weather experienced in places and seasonal changes and the effects it has on people. • To know about the types of transport used to get to other places.	• Find the British Isles on a world map or globe. • Be able to talk about different types of weather. • Recognise different types of transport.	**English** PNS: Creating and shaping texts
Lesson 9: Making a map	QCA Unit 3 'An island home' • To identify the physical and human features of a place. • To know how an island is different from the mainland.	• Know what an island and the mainland is. • Know what physical and human features are.	**English** PNS: Understanding and interpreting texts PNS: Engaging with and responding to texts
Lesson 10: Recycling in the home and school	• To know how the quality of the environment can be sustained and improved.	• Understand the term *recycling*.	**PSHE** PoS (2g) To know what improves and harms their local, natural and built environments and about some of the ways people look after them.
ICT			
Lesson 11: Creating an electronic book	QCA Unit 2A 'Writing stories: communicating ideas through text' • To enter text with spaces and use the shift key to type capital letters. • To delete and insert text to improve readability. • To use ICT appropriately to communicate ideas through text.	• That text can be entered and edited using a keyboard.	**English** PNS: Creating and shaping texts
Lesson 12: Computer art	QCA Unit 2B 'Creating pictures' • To select and use a range of graphics tools. • To select and use different techniques to communicate ideas through pictures.	• How to select tools using the mouse. • Control the mouse with a good degree of hand-eye coordination.	**Art and design** QCA Unit 2A 'Picture this!'
Lesson 13: Controlling a floor turtle	QCA Unit 2D 'Routes: controlling a floor turtle' • To enter a sequence of instructions. • To develop and record a sequence of instructions to control the floor turtle, and predict and test results.	• Be able to use directional vocabulary. • Control the floor turtle to move forwards, backwards, left and right.	**Mathematics** PNS: Understanding shape

Lesson title	Objectives	What children should know	Cross-curricular links
Lesson 14: Finding information	**QCA Unit 2C** 'Finding information' • To be able to use appropriate search techniques to find information on a CD-ROM.	• How to use key words and contents pages to find information on a CD-ROM.	**History** PoS (4a) To know how to find out about the past from a range of sources of information. **Geography** PoS (2d) To use secondary sources of information.
Music			
Lesson 15: Sound sources	**QCA Unit 2** 'Sounds interesting – Exploring sounds' • To recognise different sound sources. • To explore different sound sources. • To focus their listening.	• Names and sounds of some common classroom instruments.	**Speaking and listening** Objective 14: To listen to others in class, ask relevant questions and follow instructions.
Lesson 16: Rhythmic patterns	**QCA Unit 4** 'Feel the pulse – Exploring pulse and rhythm' • To recall and copy rhythmic patterns. • To create rhythmic patterns based on words or phrases. **QCA Unit 6** 'What's the score? – Exploring instruments and symbols' • To create a score.	• To discriminate syllables in words.	**English** PNS: Word structure and spelling
Lesson 17: Sound symbols	**QCA Unit 6** 'What's the score? – Exploring instruments and symbols' • To identify different groups of instruments. • To understand how symbols can be used to represent sounds. • To compose a class composition and create a score.	• A variety of ways to play different instruments. • That symbols can be used to represent sounds.	**English** PNS: Word structure and spelling **ICT** QCA Unit 2E 'Questions and answers'
Art and design			
Lesson 18: Reviewing artwork	**QCA Unit 2A** 'Picture this!' • To record from imagination and experience and explore ideas. • To be able to review what others have done and say what they think and feel about it.	• Describe what they like and dislike about a painting. • Mix a variety of colours using the primary colours, black and white.	**Speaking and listening** Objective 21: To use language and gesture to support the use of models/diagrams/displays when explaining.
Design and technology			
Lesson 19: Vehicle research	**QCA Unit 2A** 'Vehicles' • To know that there are many different types of vehicles with different purposes. • To know that vehicles are made up of different parts. • To know that ideas for their own designs can be obtained by looking at familiar products. • To make simple drawings and label parts.	• Names of a variety of different vehicles and what they are used for. • That ideas can be created by looking at what already exists. • How to label a diagram.	**Speaking and listening** Objective 15: To listen to each other's views and preferences, agree the next steps to take and identify contributions by each group member.
Physical education			
Lesson 20: Evaluating dance	**QCA Unit 2** 'Dance activities (2)' • To compose and perform dance phrases that express and communicate moods, ideas and feelings choosing and varying simple compositional ideas. • To watch and describe dance phrases and dances, and use what they learn to improve their own work.	• How to link dance movements together. • Suitable vocabulary for describing dance movements.	**English** PNS: Understanding and interpreting texts **ICT** PoS (5b) To explore a variety of ICT tools.

Changes Florence Nightingale made

Learning objectives
QCA Unit 4 'Why do we remember Florence Nightingale?'
● To select information from pictures of the past.
● To understand about the conditions in the Crimea.
● To know about some of the improvements made by Florence Nightingale and identify reasons for her actions.

Resources
'Florence Nightingale' Notebook file; photocopiable page 163 'Changes Florence made'; pictures of the hospital in the Crimea before and after Florence's changes; tape recorders for more confident learners.

Links to other subjects
ICT
PoS (3a) To share their ideas by presenting them in a variety of forms.
● The children will be using their ICT skills when they are asked to use a tape recorder to record their interviews.
English
PNS: Sentence structure and punctuation
● Following on from the speech bubbles activity, the children can practise putting speech into sentences using speech marks.

Starter
Open the 'Florence Nightingale' Notebook file and go to page 2. Explain to the children that the British Army was fighting in the Crimean War and talk briefly about what the soldiers would have been doing and how they may have been wounded. Tell the children about the long journey that the soldiers had to make to get to the hospitals in Scutari once they had been wounded.

Whole-class shared work
● Show the children a picture of the hospital in Scutari before Florence Nightingale arrived. Ask them to talk with a partner about what they can see.
● Review what the picture tells us about the conditions in the Crimea for wounded soldiers. List them on page 3 in the left-hand column.
● Explain that Florence and a group of nurses went to Scutari to help treat the wounded soldiers and that Florence was horrified by what she saw.
● Show a picture of the hospital in Scutari after Florence had implemented all of her changes. Ask the children to talk with a partner about what they can see now.
● Review what the picture tells us about how the conditions changed for wounded soldiers once Florence arrived. Make notes on page 3 in the right-hand column.
● Show the children page 4. Ask them to decide which time the pictures belong to: *before* or *after* Florence. Invite volunteers to come to the whiteboard and drag and drop the pictures into the correct box.
● Encourage the children to talk about why Florence made these changes, and what benefits they had for the soldiers.
● Look at page 5 and ask the children to work with a partner to think of statements to put in the two empty bubbles. Scribe the children's ideas.

Independent work
● Give each child a copy of photocopiable page 163. Ask them to think of three improvements that Florence made. Invite them to write them in the speech bubbles on the left-hand side of the picture of Florence.
● Ask: *Why do you think Florence made these changes?* Invite the children to record their ideas in the speech bubbles on the right-hand side.
● Act as a scribe for the less confident learners so that they can record their ideas.
● Extend more confident learners by challenging them to use a tape recorder to record an interview with Florence Nightingale about the changes she made in the hospital.

Plenary
● Invite some of the children to share their ideas with the rest of the class by writing their sentences on page 6 of the Notebook file.
● Discuss and evaluate the reasons that the children gave for Florence making the changes that she did. Ask them to consider how the changes Florence made in Scutari have affected our lives today.

Whiteboard tools

 Pen tray

 Select tool

The life of Florence Nightingale

Learning objectives

QCA Unit 4 'Why do we remember Florence Nightingale?'
● To find out about the life of a famous person from the past.
● To recount the main events in the life of Florence Nightingale.
● To understand why Florence Nightingale is remembered today.

Resources

'Florence Nightingale' Notebook file; photocopiable page 164 'The life of Florence Nightingale'; photocopiable page 167 'How to create an electronic book'; individual whiteboards and pens; paper; pencils. (Microsoft PowerPoint is required to produce the electronic book.)

Links to other subjects
ICT
QCA Unit 2A 'Writing stories: communicating information using text'
● The children will use their knowledge of ICT to present their work in an electronic book (see Lesson 11).
English
PNS: Understanding and interpreting texts
PNS: Creating and shaping texts
● Encourage the children to use books about Florence Nightingale as a model for their own non-fiction fact sheet or book about her life.

Whiteboard tools

Move the Screen Shade to reveal the sentences at the bottom of page 8.

  Pen tray

  Select tool

  Screen Shade

Starter

Open page 7 of the 'Florence Nightingale' Notebook file. Ask the children to list on their individual whiteboards three things that they have learned about Florence Nightingale and her work since beginning the topic. Share some of these ideas as a class and discuss them, as appropriate, in order to offer the children a general reminder about her work and her life.

Whole-class shared work

● Go to page 8. Explain that the timeline shows Florence's life from when she was born in 1820 until when she died in 1910.
● Move the Screen Shade 🖵 to reveal the sentences at the bottom of the page and ask the children to place the events in the correct place on the timeline.
● Start by ordering the events from earliest to latest and ask questions to support this process. For example: *Did this happen near the beginning or the end of her life? Did this happen before or after the Crimean War?*
● Read the events on the timeline in order. Ask the children to consider whether there are any other events that could be added to the timeline.
● Encourage the children to add these events to the timeline with a written explanation.
● Read the events on the timeline in order again to give a fuller picture of Florence's life.

Independent work

● Give each pair of children a copy of photocopiable page 164, and ask them to sequence the pictures of Florence's life.
● Encourage the pairs to work together to create a book about the life of Florence Nightingale, using the pictures as prompts.
● Suggest that each picture could represent a new chapter. Talk with the children about how they could show this in their book (for example, using a heading, beginning a new page).
● Encourage the children to illustrate their work.
● Pair less confident learners with supportive peers so that they can contribute in the same way as the rest of the class.
● Invite some children to use ICT to create an electronic book about the life of Florence Nightingale. Use the instructions on photocopiable page 167 to help you prepare a template for the children to use.

Plenary

● Invite some of the children to share their books with the class. Encourage them to evaluate whether all of the important information about Florence's life has been included.
● Play the electronic books to the class.
● Use page 9 of the Notebook file to talk about the reasons why Florence is remembered today. Encourage the children to discuss how to sort the statements into 'important' and 'not important' categories. Explain that although the statements may be true, they are not necessarily all reasons why she is remembered.

What happened during the Great Fire of London?

Learning objectives
QCA Unit 5 'How do we know about the Great Fire of London?'
● To know why the fire broke out.
● To know about the main events of the fire.
● To sequence the events correctly.
● To know what an eyewitness is.

Resources ● P
'The Great Fire of London' Notebook file; photocopiable page 165 'An eyewitness report'; a video about the Great Fire of London; a wig and long black coat similar to Samuel Pepys'; A4 paper; black pens; used teabags; line guides (optional).

Links to other subjects
Speaking and listening
Objective 24: To present work from different parts of the curriculum for members of their class.
● Invite the children to use their knowledge of the events to create a succession of freeze frames that tell the story of the fire.

Starter
Watch a video about the Great Fire of London with the children. Invite them to spend a few minutes talking about what happened during the fire with a partner, then share these ideas as a class. Write the children's ideas on page 2 of the Notebook file, and create a mind map on the subject.

Whole-class shared work
● Ask the children to recall where, when and why the fire broke out. Discuss how the baker must have felt when he realised that the fire was his fault.
● Ask the children to recall how the people tried to fight the fire and how it was eventually put out. Compare these responses and actions with how a fire would be dealt with today.
● Look at page 3 of the Notebook file and read the six statements with the children. Challenge them to put the events of the fire in order.
● Invite volunteers to come to the whiteboard to drag and drop the boxes into the correct order. Discuss how the children are making their choices.
● Ask: *Are there any people still alive today who would have been at the fire of London?* Establish that it happened far too long ago.
● Ask: *How do you think we know so much about the events of the fire?* Discuss the children's answers.
● Use page 4 to explain to the children what an *eyewitness* is. Tell the children that Samuel Pepys recorded the events of the fire in his diary.

Independent work
● Give each child a sheet of A4 paper and a black pen. Provide them with line guides if necessary. Ask the children to use the information they have gained from the video and the sequencing file to create their own eyewitness report in the form of a diary or letter.
● Share the significant events of the fire with the children again, giving them a brief reminder of when they happened.
● When the work is complete, photocopy it and invite the children to rub used teabags onto the copy to make the paper look old.
● Allow less confident learners to use photocopiable page 165 to record four facts that they can recall about the fire.

Plenary
● Carry out some hot-seating. Dress up as Samuel Pepys and invite the children to ask questions about the fire. Encourage them to ask questions that will develop their understanding of the fire.
● Allow sensible children to have a turn as Samuel Pepys and invite the rest of the class to ask him questions.
● Write down some of these questions on page 5 of the Notebook file.

Whiteboard tools

 Pen tray

 Select tool

What have we learned about the Fire of London?

Learning objective
QCA Unit 5 'How do we know about the Great Fire of London?'
● To use knowledge and understanding of the Great Fire to make a representation of it.

Resources
'The Great Fire of London' Notebook file; a painting of the Great Fire of London; individual whiteboards and pens; art materials; paper. (Microsoft Word is required to view the embedded text document in the Notebook file.)

Links to other subjects
Art and design
PoS (2c) To represent observations, ideas and feelings, and design and make images and artefacts.
● The children will be communicating their ideas about the fire of London through a piece of artwork.

Whiteboard tools
The Shapes and Lines tools can be used to build a mind map. Add scanned images of the children's work to the page by selecting Insert, then Picture File, and browsing to where you have saved the images.

 Pen tray

 Select tool

 Shapes tool

 Lines tool

Starter
Encourage the children to talk to a partner about everything that they have learned about the Great Fire of London. Show them a painting of the fire and discuss what it shows. Explain that the painting is evidence that they can use to find out more about what the fire was like.

Remind the children about the different methods they have used to find evidence about the fire (such as videos, eyewitness accounts, books, paintings). Use page 6 of the Notebook file to record some of these ideas.

Whole-class shared work
● For assessment purposes, use page 7 to create a mind map of what the children know about the fire of London at the end of the topic. If a mind map was created at the start of the topic, add to that one using a different colour. There is a link to page 2 on page 7, if a mind map was created there previously.
● Go to page 8. Read the text together, then invite volunteers to come to the board to drag and drop the appropriate missing words into the spaces provided. Press the arrow at the top of the page to check the answers and to read some additional information about the events surrounding the Great Fire.
● Repeat this activity on pages 9 to 11.
● Go to page 12. Ask the children to close their eyes and imagine that they are back in 1666, watching the fire. Encourage them to think about what they could hear, see and smell, and to share their ideas. Record some of their comments on the Notebook page.

Independent work
● Provide the children with a range of art materials and ask them to choose a medium of their choice to create a representation of the Great Fire of London.
● Encourage the children to use the factual information that they have learned to guide their work.
● Talk with the children about what they are going to include in their pictures, and why they feel that this is important.
● As an extension, when the children have completed their pictures, ask them to write a few sentences about what they have included in their picture, and why.

Plenary
● Take some of the children's work and scan it into the computer. Display the work using the whiteboard software. (The pictures can be added to page 13 as links or images.)
● Invite the children to talk about how they created their own piece of work and what it depicts.
● Encourage a discussion about whether the pieces of work show an accurate depiction of the fire. Annotate the work with some of the children's comments.
● Ask the children to consider what others may be able to learn when they look at the pieces of work on display.

What were seaside holidays like in the past?

Learning objectives
QCA Unit 3 'What were seaside holidays like in the past?'
● To sequence photographs into a time series of three time periods by identifying differences between present and past times.
● To use time-related vocabulary.
● To find out about holidays in the past from photographs.

Resources
'Seasides in the past' Notebook file; a collection of photographs of seaside holidays in the 1900s (plus a video if possible); paper; pencils.

Links to other subjects
Geography
QCA Unit 4 'Going to the seaside'
● The children will be discussing the features of places at the seaside.

Starter
Open the 'Seasides in the past' Notebook file and go to page 2. Ask the children to identify when the three main holidays from school are and what they do in these holidays. Find out who has been on a holiday to the seaside in this country and abroad. Ask these children to tell the rest of the class what they would expect to find at the seaside (such as a beach, fairground, shops, restaurants).

Whole-class shared work
● Use the Spotlight tool 🔎 to focus on the three photographs on page 3 with the children (do not show the timeline yet).
● Encourage the children to have a guess when each of the photographs was taken. Then ask them to order the three photographs from the earliest to the latest time.
● Talk with the children about when the photographs were actually taken (1900, 1950, 2000) and relate these times to other events that may be meaningful to them, such as 'when grandma was little'.
● Challenge the children to explain how they knew in which order the photographs should be. Draw out the differences between the clothing and artefacts in each photograph.
● Show the children the photograph on page 4. Explain that it is a picture of a seaside from about 100 years ago.
● Encourage the children to talk with a partner about what they can see in the photograph and answer any questions about objects in the picture that they do not recognise. Highlight and label a few of the objects.

Independent work
● Give the children a variety of different photographs of seaside holidays from the 1900s and ask them to look closely at them and describe what they see to a partner.
● Ask the children to choose one photograph and draw it at the top of a piece of paper. Beneath the drawing, ask them to write a detailed description of what they can see in the photograph.
● Ask more confident learners to work with a partner, describing and comparing photographs of the seaside today with photographs taken in the past.

Plenary
● Ask the children to share what they have found out about seaside holidays many years ago. Use page 5 of the Notebook file to record some of their responses.
● If possible, show the children a video depicting what seaside holidays were like many years ago. Once the class has finished watching it, talk briefly about the similarities and differences between seaside holidays now and then.

Whiteboard tools
Use the Spotlight tool to focus on the seaside photographs.

 Pen tray

 Select tool

 Highlighter pen

 Spotlight tool

Holiday destinations

Learning objectives
QCA Unit 4 'Going to the seaside'
● To be able to name and investigate places.
● To be able to use geographical terms.
● To know how to use maps and atlases.
● To be able to conduct a survey.

Resources
'Holiday destinations' Notebook file; photocopiable page 166 'Holiday destinations'; maps and atlases; pencils.

Links to other subjects
Mathematics
PNS: Handling data
● The children will be using their mathematical knowledge to create and interpret a block graph.

Starter
Ask the children to name the five parts that make up the British Isles. Then open page 2 of the 'Holiday destinations' Notebook file and ask the children to label the parts of the British Isles by dragging and dropping the labels into the appropriate places around the map.

Ask the children to talk about the places that they have been on holiday to in the British Isles. Determine what type of location it was – seaside, countryside or town/city.

Whole-class shared work
● Ask who has visited the seaside somewhere in the British Isles. Do the children remember the name of the place they visited? Ask them to point to it on the map on page 2, if they know where the place is located.
● Explain that maps and atlases help people to find where a place is if they don't know.
● Give an atlas to each pair of children and show them how to use it to locate the names of seaside towns in the British Isles.
● Show the children page 3 and ask them to label the seaside places. Encourage them to use an atlas to check the answers.
● Now pose a question: *Is the seaside the class's most popular holiday destination?*
● Ask: *How can we answer this question? What do you think the answer will be?* Encourage the children to carry out a survey to find the answer.
● Using page 4 to record their choices, ask each child in the class to decide whether they prefer holidays to the *seaside, countryside, town and city* or *nowhere*.

Independent work
● Give each child a copy of photocopiable page 166. Ask them to use the results of the tally on page 4 of the whiteboard to complete the table at the top of the photocopiable sheet and the block graph below it.
● Challenge the children to use their block graphs to draw a conclusion about whether the seaside is the most popular holiday destination. How do they know this?
● Extend the atlas skills of more confident learners by asking them to use the atlas to sort holiday place names into the appropriate countries.

Plenary
● Use page 5 of the Notebook file to recreate the block graph the children have been working on.
● Give the children the opportunity to explain what their block graphs tell them, and encourage them to answer the question of whether the seaside is the most popular holiday destination. Ask them to suggest reasons for their results.
● Finish off the lesson with some atlas challenges. For example, ask: *Can you find a seaside place beginning with B? Can you find a city in Scotland beginning with G?* Explain that the first pair to point to the place in their atlas scores one point.

Whiteboard tools

 Pen tray

 Select tool

Seaside features

Starter

Read a story about some characters who visit the seaside. Ask the children to talk about what the characters did and saw while they were there.

Now ask the children which seaside places they have visited, and what they did and saw while they were there. Talk about how seaside places can be very different from each other (for example, St Ives and Blackpool). If possible, show the children some photographs of different types of seaside places and talk about these. Make notes on page 2 of the Notebook file.

Whole-class shared work

- Explain the term *feature* to the children and give a few examples of seaside features, such as hotel, beach, and so on.
- Ask them to talk to a partner about the features they can see in the picture in the labelling activity on page 3.
- Challenge the children to label the features in the picture correctly.
- Give the children individual whiteboards and ask them to work with a partner to list any other features that might be found at the seaside.
- Explain the terms *human feature* and *physical feature*. Ask the children to give examples of each. Ensure that they know that human features have been created by humans, whereas physical features are natural phenomena that have always been there (or have been created by nature). Use page 4 to make notes.
- Go to page 5. Invite volunteers to sort the features into 'physical' and 'human' by dragging and dropping the labels into the appropriate side of the table.
- Add to the table any other features from the lists the children made earlier on their individual whiteboards.

Independent work

- Ask the children to draw a picture of a seaside and label its features. Give them a selection of word cards containing features that can be found at the seaside.
- Ask them to sort the features into 'human' and 'physical', and record these in a table.
- Encourage them to compare their decisions with a partner and discuss any differences they may have.
- Allow less confident learners to create and then add labels to a small-world seaside scene.

Plenary

- Go to page 6 of the Notebook file. Sit the children in a circle. Pass a bean bag around the circle and explain that only the person holding the bean bag can speak. Ask the children to alternate between giving a human seaside feature and a physical seaside feature until everyone in the circle has had a go.
- Use this as an opportunity to assess the learning that has taken place in the lesson.

Learning objectives
QCA Unit 4 'Going to the seaside'
- To investigate a place.
- To identify the features of a seaside.
- To use geographical terms.

Resources
'Seaside features' Notebook file; a small-world seaside scene; prepared sets of cards with a seaside feature written on each; bean bag; individual whiteboards and pens; story about a seaside visit; photos of seaside towns (if available).

Links to other subjects
History
QCA Unit 3 'What were seaside holidays like in the past?'
- Let the children use their knowledge of seaside features to investigate how seaside holidays and holiday destinations have changed over the last 100 years.

Whiteboard tools

 Pen tray

 Select tool

A different locality

Learning objectives
QCA Unit 5 'Where in the world is Barnaby Bear?'
● To find places on a map.
● To recognise features of a place.
● To identify types of weather experienced in places and seasonal change and the effects it has on people.
● To know about the types of transport used to get to other places.

Resources
'Holiday destinations' Notebook file; world atlases; a globe; blank postcards; a video, Big Book, CD-ROM or website about the destination to be studied; pencils.

Links to other subjects
English
PNS: Creating and shaping texts
● In this lesson the children will be writing a postcard to provide information about a destination.

Starter
Introduce Bertie Bear to the class using page 6 of the Notebook file. Explain that Bertie likes to travel all over the world and then share his holiday memories with everyone else. Tell the children the name of the country that Bertie has just visited (one that the children are about to study) and show them the location of the country on a globe.

Whole-class shared work
● Allow the children to use an atlas to locate the country, then use page 7 of the Notebook file to highlight the country on the screen.
● Using a video, Big Book, CD-ROM or website, allow the children an opportunity to find out about the country that Bertie Bear has visited.
● Ask the children to talk to a partner about what they have learned about the destination.
● Display page 8. Explain that the children are going to collate some information to help them to write a postcard from Bertie Bear while he was on holiday.
● Look again at the map on page 7. Ask: *What type of transport would Bertie have used to travel to his holiday destination?* Circle the transport on page 9.
● Invite the children to circle the prevailing weather type that Bertie would have experienced.
● Encourage them to list the things that Bertie would have needed to take with him, such as an umbrella and a passport.
● Help them to list some of the activities and attractions that Bertie may have experienced.
● Display again the postcard template on page 8 and point out where the address should be written. Address the card to the class.

Independent work
● Give each child a blank postcard and ask them to pretend that they are Bertie Bear writing a postcard from his holiday destination.
● Encourage the children to write their own address correctly on the postcard.
● Ask them to include information about the transport used; the things taken; the weather and the things seen and done. Display page 9 to help them if necessary.
● Ask the children to draw a picture of the destination on the front of the postcard.

Plenary
● Share some of the children's postcards with the class.
● Ask the children some questions about the destination. Encourage them to think about whether they would like to live there, and why.
● Ask the children to consider the similarities and differences between the destination and their own locality. Write some of their ideas on page 10 of the Notebook file.

Whiteboard tools

 Pen tray

 Select tool

 Highlighter pen

Making a map

Learning objectives
QCA Unit 3 'An island home'
- To identify the physical and human features of a place.
- To know how an island is different from the mainland.

Resources
'Island home' Notebook file; *Katie Morag* story books (written by Mairi Hedderwick and published by Red Fox); Isle of Struay maps; British Isles atlases; individual whiteboards and pens; paper; pens; map outline for less confident learners.

Links to other subjects
English
PNS: Understanding and interpreting texts
PNS: Engaging with and responding to texts
- The children will be learning about and discussing the features of a familiar story setting.

Starter
Open page 2 of the 'Island home' Notebook file. Share some *Katie Morag* stories with the children and talk about where the stories take place. Explain that the fictional Isle of Struay is based on a real Scottish island called Coll. Make notes on page 2, if required.

Show the children the map of the British Isles on page 3 and ask the children to identify Scotland on it. Give out some atlases and ask the children to use them to match the island name labels to the correct islands, on the larger Scotland map.

Whole-class shared work
- In pairs, refer the children back to the *Katie Morag* stories and ask them to create a list of features on individual whiteboards that they might find on the island (such as the Post Office, pier and bridge).
- Remind the children of the meaning of the terms *physical* and *human features*. Use page 4 to sort the features the children have listed into 'physical' and 'human'.
- Look at a map of the Isle of Struay (at the beginning of all the *Katie Morag* stories) and talk about how symbols are used to represent features. Explain that a key can be used to make it clear what each symbol means.
- Show the children the map of an island on page 5 of the Notebook file and make up a fictional name for it. Ask them to consider what features would be on the island, and how they could represent these on a map.
- Invite volunteers to come to the whiteboard and draw or insert symbols on the map to represent appropriate features.
- Clone each symbol, by selecting the Clone option from the dropdown menu, and create a key for the map.

Independent work
- Give each group a map of the Isle of Struay. Ask them to look at it closely and talk together about the different features.
- Give each child a piece of paper and encourage them to create their own map of the Isle of Struay.
- Ask the children to use symbols to define the features on the island, adding a key to show what each symbol represents.
- Supply less confident learners with a prepared outline of the island if necessary.

Plenary
- Share some of the children's maps with the rest of the class by scanning them into the whiteboard software. Ask the children to consider what features they would probably not find on a small island, such as an airport or high-rise buildings. Why is this?
- Provide opportunities for the children to consider what it would be like to live on a small island. Ask them how they think their life would be different.
- Go to page 6 of the Notebook file. Invite children to come to the whiteboard to make a list of some obvious similarities and differences between the island and their own locality.

Whiteboard tools
To copy and paste objects, select them and choose the Clone option from the dropdown menu.

 Pen tray

 Select tool

Recycling in the home and school

Learning objective
● To know how the quality of the environment can be sustained and improved.

Resources
'Recycling' Notebook file; a variety of clean, safe rubbish to be sorted; pictures of rubbish dumps and landfill sites; A4 paper; felt-tipped pens; posters and signs advertising recycling.

Links to other subjects
PSHE
PoS (2g) To know what improves and harms their local, natural and built environments and about some of the ways people look after them.
● This lesson leads nicely into a general discussion about the different ways that the children can help to look after the environment. Try linking it into a school-wide recycling project.

Starter
Open the 'Recycling' Notebook file and go to page 2. Ask the children to talk about what they do with their rubbish at home. Discuss what happens to rubbish once it has been put in the bin. Show the children some pictures of rubbish dumps and landfill sites and talk about these. Explain the environmental implications for burying or burning rubbish.

Whole-class shared work
● Ask the children if they know of any ways they could reduce the amount of rubbish that is buried or burned.
● Explain the term *recycle* – an object is recycled when it is put through a process in a factory to enable the raw material to be used again in a new object.
● Explain the term *re-use* – an object is re-used when it is used again in the same form as it was before, without being processed. Ensure that the children know the difference between the two terms.
● Explain that organic material can be composted because it rots and eventually turns into a useful product to use in the garden.
● Show the children the pictures at the bottom of page 3. Encourage them to decide whether the objects could be recycled, re-used or composted. Invite volunteers to come to the whiteboard to sort them accordingly.
● Discuss the children's choices and address any misconceptions as they arise.

Independent work
● Provide each child with a sheet of A4 paper and some felt-tipped pens.
● Show the children a range of signs and posters that promote recycling. Encourage them to talk about the messages they convey.
● Explain that they are going to make a poster to promote the importance of recycling. Talk about the use of text and images to convey a clear message.
● Ask less confident learners to sort a box of rubbish into four groups: *recycle, re-use, compost* and *waste*. Encourage them to work in groups to make a display of the rubbish by gluing it onto a large piece of paper or card.

Plenary
● Take a small sample of the children's work and scan it into the computer. Add the images to page 4 of the Notebook file. Display the work and ask the class to comment on it. Evaluate whether the posters communicate the desired message.
● Encourage positive comments from the children. Annotate the posters with some of these comments.
● Ask the children to consider what they do with their old clothes, toys and glasses. Tell them that they could donate these used items to a charity as long as they are still in a good condition. The items can then be used again by someone else who can't afford brand new things. Explain that the items could be used in this country or abroad.

Whiteboard tools
Add scanned images of children's work to the page by selecting Insert, then Picture File, and browsing to where you have saved the images.

 Pen tray

 Select tool

Creating an electronic book

Learning objectives
QCA Unit 2A 'Writing stories: communicating ideas through text'
● To enter text with spaces and use the shift key to type capital letters.
● To delete and insert text to improve readability.
● To use ICT appropriately to communicate ideas through text.

Resources ℗
Photocopiable page 167 'How to create an electronic book'; a fiction text to be used as stimulus for the children's work. Prepare a Notebook file: use Microsoft PowerPoint and the instructions on photocopiable page 167 to create a suitable template for an electronic text. Each pair of children will need to have access to a computer for this lesson. (Microsoft PowerPoint is required to create the electronic book.)

Links to other subjects
English
PNS: Creating and shaping texts
● The children are using ICT to create an electronic storybook with illustrations for a class of younger children to use.

Starter
Share a fiction text with the children as a stimulus for an extended piece of writing. Talk about the text and discuss the characters, setting and plot. Ensure that all of the children can retell the story in detail. Tell them that they are going to create an electronic book of the story for Nursery or Reception class children to use.

Whole-class shared work
● Open the prepared PowerPoint template (see Resources). Explain that the children are going to use this template to create the book. Show them how to move between the slides and then show them the first slide.
● In the top text box, demonstrate how to type in the title of the story.
● Show the children how to create a space between words by pressing the space bar once, and how to type a capital letter using the shift key.
● Invite a child to type the author's name into the bottom text box.
● Move to the second slide and explain the slide layout to the children. Highlight the *next page* buttons. Explain these only work when the slideshow is playing.
● Type *Chapter 1* into the heading box and ask the children to think about what they would like to write in the first chapter.
● Suggest a bland first sentence and invite a child to type it in, reminding them to use the space bar and shift key appropriately.
● Tell the children that you don't like your sentence and ask them to improve it by adding some more detail.
● Demonstrate how to insert or delete words in the centre of a piece of text using the mouse cursor. Stress that the whole sentence does not have to be deleted to change the middle of it.

Independent work
● In pairs, ask the children to work together to create an electronic book using the stimulus text.
● Encourage them to use the shift key and space bar appropriately.
● When the children have written a page, ask them to re-read and edit it using their new skills.
● Place some illustrations into the template before the lesson begins to support less confident learners with the retelling.
● Extend more confident learners by showing them how to insert pictures and sound into their presentations to make them into talking books (see photocopiable page 167 for instructions on how to do this).

Plenary
● Use the whiteboard to share the electronic books with some Nursery or Reception children. Ask the younger children to comment on what they thought of the books.
● Invite the children who made the books to explain to the rest of the class what ICT skills they used to create them.

Whiteboard tools

 Pen tray

 Select tool

 Highlighter pen

Computer art

Learning objectives
QCA Unit 2B 'Creating pictures'
● To select and use a range of graphics tools.
● To select and use different techniques to communicate ideas through pictures.

Resources
A simple graphics program; some photographs of firework displays. Prepare a Notebook file by inserting some photographs of firework displays into the whiteboard software. Each pair of children will need access to a computer for this lesson.

Links to other subjects
Art and design
QCA Unit 2A 'Picture this!'
● In this lesson the children will use different types of tool to create a specific effect.

Starter
Open the prepared Notebook file (see Resources) and give the children an opportunity to look at the images of the fireworks. Ask them to talk with a partner about a firework display that they have been to. Encourage them to comment on the shapes and colours that they saw. Write some of these comments around the images.

Whole-class shared work
● Explain to the children that they are going to produce a firework picture using a graphics program on the computer.
● Open a simple graphics program and briefly remind the children about how to select tools and change colours.
● Demonstrate each of the following tools (or their equivalents) in turn: straight line tool, geometric shape tool, flood fill tool and spray tool.
● Ask the children to consider how they could use the tools demonstrated to create a firework picture. Listen to their ideas.
● Suggest that they begin by using the flood fill tool to create a dark sky.
● Show them how to undo a mistake using the undo tool.
● Allow them to demonstrate their ideas to the rest of the class using the whiteboard.
● Continue to reiterate how to use each tool and talk about the effects each one creates.

Independent work
● Challenge the children to create their own firework picture using the graphics program.
● Remind them that they can use different tools to create a variety of effects. Allow them some time to experiment with these before they begin their final picture.
● Stop the children at certain points: ask them to look at the work of another person and make a constructive comment about something they like and something they would improve.
● Pair less confident learners together so that they can support each other.
● Encourage more confident learners to add a title to their work using a text tool.

Plenary
● Ask the children to save their drawings. Upload the scanned images onto a blank Notebook page so that the class can share the different pieces of artwork.
● Pause on each drawing and talk with the children about the tools that they have used to create the different effects in their pictures.
● Annotate the children's drawings as they talk about them. Ask the children to evaluate whether the tools were used effectively in each case.

Whiteboard tools
Upload scanned images by selecting Insert, then Picture File, and browsing to where you have saved the images.

 Pen tray

 Select tool

Controlling a floor turtle

Learning objectives
QCA Unit 2D 'Routes: controlling a floor turtle'
● To enter a sequence of instructions.
● To develop and record a sequence of instructions to control the floor turtle, and predict and test results.

Resources
'Controlling a floor turtle' Notebook file; photocopiable page 168 'Instruction cards' (copy this page a number of times onto card and cut it into separate cards); floor turtles; paper; pens.

Links to other subjects
Mathematics
PNS: Understanding shape
● The children will be using their knowledge of directional vocabulary to act as controller and robot in the Starter activity.

Starter
In pairs, ask one child to be a *robot* and the other child to be the *controller*. Invite the controller to give the robot simple directions to a predetermined destination. Remind the children about the directional vocabulary they will need to use in order to give accurate directions. Write key words on page 2 of the Notebook file. Discuss what *one unit forward* means.

Whole-class shared work
● Use page 3 to revise the instructions that the children have learned for programming the floor turtle. Talk with them about what these instructions actually make the turtle do. Invite them to move and turn the turtle on the screen (rotate the turtle by selecting it, then pressing and dragging the green circle).
● Explain and then demonstrate that it is possible to enter a sequence of instructions for the floor turtle to follow.
● Give each pair of children a printout of page 4 and a plain piece of paper. Ask them to work together to record the route that the turtle will need to take to get to the end of the track.
● Encourage the children to use the symbols displayed to record the results as they would be programmed into the floor turtle. Suggest that they may find it helpful to turn the printout so that they are facing in the same direction as the turtle.
● When the children have finished recording their sequence, share the correct instructions.
● Finally, invite a volunteer to come to the whiteboard to move the robot according to the instructions.

Independent work
● Organise the class into groups of four.
● For each group, mark out two different simple tracks on the floor for a floor turtle to follow.
● Ask two children from each group to work with a floor turtle on one track and two children on the other track, to develop a set of instructions.
● Invite the children to record the instructions in a way that will allow another pair to test them. Encourage them to test their programs as they write them and to modify them accordingly.
● When the pairs have finished, ask them to swap and test each other's programs.
● Ask them to give feedback to the other pair after testing.
● Give less confident learners a simpler track and provide prepared cards (from photocopiable page 168) to support their recording.

Plenary
● Make a set of instructions for moving the floor turtle around your classroom. Place the turtle on a starting spot.
● Go to page 5 of the Notebook file. Show the children your typed or written instructions (based on available space and ability) that are going to be programmed into the turtle.
● Ask the children to predict where the turtle will end up. Allow each of them to place a marker in that place.
● Once everyone in the class has placed their marker, invite a volunteer to enter the program into the turtle in order to test the children's predictions.

Whiteboard tools

 Pen tray

 Select tool

Finding information

Learning objective
QCA Unit 2C 'Finding information'
● To be able to use appropriate search techniques to find information on a CD-ROM.

Resources
CD-ROM encyclopedia suitable for children; children's encyclopedia. Each pair of children will need access to a computer for this lesson.

Links to other subjects
History
PoS (4a) To know how to find out about the past from a range of sources of information.
Geography
PoS (2d) To use secondary sources of information.
● In this lesss the children will be using a CD-ROM and encyclopedias to search for information about a place, person or event.

Starter
Show the children an encyclopedia. Talk about what it is and how to use it to find information. Look at the contents page and talk about how it is arranged in page-number order, displaying the heading for each section. Show the index page and ask one of the children to explain to the class how they would use the index to find some information about a given topic.

Whole-class shared work
● Explain that an adult encyclopedia often has thousands of pages, so it is important to know how to find the information easily.
● Show the children a CD-ROM encyclopedia and explain that it is possible for this one small disc to hold the same amount of information as lots of books.
● Open the CD-ROM encyclopedia and introduce the children to the different ways that they can find information – index, contents and keyword search.
● Explain that the index and contents pages work in a very similar way to a book, except that instead of having to turn to a given page number they just need to press on the hyperlink or button and the CD-ROM will display the appropriate page. Highlight a few hyperlinks and buttons to demonstrate this.
● Explain that a keyword search looks through all of the information held on the CD-ROM to find words that match the keyword. Make sure that the children understand the importance of typing a word correctly if a keyword search is to be successful. Highlight the keyword search box.
● Demonstrate how to use each of the techniques to find information about a relevant topic. Compare the techniques for efficiency and talk about when it is appropriate to use each of the techniques.

Independent work
● Ask the children to work in pairs to create a piece of computer-generated text about a topic of relevance.
● Encourage each pair to use the CD-ROM to find out three facts about their topic to include in their text. Suggest that they find one fact using a contents search, one using an index search and one using a keyword search.
● Use a talking encyclopedia to support less confident learners.
● If the CD-ROM program allows, show more confident learners how to highlight, copy and paste text from the encyclopedia into a word-processing program for editing (copyright permitting).

Plenary
● Ask the children to share some of the work that they have produced. Invite them to explain the three ways they found out the information using the CD-ROM.
● Set a challenge: invite one child to use a book and another to use a CD-ROM to find the answer to the same question. Talk about which medium the children prefer to use, and the advantages and disadvantages of each.

Whiteboard tools

 Pen tray

 Select tool

 Highlighter pen

Sound sources

Learning objectives
QCA Unit 2 'Sounds interesting - Exploring sounds'
● To recognise different sound sources.
● To explore different sound sources.
● To focus their listening.

Resources
'Instruments' Notebook file; a selection of percussion instruments; CD recording of Prokofiev's *Peter and the Wolf* (narrated if possible); prepared sets of cards depicting the different characters from *Peter and the Wolf*.

Links to other subjects
Speaking and listening
Objective 14: To listen to others in a class, ask relevant questions and follow instructions.
● The children must listen carefully to the sounds so that they can repeat them accurately.

Starter
Display page 2 of the 'Instruments' Notebook file. Explain to the children that they are going to hear a range of different sounds and that they must listen to them carefully and try to guess what they are.

Press the first sound button to play a sound, then allow the children time to share their guesses. Once they have done this, use the Delete button 🗙 to remove the shape to reveal what the sound actually is. Repeat this procedure for the rest of the sounds on the page.

Whole-class shared work
● Move on to page 3. Invite the children to guess the names of each instrument, then reveal the names by deleting the boxes. Talk about the sounds each instrument makes.
● Press the *play sound* button, in the centre of the page, and listen to the sound. Challenge the children to guess which instrument they can hear. When they press the correct instrument they will hear a cheer.
● Continue in the same way on pages 4 to 8 until all the instruments have been played.
● Now show the children a variety of real percussion instruments and ask them to name them. Provide them with the opportunity to hear each instrument being played.
● Next, hide the instruments behind a screen so that the children cannot see them. Play two instruments and ask the children to name the two instruments in the order they were played.
● Move on to play three, and then four, instruments in sequence.

Independent work
● Put the children into pairs. Give each pair a set of five different instruments and a screen to hide them behind.
● Ask one child to play a sequence of three different instruments for their partner to listen to.
● Challenge the second child to repeat the sequence played by their partner in exactly the same way.
● Encourage the children to consider the different ways that they could play the instruments. Vary this to add an extra challenge.
● Suggest that less confident learners begin with a sequence of two sounds, and more confident learners begin with a sequence of four sounds.

Plenary
● Play the *Peter and the Wolf* CD to the children. Explain that different instruments depict different characters in the story. Challenge the children to identify some of the instruments used for the different characters. Write their ideas on page 9 of the Notebook file.
● Give the children a set of prepared cards (see Resources). Ask them to hold up the card depicting the character that they can hear while they listen to the recording.

Whiteboard tools
Use the Delete button (or choose the Delete option from the dropdown menu) to reveal the answers on page 2.

 Pen tray

 Select tool

 Delete button

Rhythmic patterns

Learning objectives
QCA Unit 4 'Feel the pulse –
Exploring pulse and rhythm'
● To recall and copy rhythmic
patterns.
● To create rhythmic patterns
based on words or phrases.
QCA Unit 6 'What's the score?
– Exploring instruments and
symbols'
● To create a score.

Resources
'Rhythmic patterns' Notebook
file; sheets of A3 paper; pens.
Prepare some cards with
'minibeast scores' on them
(see pages 11–16 of the
Notebook file for examples);
claves; chopsticks.

Links to other subjects
English
PNS: Word structure and
spelling
● In this lesson the children
will use their syllable
discrimination skills to
establish the rhythm of a
word.

Starter
Sit the children in a circle. Work around the circle, asking the children to clap the syllables for their own name as they say it.

Open the 'Rhythmic patterns' Notebook file. Ask the children to name the fruit on page 2. Reveal the name of the fruit by using the Delete button ✖ to delete the red rectangle. Challenge them to clap the rhythm of the fruit's name. Repeat this for the fruits and vegetables on pages 3 to 9.

Whole-class shared work
● Go to page 10. Ask the children to listen to and then copy the rhythm pattern for each of the insect names. Press the orange sound button to hear the rhythm.
● Practise clapping the rhythms and help the children to realise that it takes the same time to clap *caterpillar* as it does to clap *spider*, because the claps in *spider* are longer.
● Explain the term *score* – a composition that is recorded using pictures or symbols.
● Using page 11, ask the children to listen to a sequence of rhythms by pressing the orange sound button. Challenge the children to choose the score that correctly represents the sequence. Ask them to write the answer on their individual whiteboards, then take a tally of their votes. Press the letters (a, b or c) to check the answers.
● Repeat this activity on pages 12 to 14.
● Go to page 15, play the rhythm and ask the children to drag the minibeast cards into order.
● Divide the children into four groups. Show the children page 16 and assign a score to each group.
● Give each group the opportunity to practise their score. Then invite them to perform it for the rest of the class using either claps or claves.

Independent work
● Tell the children that they are going to create their own 'minibeast' composition and record it using a score.
● Put the children in pairs. Provide each pair with claves or chopsticks and a piece of A3 paper divided into eight sections.
● Encourage the children to record their eight-bar composition using drawings of the minibeasts.
● Let less confident learners work with more confident learners to create echo compositions. The more confident learner can play two bars and the less confident learner can then echo those two bars.
● Give the children time to practise performing their compositions.

Plenary
● Invite the pairs to perform their composition by following their score.
● Encourage the audience to evaluate the performance, using the scale provided on page 17 of the Notebook file.
● Ask each pair to swap their score with another pair and give some time for them to play it. Encourage the pairs to evaluate the ease of use of the new score. If a microphone is available, you could record the children's performances using Windows® Sound Recorder.

Whiteboard tools
If a microphone is available
record the children's
compositions using Windows®
Sound Recorder (accessed
through Start>Programs>
Accessories>Entertainment).

 Pen tray

 Select tool

 Delete button

Sound symbols

Learning objectives
QCA Unit 6 'What's the score?
– Exploring instruments and symbols'
● To identify different groups of instruments.
● To understand how symbols can be used to represent sounds.
● To compose a class composition and create a score.

Resources
'Instruments' Notebook file; a variety of percussion instruments; sheets of A3 paper; pens. (Microsoft PowerPoint is required to view the embedded slideshow in the Notebook file.)

Links to other subjects
English
PNS: Word structure and spelling
● In this lesson the children will use their syllable discrimination skills to establish the rhythm of words.
ICT
QCA Unit 2E 'Questions and answers'
● Ask the children to enter data on different instruments into a basic database.

Starter
Look at a variety of percussion instruments with the children. Ask them to name the instruments. Invite some children to demonstrate the different ways that each of the instruments can be played. Encourage the children to use the correct terminology when describing how the instruments are played, such as *tap, shake, scrape* and *blow*. Make a note of key words on page 10 of the 'Instruments' Notebook file.

Whole-class shared work
● Show the children the instruments on page 11 and ask them to talk with a friend about how they are played. Once they have done this, reveal the instrument names by using the Delete button to remove the orange rectangles underneath each image.
● Go to page 12. Explain that each word describes a way that an instrument can be played.
● Ask the children to name two instruments that belong in each of the four groups (*tap, shake, scrape* and *blow*). Write these into the spaces provided.
● Give each child an instrument and ask them to sort themselves into four groups according to how they are going to play it.
● Show the children page 13. Explain which group each symbol represents.
● Tell the children that the symbols are going to appear on the screen in a sequence, and that their group should play their instruments only when their symbol is showing. Explain that this is called a *score*.
● Open the slideshow presentation on page 14 and press the play button. Help the children to perform at the correct times.

Independent work
● Explain to the children that they are going to create their own composition for the class orchestra and record it using a score.
● Supply each child with a sheet of A3 paper divided into eight sections.
● Remind the children of the groups of instruments that are available to them, and encourage them to think of a symbol to use to represent each group.
● Encourage the children to record their eight-bar composition using these symbols.
● Support less confident learners with their work, by allowing them to work in pairs or with an adult scribe to record their score.
● Challenge more confident learners by asking them to consider whether they want each bar to be quiet or loud, slow or fast, and how they could show this on their score.

Plenary
● Explain that every orchestra needs a conductor who tells them when to play. Show the children how to use hand signals to show each group of instruments when they should play and stop.
● Encourage each group to choose one of their members to use their scores and be the conductor to lead the rest of the group.
● Evaluate each performance as a class. Page 15 of the Notebook file can be used as part of the evaluation process.

Whiteboard tools
Use the Delete button to reveal the names of the instruments on page 11.

 Pen tray

 Select tool

 Delete button

Reviewing artwork

Learning objectives
QCA Unit 2A 'Picture this!'
● To record from imagination and experience and explore ideas.
● To be able to review what they and others have done and say what they think and feel about it.

Resources
Paper; powder paints; small parts of pictures cut from magazines or birthday cards. Prepare a Notebook file by inserting pictures of two paintings by well-known artists (copyright permitting) onto a blank page (there is a good selection of examples in the Arts folder under My Content in the Gallery).

Links to other subjects
Speaking and listening
Objective 21: To use language and gesture to support the use of models/diagrams/displays when explaining.
● The children are given the opportunity to discuss, evaluate and reflect upon their artwork.

Whiteboard tools
Use the Spotlight tool to reveal parts of a painting on the screen. Upload scanned images of the children's work to the Notebook page by selecting Insert, then Picture File, and browsing to where you have saved the images.

 Pen tray

 Select tool

 Spotlight tool

 Gallery

Starter
Look at a painting by a well-known artist using the prepared Notebook file (see Resources). Reveal parts of it at a time with the Spotlight tool.

Ask the children to discuss whether they like the painting or not. Ensure that they offer sensible reasons for their answers. Explain that it is acceptable to have different opinions about artwork as long as the opinion can be explained. Talk about the colours and shapes used in the painting and the effects that they create.

Whole-class shared work
● Reveal a part of the second painting on the whiteboard screen.
● Ask the children to take a close look at the part image and encourage them to discuss with their partner what they can see. What do they think the whole image shows?
● Encourage them to look closely at the colours in the image and discuss with a partner how they could mix these colours using powder paint. Ask them to share their ideas with the rest of the class.
● Revise how to mix particular colours and make lighter and darker shades using powder paints.
● Look at the whole of the second painting and discuss what you see together.

Independent work
● Give each child a part of an image from a magazine, photograph, birthday card or print of a painting. Ask them to stick it into the centre of a larger piece of paper.
● Invite the children to use powder paints to extend the part image to fill the larger piece of paper.
● Encourage them to use their imagination to decide what might be beyond the crop of the image.
● Ask them to name their piece of work before and after they extend it. Talk to them about their choices.
● Stop the children regularly: encourage them to reflect on their work so far and whether they are achieving the desired results.
● Encourage the children to use their peers to evaluate their progress.

Plenary
● Take some of the children's work and scan it into the computer. Display the work on a blank Notebook page using the whiteboard software.
● Show one piece of work. Tell the children that they have one minute to discuss with a partner something that they like about it and something that they think could be improved. If you wish, you could use the Timer from the Gallery to time them while they do this.
● Discuss the choice of expansion that the artist has made and whether there were any other ideas that could have been pursued instead. Write some of the children's comments next to the image on the whiteboard.
● Repeat this procedure for each of the examples of the children's artwork that you have uploaded into the Notebook file.
● Ask the artists whether they had any particular successes or difficulties with their pieces.

Learning objectives
QCA Unit 2A 'Vehicles'
● To know that there are many different types of vehicles with different purposes.
● To know that vehicles are made up of different parts.
● To know that ideas for their own designs can be obtained by looking at familiar products.
● To make simple drawings and label parts.

Resources
'Vehicles' Notebook file; photocopiable page 169 'Vehicle research'; a variety of different toy vehicles; individual whiteboards and pens.

Links to other subjects
Speaking and listening
Objective 15: To listen to each other's preferences, agree the next steps to take and identify contributions by each group member.
● Encourage the children to listen to each other's views and preferences as they investigate their vehicles.

Vehicle research

Starter
Open page 2 of the 'Vehicles' Notebook file. Ask the children to name some of the vehicles on the page and encourage them to talk about how the vehicles travel. Discuss who might use each of the vehicles, and why.

Ask the children to identify which vehicle it would be best to use for particular purposes. Then select the blue rectangle in the top right-hand corner of the page and move it underneath each vehicle to reveal its name.

Whole-class shared work
● Tell the children that they are going to find out more about wheeled land vehicles so that they can design and make a model of their own.
● Using page 3, ask the children to vote where each vehicle should be placed by writing the letter on their individual whiteboards and holding their boards up when you say *Show me*. Take a tally of their votes. Then invite volunteers to come to the board to sort the vehicles by dragging and dropping them into the appropriate boxes. Look closely at the ones that travel on land using wheels.
● Explain that it is important to look at vehicles that already exist to find out how they work and to generate ideas to use on their own vehicle.
● Let the children each examine a toy car. Ask them to focus on the wheels and axles (including the underside) and encourage them to talk about how the wheels turn.
● Display page 4. Invite children to come to the board and label the parts of the vehicle by dragging and dropping the labels into the appropriate position.
● Explain that it is important to design a vehicle that is suitable for its purpose. For example, a family of four going on holiday would not find an ice-cream van a useful vehicle!
● Go to page 5. Ask the children to choose a vehicle to discuss with a partner. Encourage each pair to decide who would use the vehicle they have chosen, and what they would use it for.
● Make notes of the children's ideas under each vehicle.

Independent work
● Put a selection of toy vehicles on each table. Invite the children to choose the one that they would like to research.
● Provide each child with a copy of photocopiable page 169. Ask them to draw and label the vehicle as accurately as possible.
● Encourage the children to consider who might use the vehicle, and why. Ask them to record their ideas on the photocopiable sheet.

Plenary
● Ask the children to tell a partner what they have found out about vehicles today. Invite them to share their ideas and record some of their comments on page 6 of the Notebook file.
● Work with the children to decide on three different briefs that they would like to use when designing their own vehicles in the future (such as a car for a family with three children, a sofa delivery truck, and so on).

Whiteboard tools
 Pen tray

 Select tool

Evaluating dance

Learning objectives
QCA Unit 2 'Dance activities (2)'
● To compose and perform dance phrases that express and communicate moods, ideas and feelings, choosing and varying simple compositional ideas.
● To watch and describe dance phrases and dances, and use what they learn to improve their own work.

Resources
A digital video recorder; music to fit the theme of bubbles; bubble blower. Prepare a Notebook file: on the first page write the title 'Words to describe bubbles', and on the second page write 'Successes' and 'Difficulties'.

Links to other subjects
English
PNS: Understanding and interpreting texts
● Suggest that the children add the words they think of to describe the bubbles to their vocabulary lists.
ICT
PoS (5b) To explore a variety of ICT tools.
● Invite the children to use their acquired skills in using a digital video recorder to share information about another topic in the curriculum.

Whiteboard tools
To upload the children's digital video recordings, open SMART Video player from the SMART Board tools menu. Select File, then Open, and browse to where you have saved the video file on your computer. Your video will play in the SMART Video player window. Take a screen shot of a frame with the Image Capture tool in the toolbar of this window.

 Pen tray

 Select tool

 Gallery

Starter
In the hall, ask the children to think about the way in which bubbles form, move and burst. Blow some bubbles for the children to watch and ask them to suggest words to describe their movements (such as *shimmer, stretch* and *pop*). Pick out a few of the more interesting words that the children suggest and write them on the first page of your prepared Notebook file (see Resources). Encourage the children to think of a dance movement to illustrate the words.

Whole-class shared work
● Play the children a simple piece of music that fits the theme of bubbles. Encourage them to listen carefully to the tempo of the music as well as any changes in the music that they need to respond to.
● Next, ask the children to compose a short dance piece that shows a bubble being blown up, shimmering and floating around the room in the breeze, falling slowly to the ground, then finally popping.
● Allow the children a few minutes to experiment with their ideas while the music is playing.

Independent work
● Put the children into pairs. As one of the pair performs the dance, the other uses a digital video recorder to record the performance.
● In the classroom, save the digital videos onto the computer (see Whiteboard tools, below, for advice on how to do this) and view some of the children's dances on the whiteboard.
● Show one of the dances and tell the children that they have one minute to discuss with a partner something that they like about it and something that they think could be improved. If you wish, you could use the Timer from the Gallery 🖾 to time them while they do this.
● Discuss the choice of movements that the dancers made. Let the children suggest other ideas that they could pursue instead, if necessary.
● Ask the dancers whether they feel that they had any particular successes or difficulties during their performance. Write these on the second page of your prepared Notebook file.
● In the hall, ask the children to use the evaluations of themselves and others to try to improve their performances.
● Record the performances again, in the same way as before.

Plenary
● Save the second set of digital videos onto the computer. Show a dance and tell the children that they have one minute to discuss with a partner two things that they feel have improved since the last performance.
● Discuss again the choice of movements that the dancers made, and how they have changed since the last performance.
● Ask the dancers whether they feel they had any particular successes or difficulties during their second performance. Write these on the third page of your Notebook file and discuss the improvements.

Changes Florence made

...because

...because

...because

Illustration © Mark Brierley / Beehive Illustration

The life of Florence Nightingale

Florence improved the conditions for the soldiers in the Crimea.

Florence was taught at home by her father.

Florence was awarded the Order of Merit.

Florence decided she wanted to be a nurse.

Florence opened a training school for nurses.

ST THOMAS HOSPITAL

Florence learned how to be a nurse in Germany.

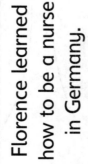

KAISERSWERTH KRANKENHAUS

Florence made many hospitals cleaner and safer.

Florence died in 1910.

FLORENCE NIGHTINGALE
1820 – 1910

Florence went to the Crimean War in 1854.

Florence was born on 12 May 1820.

Illustrations © Mark Brierley / Beehive Illustration

▪ S C H O L A S T I C
w w w . s c h o l a s t i c . c o . u k

An eyewitness report

● Write down four things that Samuel Pepys might tell you about the fire if you could interview him today.

Illustration © Mark Brierley / Beehive Illustration

Holiday destinations

	seaside	countryside	town or city	nowhere
Number of children				

Our favourite holiday destinations

18				
17				
16				
15				
14				
13				
12				
11				
10				
9				
8				
7				
6				
5				
4				
3				
2				
1				
	seaside	countryside	town or city	nowhere

◀ SCHOLASTIC
www.scholastic.co.uk

How to create an electronic book

■ Create a simple electronic book using the templates provided with Microsoft PowerPoint:

1. Open PowerPoint and press Ctrl+N to create a new blank presentation.
2. Click Format on the top menu bar then choose Slide Layout. From the Slide Layout options, choose the Title Slide layout for the first page.
3. Press Ctrl+M to insert a new slide and then choose an appropriate text and content layout from the Slide Layout options for this page.
4. Insert duplicate slides until there are an adequate number of pages.
5. It is possible to insert any type of digital image (copyright permitting) into the content box using the buttons so the children can insert clipart, a digital photograph or movie, a scanned image or their own drawing created in a graphics package.
6. Save the slideshow.

■ Add buttons to turn the pages backwards and forwards like a real book:

1. Add a backwards and forwards arrow to the bottom of the page using AutoShapes, which can be found in the Drawing toolbar.
2. Right-click on the backwards arrow and choose Hyperlink from the menu.
3. Press the button to link to a 'Place in This Document' and then select 'Previous slide' from the list.
4. Right-click on the forwards arrow and choose Hyperlink from the menu.
5. Press the button to choose to link to a place in this document and then select 'Next slide' from the list.
6. A hyperlink can be added to any text or image. This means that the same process can easily be applied to create links to a glossary page or links from a contents page.

■ Add sound to create a talking book:

1. Open the Windows® Sound Recorder program. It can be found under 'Accessories' and then 'Entertainment' in the Start menu.
2. Using a microphone connected to the computer, let the children record their voices and save each sound file.
3. When all of the voices have been recorded, open the PowerPoint file and go to the first page the sound is to be added to.
4. Click Insert on the top menu bar, choose Movies and Sounds then choose Sound from File. Choose the sound that you wish to insert from the file menu.
5. Select the facility for the sound to play when clicked. The sound should now play when the loudspeaker icon is double-clicked.

Instruction cards

(1)	(2)	(3)
(4)	(5)	(6)
(7)	(8)	(9)

  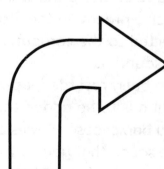 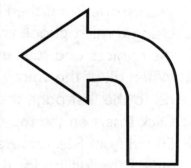

SCHOLASTIC
www.scholastic.co.uk

Vehicle research

What type of vehicle is it? _____

Who uses the vehicle? _____

What is the vehicle used for? _____

_____

_____

_____

Useful words

| aerial | headlight | axle | indicator | steering wheel |
| chair | chassis | wheel | door | windscreen |

Whiteboard diary

Teacher's name: _____

Date	Subject/ Objective	How was the whiteboard used?	Evaluation

SCHOLASTIC
www.scholastic.co.uk

Whiteboard resources library

Teacher's name: _____

Name of resource and file location	Description of resource	How resource was used	Date resource was used

Using your SMART Board™ interactive whiteboard

This brief guide to using your SMART Board interactive whiteboard and Notebook software is based on the training manual *SMART Board Interactive Whiteboard Masters Learner Workbook* © SMART Technologies Inc.

Your finger is your mouse

You can control applications on your computer from the interactive whiteboard. A press with your finger on a SMART Board interactive whiteboard is the same as a click with your mouse. To open an application on your computer through the interactive whiteboard, double-press the icon with your finger in the same way that you would use a mouse to double-click on your desktop computer.

The SMART Pen tray

The SMART Pen tray consists of four colour-coded slots for Pens (black, red, green and blue) and one slot for the Eraser. Each slot has a sensor to identify when the Pens or the Eraser have been picked up. You can write with the Pens, or with your finger, as long as the pen slot is empty. Likewise, if you remove the Eraser from the slot you can use either it or your hand to erase your digital ink.

   The Pen tray has at least two buttons. One button is used to launch the On-screen Keyboard and the second button is used to make your next touch on the interactive whiteboard a right-click. Some interactive whiteboards have a third button, which is used to access the Help Centre quickly.

The On-screen Keyboard

The On-screen Keyboard allows you to type or edit text in any application without leaving the interactive whiteboard. It can be accessed either by pressing the appropriate button in the Pen tray, or through the SMART Board tools menu (see page 173).

   A dropdown menu allows you to select which keyboard you would like to use. The default Classic setting is a standard 'qwerty' keyboard. Select the Simple setting to arrange the keyboard in alphabetical order, as a useful facility for supporting younger or less confident learners. A Number pad is also available through the On-screen Keyboard.

   The Fonts toolbar appears while you are typing or after you double-press a text object. Use it to format properties such as font size and colour.

On-screen Keyboard

Floating tools toolbar

The Transparency layer

When you remove a Pen from the Pen tray, a border appears around your desktop and the Floating tools toolbar launches. The border indicates that the 'transparency layer' is in place and you can write on the desktop just as you would write on a transparent sheet, annotating websites, or any images you display. The transparency layer remains in place until all the Pens and the Eraser have been returned to the Pen tray. Your first touch of the board thereafter will remove the border and any notes or drawings you have made.

Ink Aware applications

When software is Ink Aware, you can write and draw directly into the active file. For example, if you write or draw something while using Microsoft Word, you can save your Word file and your notes will be visible the next time you open it. Ink Aware software includes the Microsoft applications Word, Excel, PowerPoint; graphic applications such as Microsoft Paint and Imaging; and other applications such as Adobe Acrobat. Ensure that the SMART Aware toolbar is activated by selecting View, then toolbars, and checking that the SMART Aware toolbar option is ticked.

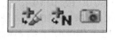

Aware tools

When you are using Microsoft Word or Excel, you will now notice three new buttons that will be either integrated into your current toolbar (as shown on the left), or separated as a floating toolbar. Press the first button to insert your drawing or writing as an image directly into your document or spreadsheet. The second button converts writing to typed text and insert it directly into your document or spreadsheet. Press the third button to save a screen capture in Notebook software.

When you are using Microsoft PowerPoint on an interactive whiteboard, the SlideShow toolbar appears automatically. Use the left- and right-hand buttons on the SlideShow toolbar to navigate your presentation. Press the centre button to launch the Command menu for additional options, including access to the SMART Floating tools (see page 175), and the facility to save notes directly into your presentation.

SlideShow toolbar

SMART Board tools

The SMART Board tools include functions that help you to operate the interactive whiteboard more effectively. Press the SMART Board icon at the bottom right of your screen to access the menu.

- SMART Recorder: Use this facility to make a video file of anything you do on the interactive whiteboard. You can then play the recording on any computer with SMART Video player or Windows® Media Player.
- Floating tools: The features you use most are included in the Floating toolbar. It can also be customised to incorporate any tools. Press the More button at the bottom-right of the toolbar and select Customise Floating Tools from the menu. Select a tool from the Available Tools menu and press Add to include it.
- Start Centre: This convenient toolbar gives you access to the most commonly used SMART Board interactive whiteboard tools.
- Control Panel: Use the Control Panel to configure a variety of software and hardware options for your SMART Board and software.

See page 175 for a visual guide to the SMART Board tools.

Using SMART Notebook™ software

Notebook software is SMART's whiteboard software. It can be used as a paper notebook to capture notes and drawings, and also enables you to insert multimedia elements like images and interactive resources.

Side tabs

There are three tabs on the right-hand side of the Notebook interface:

Page Sorter: The Page Sorter tab allows you to see a thumbnail image of each page in your Notebook file. The active page is indicated by a dropdown menu and a blue border around the thumbnail image. Select the dropdown menu for options including Delete page, Insert blank page, Clone page and Rename page. To change the page order, select a thumbnail and drag it to a new location within the order.

Gallery: The Gallery contains thousands of resources to help you quickly develop and deliver lessons in rich detail. Objects from the Gallery can be useful visual prompts; for example, searching for 'people' in an English lesson will bring up images that could help build pupils' ideas for verbs and so on. Objects you have created yourself can also be saved into the Gallery for future use, by dragging them into the My Content folder.

The Search facility in the Gallery usually recognises words in their singular, rather than plural, form. Type 'interactive' or 'flash' into the Gallery to bring up a bank of interactive resources for use across a variety of subjects including mathematics, science, music and design and technology.

Attachments: The Attachments tab allows you to link to supporting documents and webpages directly from your Notebook file. To insert a file, press the Insert button at the bottom of the tab and browse to the file location, or enter the internet address.

Objects in Notebook software

Anything you select inside the work area of a Notebook page is an object. This includes text, drawing or writing, shapes created with the drawing tools, or content from the Gallery, your computer, or the internet.

(ii)

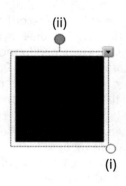

(i)

Manipulating objects: To resize an object, select it and drag the white handle (i). Use the green handle (ii) to rotate an object. To adjust the properties of a selected object, use the dropdown menu.

- Locking: This sub-menu includes options to 'Lock in place', which means that the object cannot be moved or altered in any way. Alternatively you can choose to 'Allow Move' or 'Allow Move and Rotate', which mean that your object cannot be resized.
- Grouping: Select two or more objects by pressing and dragging your finger diagonally so that the objects are surrounded by a selection box. Press the dropdown menu and choose Grouping > Group. If you want to separate the objects, choose Grouping > Ungroup.
- Order: Change the order in which objects are layered by selecting 'Bring forward' or 'Send backward' using this option.
- Infinite Cloner: Select 'Infinite Cloner' to reproduce an object an unlimited number of times.
- Properties: Use this option to change the colour, line properties and transparency of an object.
- Handwriting recognition: If you have written something with a Pen tool, you can convert it to text by selecting it and choosing the Recognise option from the dropdown menu.

Tools glossary

Notebook tools
Hints and tips
● Move the toolbar to the bottom of the screen to make it more accessible for children.

● Gradually reveal information to your class with the Screen Shade.

● Press the Full screen button to view everything on an extended Notebook page.

● Use the Capture tool to take a screenshot of work in progress, or completed work, to another page and print this out.

● Type directly into a shape created with the Shapes tool by double-pressing it and using the On-screen Keyboard.

	Pen tray		Lines tool
	Next page		Shapes tool
	Previous page		Text tool
	Blank Page button		Fill Colour tool
	Open		Transparency tool
	Save		Line properties
	Paste		Move toolbar to the top
	Undo button		
	Redo button		Capture tool
	Delete button		Area Capture tool
	Screen Shade		Area Capture 2
	Full screen		Area Capture 3
	Select tool		Area Capture (freehand) tool
	Pen tool		
	Highlighter pen		Page Sorter
	Creative pen		Gallery
	Eraser tool		Attachments

SMART Board tools
Hints and tips
● Use the SMART recorder to capture workings and methods, and play them back to the class for discussion in the Plenary.

● Adjust the shape and transparency of the Spotlight tool when focusing on elements of an image.

● Customise the Floating tools to incorporate any tools that you regularly use. Press the More button at the bottom right of the toolbar and select Customise Floating Tools from the menu.

Press the SMART Board icon at the bottom right of your screen to access the **SMART Board tools** menu (shown right).

The **Start Centre** (shown below), is reached through the SMART Board tools menu.

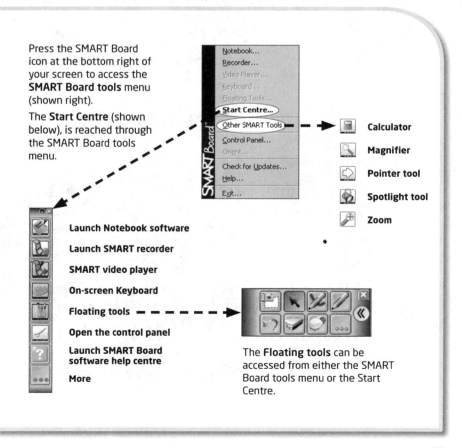

Launch Notebook software

Launch SMART recorder

SMART video player

On-screen Keyboard

Floating tools

Open the control panel

Launch SMART Board software help centre

More

The **Floating tools** can be accessed from either the SMART Board tools menu or the Start Centre.

![SCHOLASTIC]

Also available in this series:

ISBN 978-0439-94536-3	ISBN 978-0439-94537-0	ISBN 978-0439-94538-7

ISBN 978-0439-94539-4	ISBN 978-0439-94540-0	ISBN 978-0439-94541-7	ISBN 978-0439-94542-4

New for 2007-2008

ISBN 978-0439-94546-2	ISBN 978-0439-94523-3	ISBN 978-0439-94508-0

To find out more, call: 0845 603 9091
or visit our website www.scholastic.co.uk